Dating
Techniques
for the
Archaeologist

The MIT Press

Cambridge, Massachusetts

and London, England

Dating
Techniques
for the
Archaeologist

Coedited by
Henry N. Michael
and
Elizabeth K. Ralph

Copyright © 1971 by
The Massachusetts Institute of Technology
This book was designed by The MIT Press Design Department.
It was set in IBM Univers
by Williams' Graphic Service
printed on Warren's Old Style Offset
by American book-Stratford Press, Inc.
and bound in Roxite B-Vellum
by American book-Stratford Press, Inc.
in the United States of America.
ISBN 0 262 13074 2 (hardcover)
Library of Congress catalog card number: 79-153296

## Contributors

Froelich Rainey
Museum Applied Science Center for Archaeology
University Museum, University of Pennsylvania
Philadelphia, Pennsylvania

Elizabeth K. Ralph
Museum Applied Science Center for Archaeology
University Museum, University of Pennsylvania
Philadelphia, Pennsylvania

Henry N. Michael
Museum Applied Science Center for Archaeology
University Museum, University of Pennsylvania
Philadelphia, Pennsylvania

Václav Bucha
Geophysical Institute of the Czechoslovakian Academy
of Sciences, Prague

John Winter
Museum Applied Science Center for Archaeology
University Museum, University of Pennsylvania
Philadelphia, Pennsylvania

Henry Faul and Günther A. Wagner
Department of Geology
University of Pennsylvania
Philadelphia, Pennsylvania

Henry Faul
Department of Geology
University of Pennsylvania
Philadelphia, Pennsylvania

Joseph W. Michels and Carl A. Bebrich
Department of Anthropology
The Pennsylvania State University
University Park, Pennsylvania

# Foreword                    Froelich Rainey

Several American archaeologists undoubtedly will recall an evening at the Wenner Gren Foundation in New York, just over 20 years ago, when Willard Libby and Aristide de Grosse proposed an experiment with radioactive carbon-14 in an attempt to develop a system for absolute dating of prehistoric events. That was shortly after atomic explosions became reality and before atomic-nuclear research developed a new order of technology. It is no wonder that the two languages of physics and archaeology were mutually almost unintelligible at that time. Certainly we archaeologists had a very vague idea of the nature of atomic-nuclear phenomena, and I am sure the physicists were impatient with our uncertainty about the sequence of prehistoric events. However, at that point four of us agreed to work with the Chicago Laboratory to find organic materials of known age in order to test the theories of $C^{14}$ dating; during the next several years we learned much about the speculative, experimental nature of the "hard" sciences. It was impressed upon us that there was never a yes-or-no, black-or-white answer. Absolute $C^{14}$ dates were "probabilities" dependent upon many uncertain factors in the system, human failures in collecting and recording data, and the reliability of the fundamental assumptions about the nature of radioactive materials. Many archaeologists at that time (and, I fear, some to this day) assumed that such a scientific technique must be either right or wrong, a success or a failure, dependable or useless.

More than two decades of research in $C^{14}$ dating have now refined and improved the method so that much more precise dates can be determined, given adequate organic materials and taking into account several correction factors now known to be necessary.* But there are still uncertainties that leave any $C^{14}$ date a question of "probability." This is a very familiar conception in all archaeological research, and we hope this handbook on methods for dating archaeological materials will help to make it clear to all "diggers" that the results of scientific methods of dating are very much like other data utilized by them.

*Over the major part of these two decades much of the research done in MASCA (Museum Applied Science Center for Archaeology) has been supported by the National Science Foundation. In addition to radiocarbon investigations, dendrochronological and thermoluminescence studies were supported.

Dates derived from $C^{14}$ and those derived from several other new methods of nuclear-atomic dating are not of equal validity. Many dates long accepted in archaeological literature are now known to be grossly incorrect. Others are completely unreliable and some are clearly meaningless. Under these circumstances any statistical organization or systemization of published dates can have but very little realistic significance. With our current knowledge of atomic-nuclear dating, the determination of a "highly probable" prehistoric date is a most sophisticated process— certainly not something turned out automatically from a "magic box."

With all the uncertainties in the various methods of atomic-nuclear dating, radiocarbon dating has at least been so far accepted by all archaeologists so that one seldom sees an archaeological report without some reference to $C^{14}$ dating. In fact it has gradually brought about a revolution in our concept of human events. The end of the Ice Age has been brought forward in time, the beginning of urbanization has been pushed back, many of our assumptions about the origin of civilizations in different continents have been changed, and time scales in most regions have been altered. Other types of atomic-nuclear dating are demonstrating that the origins of man go much farther back in time than we supposed. All this dramatically affects man's time perspective and his conception of human history. But this development in archaeology is not unique. Spectacular developments in atomic-nuclear research since the Second World War have altered our whole perspective of the universe, both the macrocosm and the microcosm, our view of matter and energy, and the nature of life. Certainly in part this change has come about because of very great refinements in techniques for measuring time and space, something we are now all keenly aware of since men have landed upon the moon.

It is difficult at this stage to measure the effect of changing perspectives in so many fields of research, simply because those changes are so recent and proceed so rapidly. But the new perspective in human events must somehow have a significant bearing upon the ways of measuring, with accuracy, the many stages or episodes in the unique history of the human species, the rates of development and change, and the accelerating crescendo of events which leaves the future of the species in doubt.

As an example, these dating techniques now tend to show that the hominid hunter Austrolopithecine originated long before any of us expected (probably up to 4 million years ago) and that his development toward true man was extremely slow. There is also some evidence that true man (Homo sapiens like ourselves) may be much older than we thought) perhaps 500,000 years. Likewise the evolution of tools is now seen as much slower than was supposed, some stages lasting for hundreds of thousands of years. But with the end of the Ice Age, when man in general could no longer live by hunting large animals, we now know that very quickly he invented domestication of plants and animals, began living in towns, and laid the foundation for civilization. Potassium-argon and fission-track dating vastly extended the age of man, while $C^{14}$ and thermoluminescence dating pushed back the beginning of civilization and sharply reduced the period of change from hunter to urban dweller. Thus the dating techniques at least demonstrate the varying rates of acceleration and allow us to see the fantastic acceleration of the past century more clearly. All this also serves to point out that we are still biologically hunters, physically adapted to a rugged environment and the natural world rather than to the synthetic environment so recently created by technology.

There is another significant aspect of these scientific methods of dating the past and other new scientific methods developed during the past 25 years. In archaeology the preceding two generations saw such men as Flinders-Petrie and Koldeway organizing field research on a precise, systemized basis with very careful recording of details and painstaking interpretation of archaeological remains. In one sense systemization (often referred to as scientific archaeology) was completed by such men as Sir Mortimer Wheeler about twenty years ago. The trend since then appears to be toward the development and application of science (in the more restricted sense), toward field research as well as analysis of materials in the laboratory, and toward interpretation of the data. This trend probably began with $C^{14}$ and continues with electronic search equipment, elaborate gear such as side-scanning sonar for undersea archaeology, atomic-nuclear methods for material analysis, and computerized interpretation.

Such techniques do not make archaeology a science, any more than did the systemization of the past generations, but it is apparent that they will have an increasing effect upon the way archaeologists think. A logical and well-reasoned conclusion, even though based upon many hypotheses not subject to proof, still is convincing to most archaeologists. But familiarity with the experimental point of view characteristic of scientists already affects many of the younger generation. They are more skeptical of conclusions based largely upon logic and seek ways to demonstrate, in some objective manner, factual proof. For example, the chronology of the Bronze and Iron Ages in the Mediterranean, based upon king lists, interpretation of fragmentary texts, sequence of pottery types, and a few correlations with our own calendar worked out by astronomers, is now being reexamined with the aid of $C^{14}$ and thermoluminescence, because the logical reasoning lying behind that chronology in many cases could not be proved in any factual sense. Even though the dates achieved through these scientific techniques are also only "probabilities," they are cast in an objective, mathematical, experimental framework that makes them more acceptable from the contemporary point of view.

One of the few exceptions to the "probabilities" mentioned in the preceding paragraph is the relationship of accurately dated wood samples and radiocarbon analyses of these. The discovery of deviations between dendrochronological and radiocarbon dates has been vigorously pursued over the past decade and has resulted in the formulation of "correction factors" that enhance the value of archaeological radiocarbon dates (see chapters 1 and 2). Conversely, obsidian dating still depends on local soil and temperature conditions, and the results from one site cannot be applied generally throughout the world, even though much improvement has been seen in the past few years.

The scientific techniques for more precise ordering of human events are already redirecting much of the past concern with chronology toward other aspects of the human story. There is now apparently increased interest in reconstructing the material and intellectual culture of past ages, the rates of cultural change on different continents, the processes of cultural change, and so on. Such changing interests demand additional scientific tools, such as computers, and accelerate the development and adaptation of other techniques. Probably future generations of diggers will look back upon this one as the one responsible for the adaptation of scientific technology and a new trend in archaeology.

The present handbook on dating techniques is the first of a series to be produced under the auspices of the Applied Science Center for Archaeology at The University Museum in Philadelphia. We are deeply grateful to all of those people from many institutions who are now involved in preparing the handbooks. Certainly they must be revised and reissued regularly, to judge from the past rate of change and improvement, and they are published in the present form with that in mind. They are of course intended for the use of professional archaeologists, and we hope for comment on how future revised handbooks can be improved.

## Acknowledgments

The assembling of original materials in this handbook involved the expertise of many people. The tasks of the editors have been considerably lightened by the aid of several individuals connected directly with the Museum Applied Science Center for Archaeology or with the University Museum, and the University of Pennsylvania. Jeanette Flamm and Francesca Giegengack, research librarians at MASCA, carried on the complex correspondence with the various authors and were particularly effective in tracing obscure references in many languages. Eric Parkinson of the University Museum and Joseph Guerrero, Jr., of the Physics Department have skillfully redrawn some of the graphs and maps and have created many from the raw data provided them. The photographic work in connection with the numerous graphs, tables, sketches, and photographs proper was ably done by George M. Quay and William Clough, both of the University Museum. The chores of typing and seemingly endless retyping were the lot of the patient foursome of Lillian Faison, Emily Falcone, Ruby Schmid, and Elpida Kohler. To all go our profound thanks.

**Henry N. Michael and Elizabeth K. Ralph**
Museum Applied Science Center for Archaeology (MASCA)
University Museum, University of Pennsylvania
Philadelphia, Pennsylvania

Philadelphia, November 1970

# 1 Carbon-14 Dating   Elizabeth K. Ralph

## 1.1
### Introduction

The fortunes of radiocarbon (carbon-14, $C^{14}$, or C-14) dating might be compared with those of the stock market. There have been ups and downs. Twenty years ago there was some reluctance to accept $C^{14}$ dates; then, as thousands of such dates were accumulated and comparisons were made with other chronological techniques, there began to be almost universal acceptance of radiocarbon dating. More recently, significant discrepancies between $C^{14}$ results and artifacts of known ages have been found for some segments of time, and the "doubting Thomases" have again become active to a certain extent. In this chapter the problems and uncertainties are explained, but the main emphasis is on the practical and technical aspects of $C^{14}$ dating—the collection of appropriate samples, the pretreatments, the physical methods of dating—and the processing and publication of the data. Means of correcting for the discrepancies are being found, and we expect that $C^{14}$ dating will be useful for many years to come.

## 1.2
### Summary of the Development of the Method

Shortly after the discovery of artificial radioactivity, the existence of natural "cosmic radioelements" was anticipated by A. V. Grosse (1).*
More than a decade later, in 1947, W. F. Libby in collaboration with Grosse and others (2) demonstrated that natural $C^{14}$ does exist. The proof was established by enriching methane from sewage gas in thermal diffusion columns. With this encouragement, Libby and his students then pioneered in the development of greatly improved techniques for the detection of this low-level radioactivity that enabled them to measure $C^{14}$ without enrichment. They used a screen-wall counter developed by Libby (3) and a surrounding ring of anticoincidence counters, all enclosed in a massive shield of iron. These improvements led to the reduction of the background of unwanted counts below the level of natural $C^{14}$ and hence to its detection without enrichment.

   The technique of counting $C^{14}$ as solid carbon with mechanical shielding of iron in combination with the more effective electronic

*Numbers in parentheses refer to the notes at the end of each chapter.

shielding consisting of an anticoincidence ring of cosmic-ray counters surrounding the carbon counter is now well known (4). In 1949, little was known about gas-proportional or about scintillation counting, but geiger counting of solids was in vogue. Therefore, it was logical to convert samples to solid carbon—the element itself, not even a compound—which therefore contained as much carbon as possible per mole. This method was used by Libby and in other laboratories for more than five years. However, there were two basic weaknesses in solid carbon counting: first, self-absorption which reduces the counting efficiency and second, liability to contamination, especially from fallout. For these reasons workers began to experiment with gas-counting techniques and a few with scintillation detection.

## 1.3
### Explanation of the Method

Before we consider present-day techniques in detail, we must understand why the existence of natural $C^{14}$ provides a method of dating. First of all, where does it come from? It is formed in the upper atmosphere by the reaction of ordinary nitrogen ($N^{14}$) with neutrons (n):

$$N^{14} + n \rightarrow C^{14} + H'.$$

Since there is an abundant supply of nitrogen, one notes that the constancy of this production is dependent upon the supply of neutrons. The neutrons are produced by cosmic rays, and the quantity is dependent upon the cosmic-ray intensity and therefore also upon the intensity of the magnetic field of the earth—when the field is stronger, fewer cosmic rays reach the upper atmosphere. After production of the $C^{14}$, it becomes approximately one part in $10^{12}$ parts of our atmospheric carbon dioxide (a very small amount). This in turn is in equilibrium with terrestrial life and with the oceans, the largest reservoirs of carbon. For dating we must assume that the balance among the reservoirs has remained constant, and that the mixing rate of the entire atmosphere is rapid with respect to the average life of an atom of $C^{14}$—8033 years.

That all of these conditions are fulfilled within a precision of approximately 10 percent was first demonstrated by Arnold and Libby (5), and a surprisingly accurate estimate of the worldwide distribution of natural

C$^{14}$ was made by Anderson and Libby (6). The present best estimate of the mean specific activity of C$^{14}$ in equilibrium with the biosphere is 13.56 ± 0.07 disintegrations per minute per gram, abbreviated dpm/g (7).

Due to the mechanism of photosynthesis, all living vegetation is in equilibrium with this atmospheric C$^{14}$O$_2$, and almost all forms of terrestrial life that consume this vegetation contain the same amounts of C$^{14}$. An equilibrium balance between intake and radioactive decay is achieved. However, as soon as an organism dies, it no longer "breathes" and it ceases to acquire additional C$^{14}$ from the atmosphere. Its radiocarbon content therefore begins to decrease, and its rate of radioactive decay is dictated by the half-life of C$^{14}$. It decays back to N$^{14}$ by emission of a beta particle:

$$C^{14} \rightarrow N^{14+} + \beta^-.$$

The accuracy of dating is therefore dependent also upon the precision with which the half-life is known. In 1951 the best estimate of the half-life of C$^{14}$ was 5568 ± 30 years (8, 9, 10, 11, 12), and this value continues to be used for the calculation of dates published in Radio-carbon. However, the present best estimate, as a result of three more recent determinations, is 5730 ± 40 years (13). The latter was accepted as the most probable value at the Fifth Radiocarbon Dating Conference held in Cambridge, England, in 1962. Even though there has been some uncertainty in the exact value of the half-life, it is fortuitous that it is neither too short nor too long. Because of this, the simple element carbon, found universally on earth, provides a tracer for age determination for the period of greatest interest to archaeologists, Pleistocene geologists, and many others.

We now turn our attention to the datable materials and the specific techniques for dating them.

## 1.4
### Samples for C$^{14}$ Dating

In general, organic carbon samples are to be preferred over inorganic. Yet it is important to consider the possible sources of error or contamination for each type of sample. In the following discussions of specific types, the quantities required (about 6 grams of carbon) are sufficient for large 8-liter counters filled to a pressure of one atmosphere. Many laboratories are equipped with small counters and can process correspondingly smaller samples, but with some loss in counting precision.

### 1.4.1
### Charcoal and Wood (25 grams required)

These are the carbon-containing materials found most commonly in archaeological excavations. There is little likelihood of contamination except for finely divided charcoal that has been exposed to certain percolating groundwaters which may cause adsorption by the charcoal of humic acids. The most important consideration is the age of the wood, whether charred or uncharred. We call this the post-sample-growth error (14). It might be more appropriate to call it the pre-sample-growth error because it is the growing of the tree before it was cut for use with which we are concerned. If the sample provided for $C^{14}$ dating has been taken from the center, that is, from the pith of a large log, or if this is all that remains of the wood, the date will represent the time that the tree started to grow and not the time of its use for construction or other purpose. In the extreme case of trees as old as the bristlecone pines this error could amount to more than 4000 years. However, with most large trees it is of the order of 100 to 200 years.

### 1.4.2
### "Short-lived" Samples (25 grams required)

Because of the possibility of the post-sample-growth error of wood, so-called "short-lived" materials are often to be preferred. These materials include grains, other seeds, nutshells, grasses, twigs, cloth, paper, hide, burned bones, and any others encountered by the excavator that consist mostly of organic carbon and are likely to have grown and died very shortly before use. These materials, except for bones, are equally suitable whether charred or uncharred. As with wood and charcoal, these sample types are unlikely to have become contaminated.

### 1.4.3
### Organic Matter Mixed with Earth (50 to 300 grams required)

In the field it is frequently impossible to separate a sufficient quantity of charcoal (or other suitable material) from the earth with which it is mixed. It is best to try to remove as much earth as possible from the sample at the site because it will be even more difficult to separate after it has been packed and shipped. The quantity required will depend upon the proportion of organic matter present. To obtain a reliable date, the sample must contain at least 1 percent of organic carbon and this preferably in the form of visible pieces. Occasionally samples are received in the laboratory that to the excavator looked darker than the surrounding earth, but when dry lose this "darkness." Usually, these contain negligible organic carbon.

### 1.4.4

### Peat (50 to 200 grams required)

The composition of peat varies widely so that it is best to collect a large sample. Many reliable dates have been obtained with peat, but for archaeological dating it is especially important to make sure that each peat sample represents the time of occupation in question. Also, the freer the sample is of intrusive rootlets, the more reliable the date.

### 1.4.5

### Ivory (50 grams required)

In most cases the carbon in ivory is firmly fixed so that there is little danger of contamination. Tusks more than 40,000 years old have been found in such good condition that it has been suspected that they might have come from modern elephants (15). Incidentally, the growth patterns of mammal tusks are the opposite from those of trees: the inner part is the youngest and the outer, the oldest. Elephant or walrus ivory seems to be more reliable as a dating material than are antlers. In one comparison of contemporaneous samples from the Arctic, a region where in general problems of contamination are particularly severe, antler was found to be 25 percent younger than ivory (16).

### 1.4.6

### Bones

If bones have been heavily charred shortly after the time of death, reliable dates may be obtained without special treatment. Dependent upon the degree of charring, up to 300 grams may be required. Slight charring is not sufficient. The carbon content in bones is very low, mostly inorganic, and contained in a very porous structure. Only heavy charring fixes the carbon so that it is not subject to alteration. Com-

parisons between charcoal and bone samples in a Tiahuanaco series
from Bolivia (17) showed that the bones were contaminated with
younger carbon from groundwater; this made a difference in age of
500 years. Another test (18) showed bones to be 1000 years younger
than contemporaneous charcoal samples. There is a small fraction of
organic (and hence more stable) carbon in bones which is called collagen (19, 20, 21). The amount present tends to decrease with age and
with conditions of oxidation, and it may be as low as 2 percent after
the passage of time. Therefore at least 1 kg of bones should be submitted to the laboratory. The collagen fraction, however, does seem to
give reliable dates.

### 1.4.7

### Shells (100 grams required for inorganic fraction)

With shells the problems are similar to those with bones, but more
severe. Most of the carbon is found in the form of calcium carbonate, as
calcite and aragonite, which are subject to exchange, especially with
older limestone from groundwater. The problem of exchange seems to
be worse with terrestrial than with marine shells. Experiments with
snail shells by Rubin et al. (22) indicated that aquatic snail shells in the
presence of an excess of calcium carbonate enriched in $C^{14}$ could take
up 10 percent additional $C^{14}$, and terrestrial snail shells, under the
same conditions, 12 percent.

If the shells have not exchanged with ground or other waters, there is
also the problem of possible natural enrichment in comparison with
wood or other organic samples used for calibration. Conflicting measurements have been obtained. Some workers report enrichment factors
of 1.06 for the $C^{14}/C^{12}$ ratio in carbonates with respect to wood,
whereas others have reported negligible differences. These problems are
discussed by Rafter (23). The lack of consistency in experimental results is probably due in large part to the fact that tests in various laboratories have not been made with the same species exposed to the same
conditions of exchange, and thus contamination.

With shells it is possible to extract a small organic fraction, conchiolin, which is present in amounts of 1 to 2 percent in modern
shells (19). Several kilograms of shells would be required for this. The
problem remains, however, of the appropriate standard for age calcula-

tion, especially for marine shells that may have derived their carbon from organisms in equilibrium with older seawater.

**1.4.8**

**Sediments, Lake Marls, Deep-Sea and Lake Cores**

After discussing the problems inherent in shells, it may seem surprising that many acceptable dates have been obtained from the carbonate fractions of sediments, deep-sea cores, lake marls, and similar materials. A study of contemporaneous pairs of organic and carbonate samples by Olson and Broecker (24) gave the results shown in Table 1.1. One sees that there is no significant difference between the organic and inorganic fractions from these three sites.

However, one must consider a problem similar to that of the post-sample-growth error in terrestrial woods. In a study by Deevey et al. it was shown (25) that freshwater aquatic plants that utilize bicarbonate from ancient limestone as a source of photosynthetic carbon can be markedly depleted in C$^{14}$. Both animal and plant material from the marl-forming hard waters of Queechy Lake in Connecticut gave fictitious ages as much as 2000 years too old.

In a recent study of lake sedimentation rates and lake varve chronology, Stuiver (26) found that corrections for the C$^{14}$ deficiencies of various lakes varied from 200 to 600 years.

Another type of uncertainty was found by Eriksson, Olsson and others (27, 28, 29) in dating cores from Mediterranean Sea sediments. They found that sediment fractions smaller than 44 microns contain a considerable amount of old material and that the error could be as great

Table 1.1. Results of Carbonate Fractions.

| Locality | Sample type | C$^{14}$ age (5568 half-life) |
|---|---|---|
| Vancouver delta sands | wood | 11,850 ± 250 |
| | shells | 12,000 ± 250 |
| Great Salt Lake core | organic | 26,300 ± 1100 |
| | carbonate | 25,300 ± 1000 |
| Glacial deposits, Denmark | wood | 10,890 ± 240 |
| | lake marl | 10,930 ± 300 |

as 10,000 years. Precautions must be taken against contamination of the samples by atmospheric carbon dioxide during the preparation process in the laboratory.

### 1.4.9
### Pottery and Iron (2 to 5 kilograms)

Under certain conditions both pottery and iron contain organic carbon from sources contemporaneous with the time of their manufacture. In dating three types of sherds from South America (tempered with cariapé, charcoal, and cauixi) it was found that if the organic carbon content was 1 percent or more, the $C^{14}$ dates tended to agree with normal control samples or with the archaeologists' estimates of their ages (30). A more complete comparison of carbon from sherds and charcoal samples by Taylor and Berger (31) showed general agreement between the two types, but in a comparison of wattle-and-daub samples with charcoal there was poor agreement (two of three comparisons were discordant). In both studies, organic carbon contents were found to be variable and unpredictable.

Some types of irons, such as those of meteoritic origin, cannot be dated by $C^{14}$, and in all cases one must have some knowledge of what the fuel (the source of the carbon) was likely to have been. Also, a special high-temperature furnace is required in the laboratory for the combustion of the carbon contained in the iron. Successful dating of a series of iron artifacts and also of iron and copper slags in the Yale laboratory has been reported by Van der Merwe (32).

### 1.5
### Collection, Packaging, Labeling, and Description of Samples

### 1.5.1
### Collection

It seems presumptuous for a physical scientist to describe to an archaeologist how to collect a sample, but an attempt must be made to answer the questions that occur most frequently.

One of the most common queries is whether or not the sample should be touched by hand. Obviously, with a large piece of wood, ivory, or other object from which surface dirt can easily be removed, it makes no difference. Caches of grain and other "short-lived" materials are frequently found in pots. These can usually be poured or scraped out into suitable containers without any contact by hand.

Probably small bits of charcoal mixed with earth cause the most difficulty. Naturally, one would want to use a clean trowel, spatula, or tweezers to remove the charcoal, but if suitable tools are not available to collect and to separate an adequate sample from the earth, I would recommend picking out the charcoal by hand rather than leaving it mixed with large quantities of earth. It is better to separate as much of the organic materials as possible in the field rather than after it has been packaged and shipped and consequently become more thoroughly broken and mixed.

As with any sample removed in the course of excavation, it is important that its stratigraphic position be observed carefully and recorded. If a sample of carbon is not related to an occupational level or feature of geological or other interest, there is usually no reason to date it. Also, one has to beware of intrusions. For instance, a mouse hole penetrating through occupational layers might easily result in causing an error much greater than an error brought about by a few fingerprints or a whiff of modern dust.

Samples from museum collections will have been handled many times. There is also the possibility that they may have been contaminated by impregnation with other carbon-containing coatings or preservatives.

## 1.5.2

### Packaging and Labeling

Plastic (polyethylene) bags are probably the best for packaging samples. Bags 0.1 mm (0.004 inch) thick are sufficiently strong, but thinner ones may be used, especially in multiple layers. They may be sealed with Scotch electrical tape No. 33 or any other tape that adheres well. If the samples are solid and not crumbling, they may be wrapped in aluminum foil, or even cloth or paper.

Various other containers such as metal medicine or food boxes, etc., may be used. Glass jars should be avoided, if possible, because if they break in shipment the sample will become mixed with modern packing material.

It is better to dry most types of terrestrial samples at the site, if possible. If this is not possible, they should be shipped as soon as practical and the laboratory warned that they are wet. This is especially important for samples from Arctic regions. In one instance, when samples from Alaska were stored in the laboratory for a year without attention, we found more newly formed white mold in the bags than ancient charcoal.

For the handling and sorting of wet cores, someone with experience should be consulted. For example, for deep-sea cores, see Olsson et al. (29).

Each sample must be labeled with at least an identifying number on the outside of the plastic bag or other container. Labels on small pieces of paper put inside with damp charcoal frequently become illegible. The label should contain only one number plus any special description the collector wishes to add.

### 1.5.3
#### Information Sheets

A sample information sheet is reproduced in Table 1.2. It includes the items of information that are required for publication of all $C^{14}$ dates in Radiocarbon (published by the American Journal of Science, Yale University).

A separate information sheet should be filled out for each sample and this should include the same number that appears on the corresponding label. Any other pertinent information may be added to this sheet.

If possible, the sheets should accompany the samples or be sent by airmail ahead of time. They are the collector's greatest assurance that his samples will not be ignored, misplaced, or mixed up in the laboratory. (It is recommended that the excavator keep duplicate copies.)

One can easily imagine the confusion in the laboratory when a large series of samples arrives in small batches at various times brought from overseas by different couriers, followed by a letter from one of the excavators with a list of numbers that does not match the sample labels, and finally the information sheets arrive (perhaps filled out by some other excavator) with a third set of numbers. This has actually happened.

**Table 1.2** Sample information sheet.

Radiocarbon Laboratory, Department of Physics
University of Pennsylvania
Philadelphia, Pennsylvania 19104

The information requested below must accompany each sample submitted.

1. Descriptive name of site and sample, and brief explanation of significance of each.

2. Sample material. Scientific name (and name of person so identifying) is preferred; otherwise, give popular name.

3. Precise geographic location, including latitude and longitude to nearest minute.

4. Occurrence and stratigraphic position within site; cultural and/or geologic associations; and stratigraphic and chronologic position of this sample relative to others from this site. Include sketch, if necessary.

5. Factors affecting validity of date, such as rootlets, intrusions, possible humic contamination, groundwater percolations, preservatives, etc.

6. Any further explanation felt necessary.

7. Name of collector and date of collection.

8. Name and institutional affiliation of submitter.

9. Reference to relevant publications. Include complete title, publication, pagination, etc.

10. Comment by submitter and/or collector, comparing sample with other dates and sites, etc. Sample numbers and references must be complete.

## 1.6

### Pretreatments

Pretreatments are done in the $C^{14}$ laboratory, but it is important for the submitter to know what contaminants are likely to be present and which ones can be removed.

### 1.6.1

### Mechanical Sorting and Cleaning of Terrestrial Samples

The first step in the laboratory is to give each sample a number and record its field number and any other essential identifying information in the laboratory log book. It is then examined under good light. If the sample is a large, solid piece, its outer surfaces are cleaned mechanically and it is then cut up into small chips or slivers (for wood), roughly 1 x 1/2 x 1/4 cm or smaller. If it is already fragmented or if it consists of finely divided charcoal or other bits of materials, it is examined very carefully for intrusive rootlets, stones, and other obvious impurities. These are removed with tweezers insofar as possible.

The sample is then weighed and the requisite amount is selected for subsequent chemical treatment. At this time, its number, site, name, description, and weight are recorded on a processing sheet (Table 1.3). From this point on, each step in its treatment and the date on which it took place will be recorded on this sheet.

### 1.6.2
### Standard Chemical Treatments for Organic Samples

In most laboratories all organic samples are treated with cold (or hot) 3N hydrochloric acid (HCl) by the simple process of putting them into beakers and pouring the acid over them. The HCl removes inorganic carbon contaminants such as limestones and shells; the length of treatment and amount of HCl required depend upon the nature of the sample. For clean wood one hour is sufficient, but for bits of charcoal mixed with a lot of earth or shells several days, with occasional stirring, will be required. Termination of effervescence indicates completion of the reaction. The HCl is then filtered off, usually in a Büchner funnel with aspirator suction, and the sample is rinsed thoroughly with distilled water while still in the funnel. If there is no reason to suspect humic acid contamination, the sample is then dried in an oven at 100° C or less, and it is ready for combustion.

If it is known that the sample has been subjected to percolating groundwaters, and especially if it consists of finely divided charcoal, which is a good adsorber, it may be contaminated with humic acids from decaying humus of more recent age. In this case it must then be treated with a boiling solution of 2-percent sodium hydroxide (NaOH) for half an hour. It should not be left in this solution longer than necessary because there is the possibility of slow exchange with atmospheric carbon dioxide while the sample is in an alkaline solution. For this reason, also, it should be filtered, rinsed, and reacidified with HCl as rapidly as possible—although with finely fragmented samples the filtering is usually slow and difficult. The sample may be centrifuged rather

**Table 1.3** Sample processing sheet.

No.                                          Special Procedures:

Name:

Description:

Date:                    Pretreatment:


Combustion:

Grams                         Am't $CO_2$


CaO Purification:


Counter Filling:

Counter Pressure Counter Temperature Xs Storage


Storage:

than filtered, but this is also time consuming. To check whether or not humic acid contamination was present, the filtrate from the NaOH solution can be saved and the humus fraction precipitated with acid. If not enough humus was present for subsequent counting, an alternate way of processing is to divide the sample in half after the original HCl treatment, and treat only half of it with NaOH. This latter procedure is frequently followed when not all samples in a series are large enough for the treatment for humic acids. Several of the largest ones may be halved and the $C^{14}$ dates of the pairs compared. It should be pointed out that even if no contamination is present, about half of the sample is usually dissolved by the NaOH, so that double-sized samples are required as a minimum. Caution must be exercised in the treatment of peat with NaOH because if the peat is not "woody," it may dissolve completely.

Even though the humic treatment does require larger samples, it should be carried out with the suspected materials whenever possible. This is especially true for very old samples in which even a very slight amount of contamination would cause a large error in the $C^{14}$ date.

### 1.6.3
#### Inorganic Samples

Inorganic carbon samples, such as shells, are soluble in acids. They are therefore cleaned mechanically and examined carefully (this may be supplemented by X-ray analysis) for changes of the crystal structure due to weathering or other processes. These are more apt to occur on the outer surfaces so that it is usually best to leach away up to 50 percent of the sample with diluted HCl. Even if no deterioration is apparent, a light leaching to remove surface contamination is advisable.

Since carbonates can exchange with carbon dioxide in the air, bicarbonates in water, and so on, contamination is a much more serious problem than in the case of organic samples. It may be especially severe with particles of small grain size. Therefore samples, when whole, should not be broken up until the last minute and should be stored in dry air free of carbon dioxide or in a vacuum. Specific experiments related to the contamination of foraminifera and mollusk shells are reported by Olsson et al. (29).

## 1.6.4

### Special Pretreatments of Organic Samples

If the desired sample consists of charcoal and is mixed with contaminating plant matter that is impossible to remove physically, the rootlets and similar materials may be removed chemically. There are a number of ways to do this, but the one that has been tried and tested most successfully includes the following steps (33):

1. Treat with HCl as usual.
2. Boil in 15 percent NaOH for 1 hour, filter, and wash on glass paper.
3. Add 150 ml of sodium hypochlorite (NaOCl, Chlorox) to the sample in 200 ml of 6N HCl under constant stirring. Boil 20 minutes and filter.
4. Nitrate the residual cellulose for 10 minutes with 400 ml of a 1:1 mixture of concentrated nitric and sulfuric acids. Wash sample.
5. Leach with nine 200-ml portions of acetone.
6. Aerate the remaining carbon and inorganic material (if present) with an aspirator, wash with distilled water, and dry in an oven.

It has been demonstrated that this method achieves complete removal of the contaminants, but there is some possibility, to which one should be alerted, of obtaining dates erroneously old, possibly due to fractionation.

For certain experiments it may be desirable to remove the lignin from wood and retain only the cellulose. Wilson (34) has described one way to do this, which I summarize as follows:

A "double" sample (40 g) of ground wood is first extracted with an organic solvent such as methylene chloride in a soxhlet extractor. It is then dried and the lignin removed by oxidation with sodium chlorite in acetic acid. To the residue in 1 liter of water, heated on a water bath at 60° to 70° C, first sodium chlorite (30 g) and then glacial acetic acid (10 ml) are added. The mixture is stirred, and after one hour and two hours, respectively, the additions of sodium chlorite and glacial acetic acid are repeated until the evolution of chlorine ceases. The white, pulpy mass of cellulose that remains is then filtered, washed thoroughly, and dried.

The inorganic and organic fractions of bones may be separated by treatment with cold dilute (less than 1N) HCl at reduced pressure (19, 20). The inorganic carbon is evolved as $CO_2$ (and may be collected) whereas the collagen remains largely insoluble. This same procedure may be used for the separation of conchiolin in shells.

For bones, if humic acid contamination is suspected or if the sample is very old, the collagen should be treated with NaOH <u>after</u> separation. The standard pretreatment with NaOH is ineffective on whole bones, because humic acids are rendered insoluble in basic solutions in the presence of calcium ions (21).

## 1.7
### Laboratory Methods

After the various pretreatments have been completed, the next step is the actual conversion of the sample to a compound suitable for counting the radioactive $C^{14}$. In brief, the techniques now in use are the gas-proportional counting of carbon dioxide, methane, or acetylene, or the liquid scintillation counting of benzene. The methods for preparing and counting these compounds are described in section 1.12 (p. 29).

## 1.8
### Age Calculation and Statistical Uncertainty

Let us assume for the moment that the half-life is known to our satisfaction and that the production rate of $C^{14}$ is constant. If we ignore other factors, terrestrial creatures and plants in equilibrium with the atmosphere will have a constant amount of $C^{14}$. (This is not absolutely true, especially for the past 100 years, during which the atmospheric $C^{14}$ was first depleted by the combustion of inert fossil fuels and then augmented by nuclear-bomb explosions.) This static condition persists until the subject dies, at which time its $C^{14}$ is no longer replenished and it decays only. Since this is the decay of a radioactive element, it follows the familiar exponential decay equation:

$$I = I_0 e^{-\lambda t} \tag{1.1}$$

where

$I$ = activity of the sample when measured.

$I_0$ = original activity of the sample (this value is obtained from samples of known age, approximately 100 years old, but corrected for zero age).

$\lambda$ = decay constant = $0.693/T_{1/2}$ with $T_{1/2}$ the half-life.

$t$ = time elapsed.

If we feed the value of the half-life into this equation (5568 years in this case), we have the simple formula

$$t = \log \frac{I_0}{I} \times 18.5 \times 10^3 \text{ years} \tag{1.2}$$

for routine age calculations.

Not so obvious in these simple equations is the fact that radioactive disintegration is a random process. One cannot predict when any particular atom will decay; one can say only that after a certain length of time, on the average a certain quantity will have disintegrated. In radioactive parlance this uncertainty is quoted in terms of statistical deviation. For uniformity in radiocarbon dating, it has been customary to quote the standard statistical deviation (or one sigma) with each date. This so-called one-sigma tolerance means that there is the probability in two times out of three that the date lies within the range quoted. If the one-sigma tolerance is doubled, then there is greater assurance that the true date lies within such a range—specifically 21 times in 22.

In most laboratories the tolerance quoted includes the statistical uncertainty inherent in the counting of the unknown sample, of the background, and of the calibration samples. Since at the moment we have neglected other possible discrepancies between radiocarbon and true ages, this is the minimum uncertainty and it cannot nor may not be ignored in quoting $C^{14}$ dates.

Frequently, samples are counted overnight for 1000-minute intervals, and each sample is counted at least twice. If the second count is made a week after the first, this provides a check on possible radon contamination. Since the half-life of radon is only 3.82 days, it will have decayed a measurable amount by the second week. In our laboratory, if the two counts are not statistically consistent, the sample is then counted one or more times. Our method of statistical analysis has been explained in detail in Satterthwaite and Ralph (35). A specific example, including an age calculation, is given here:

The first step is to determine the average total counting rate ($\bar{n}_t$) and the average net counting rate ($\bar{n}_n = \bar{n}_t - b$), where b is the background counting rate—an average of all of the once-a-week checks, usually for a period of 10 weeks (unless there has been a shift in background). These are set forth in Table 1.4.

**Table 1.4. Counting rates.**

| Date | Counter | $n_t$ | $n_n$ | $n_n - \bar{n}_n$ | $(n_n - \bar{n}_n)^2$ |
|------|---------|-------|-------|-------------------|----------------------|
| 5/1/69 | I | 22,623 | 13,085 | − 131 | 17,161 |
| 5/9/69 | I | 21,377 | 13,346 | + 130 | 16,900 |
| | | $\bar{n}_t = 22{,}000$ | $\bar{n}_n = 13{,}216$ | $\Sigma = -1$ | $\Sigma = 34{,}061$ |

The chi-square test is then applied, where

$$\chi^2 = \frac{\Sigma(n_n - \bar{n}_n)^2}{\bar{n}_t} = \frac{34{,}061}{22{,}000} = 1.55.$$

From a table of chi-square factors (36), we find $P(\chi^2) \geqslant 0.2$. The criterion for standard statistical consistency is that $P(\chi^2)$ be $> 0.1$. Therefore, these two counts pass the test, and since they are consistent, the statistical deviation of the average, $\sigma_s$, equals $\sqrt{(\bar{n}_t + b)_N}/N$, where N equals the number of counting runs. In this example,

$$\sigma_s = \frac{\sqrt{(22{,}000 + 8785)2}}{2} = 124.$$

(Note that in this case there was a shift in background between the two counts. This was due to the replacement of a geiger counter which became faulty after May 1, 1969.) During this counting interval in May, the average zero-age ($I_0$) counting rate, based on the 16 consistent measurements of our 100-year-old oak calibration sample, was

$$I_0 = 31.666 \pm 0.054.$$

Next, we divide $\sigma_s$ by 1000 (the standard counting time) and add the sum of the squares of $\sigma_s/1000$ and 0.054, and take the square root:

$$\sigma_t = \sqrt{(0.124)^2 + (0.054)^2} = 0.135.$$

We then subtract and add $\sigma_t$ from $\bar{n}_n$ and calculate the maximum and minimum ages from the formula $t = \log(I_0 /I) \times 18.5 \times 10^3$. With the use of a desk calculator and tables of logarithms, our worksheet appears as follows:

13.216
 .135

| 13.081 | 2.4208 | .38396 | 7103.3 (maximum age) |
| 13.351 | 2.3718 | .37507 | 6938.8 (minimum age) |
| | | | 164.5 (difference) |

164.5/2 = 82

6939 + 82 = 7021 = B.P. (before present) age

We next subtract 19 years (in 1969) from this to standardize the age to B.P. 1950, and then subtract 1950 to find its A.D.-B.C. age. To convert the date to the 5730 half-life, we multiply the B.P. age by 1.03, and obtain the following dates:

| Half-life | B.P. 1950 | A.D.-B.C. |
|---|---|---|
| 5568 | 7002 ± 82 | 5052 ± 82 B.C. |
| 5730 | 7213 ± 84 | 5263 ± 84 B.C. |

## 1.9
## Interlaboratory Calibration and Mass-Spectrographic Measurement of $C^{13}/C^{12}$

Our calibration sample on which $I_0$ is based consists of a section of tree-ring-dated white oak. From this we select samples that span no more than 10 tree rings in the range of 110 to 130 years B.P. From the counting rate I and the known age t we obtain $I_0$ from equation 1.2.

For interlaboratory calibration, however, a sample that could be made in bulk with a specific amount of $C^{14}$ was desirable. The National Bureau of Standards provided this in the form of oxalic acid (NBS no. 4990). From the measurement of this and wood calibration samples in the range of A.D. 1840 to A.D. 1860, it has been found in many laboratories that the age-corrected wood samples have activities equal to 95 percent of the oxalic acid standard sample. An absolute calibration of the oxalic acid standard and of the Heidelberg reference sample was also made (7).

Radiocarbon contains a list of all laboratories and, starting with volume 11 in 1969, an index of all sample numbers. In 1967, the editors of Radiocarbon published a comprehensive index of all radiocarbon dates published between 1950 and 1965, including lists of published references, the original $C^{14}$ dates, and possible corrections of the dates that need be made since publication.

Annual subscription rates for Radiocarbon, available only by volume, are $30.00 for institutions and $20.00 for individuals. All correspondence and manuscripts should be addressed to the Managing Editor, Radiocarbon, Box 2161, Yale Station, New Haven, Connecticut 06520.

**1.10.2**

**McBee Edge-Punched Cards**

Dr. Frederick Johnson, formerly of the Peabody Museum, Andover, Massachusetts, and one of the members of the original radiocarbon committee, who was influential in organizing conferences in the 1950s, especially the two held at Andover, Massachusetts, in 1954 and 1956, undertook the tedious task of putting all $C^{14}$ dates on individual punched cards. This included the first dates that were published in Science and elsewhere, with unstandardized and often incomplete information.

The type of card chosen is the McBee Edge-Punched card. Individual cards can be retrieved with the help of four knitting needles. Retrieval categories are: latitude and longitude to the exact degree or general area, age of the sample, dating method, laboratory sample number, and primary (and secondary) scientific field that the measurement represents such as archaeology, geology, geophysics, oceanography, contemporary problems, or miscellaneous. In practice we have found it convenient to sort the cards as they arrive, to separate archaeology and geology, and to file them by the regions of the world which they represent. After this preliminary sorting it is not always necessary to use the knitting needles nor to hunt through thousands of cards for a particular date.

For the past few years, the task of publishing these cards has been taken over by Mr. John C. Ramsden, and the cards may now be ordered from Radiocarbon Dates, P. O. Box 22, Braintree, Massachusetts. They are published in volumes of 1000 cards, and the cost is $125 per volume. So far 6000 (or 6 volumes) have been published per year, but this quantity may be reduced to 4000 or 3000 as the publisher catches up with the backlog.

Two types of half-subscriptions which cost $62.50 per volume may be ordered. The division may be made between archaeological versus geological dates, or by east versus west longitude. A quarter-subscription which may be ordered at slightly greater cost ($37.50 per volume) consists of only one of the categories of the two divisions listed above.

## 1.11
## Interpretation of C$^{14}$ Dates
### 1.11.1
### Basic Assumptions

We now return to the fundamental assumption which was mentioned briefly in the beginning of this chapter—namely, that the biospheric inventory of C$^{14}$ has remained constant during the past 50,000 years or so. We know now that this assumption is not precisely true. Up-to-date papers and discussions of most of these problems were reported at the Twelfth Nobel Symposium held in Uppsala, August, 1969 (40). Some of the interpretations which now follow were also published previously by Ralph and Michael (41) and by others.

Fortunately, numerous experiments (42, 43, and others) have demonstrated that the mixing rate of C$^{14}$ in the atmosphere is rapid—of the order of two years even between hemispheres—so that we can consider the atmosphere as a whole. A recent study by Haugen (44) in which he compared major trends in tree-ring indices for Alaska, the Urals, Scandinavia, and Labrador resulted in highly significant correlations among these areas from A.D. 1650 on, and supports the proposition of a rapid mixing rate. Incidentally, this demonstrates also that the C$^{14}$ date for a particular age will be the same all over the world.

It is more difficult to obtain a precise assessment of the constancy of the cosmic-ray intensity since we are looking for comparatively small variations in C$^{14}$ contents. Studies of the decay series of nuclides in meteorites indicate that there have been no major changes in cosmic-ray intensity during the past 300,000 years (45); Crèvecoeur (46) has extended this period to 5 million years. For more recent time ranges (less than 2000 years), a study of $Ar^{37}/Ar^{39}$ ratios in iron meteorites by Fireman and Goebel (47) indicates that the cosmic-ray flux near 1 AU (AU = average distance between earth and sun), did not differ significantly in the spring of 1969 from the previous several hundred years. The accuracy of measurement of these ratios was 5 percent—much better than most previous determinations of isotopic ratios in meteorites. However, the basic difficulty has been that the orbits in space of the meteorites have been unknown and that the cosmic-ray flux received varies with distance from the sun. Fortunately, this difficulty will soon be overcome because tracking stations set up in seven middlewestern states in 1964 have at last recorded the trajectory of a meteorite which fell near Lost City, Oklahoma, on January 3, 1970 (48). When this and others have been studied, more will be known about the constancy of the cosmic-ray intensity.

Numerous attempts have been made to correlate short-term $C^{14}$ fluctuations with sunspot activities and cycles. Results have given correlations both negative (49, 50) and positive (51, 52). The difficulties are that the $C^{14}$ fluctuations in the A.D. era are small and difficult to establish and that the sunspot data prior to A.D. 1750 are scarce and unreliable.

Another important factor is the constancy of the magnetic field of the earth in past times. The strength of the magnetic field affects the intensity of cosmic rays which reach the upper atmosphere to react with nitrogen. Fortunately, quantitative measurements can be obtained by measurements of remanent magnetization in fired ceramics. These are described by Bucha in chapter 3.

Since the experimental evidence now indicates that the changes are cyclic (at least for one cycle), the exponential solution suggested by Elsasser, Ney, and Winckler (53) is inadequate. Nevertheless if reasonable boundary conditions are used and the magnetic and $C^{14}$ changes are assumed to be worldwide, the solution for a cyclic relationship can be found. Enough measurements have been accumulated, however, to indicate that the changes in magnetic intensity are very likely worldwide (see chapter 3).

In regard to changes in equilibrium conditions which affect atmospheric, terrestrial, and oceanic content, it is more difficult to obtain precise results. The carbon dioxide content of the atmosphere, which consists roughly of $10^{-12}$ parts of $C^{14}O_2$, is in equilibrium with that on the surface of the earth. For land-based life this is adequate information, but the largest reservoir—the ocean—has a more complicated structure and is not necessarily in equilibrium throughout its depth. The atmospheric $C^{14}O_2$ is in equilibrium with surface ocean waters, but the balance between the surface and deep waters is affected by the varying mixing rates and solubilities. All of these rates are affected by temperature and circulation patterns. These problems were discussed at the Twelfth Nobel Symposium (40) as well as earlier.

### 1.11.2

### Radiocarbon versus True Ages

We may not have direct and precise methods to measure the constancy of production of $C^{14}$, its subsequent equilibrium, and its absolute decay rate, but we can evaluate radiocarbon years in terms of true ages by means of samples of known age. Additionally, these measurements may shed some light upon the basic causes of possible discrepancies. Dendrochronology provides a source of samples of known age. The tree-ring dating of the long series of sequoias and bristlecone pines which have been used in these studies is described by Michael in chapter 2. The $C^{14}$ dating of these dendrochronological samples has been done with great care and with the highest precison attainable, including the measurement of $C^{13}/C^{12}$ ratios to correct for possible natural or laboratory fractionation. The results of about 185 determinations made in the radiocarbon laboratory at the University of Pennsylvania are plotted in Fig. 1.1.*

We see a definite oscillation in the range of A.D. 1700 to A.D. 1500, then a good correspondence on the average between $C^{14}$ and tree-ring ages from A.D. 1500 to 500 B.C. However, toward the beginning of the first millennium B.C. the departure becomes pronounced and the magnitude at 5000 B.C. is +750 years; that is, $C^{14}$ dates are approximately 10 percent too young.

It is tantalizing at the moment not to have tree-ring dated samples

*We acknowledge with gratitude financial support from the National Science Foundation for our known-age dating program. This has been supported since 1957 with NSF grants G-3281, G-5608, G-14094, GP-405, GP-3778, GA-993, and GA-12,572.

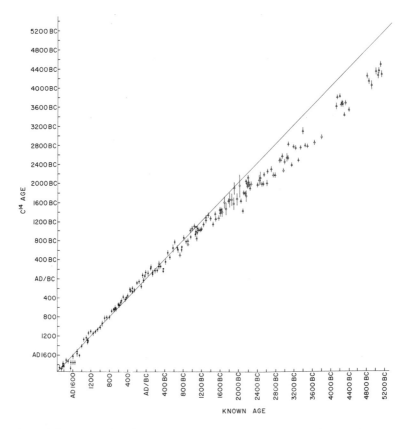

**Fig. 1.1** Carbon-14 dates for all sequoia and bristlecone pine tree-ring samples processed by the Radiocarbon Laboratory at the University of Pennsylvania. Dates for sequoia samples are shown as solid dots. Bristlecone pine samples are represented by open symbols—triangles for those counted at the University of Pennsylvania, and circles for the ten samples counted by Isotopes, Inc. Carbon-14 dates have been calculated with the 5730 half-life and have been corrected for possible isotopic fractionation by means of $C^{13}/C^{12}$ ratios.

extending back another 3000 years, because if these changes in $C^{14}$ inventory were cyclic, it may well be that the atmosphere contained an amount comparable to that of 100 years ago at certain times and that it was depleted at other times. At any rate, it now appears that these changes are due in part to the changes in magnetic intensity* and that

*Parenthetically, it should be noted that in Bucha's Fig. 3.21 (page 94), the scale of the $C^{14}$ deviations has been adjusted arbitrarily to approximate the amplitudes of the changes in magnetic intensity. According to our calculations, based

they have been influenced also by climatic changes, especially by the warming of the oceans since the end of the Wisconsin glacial period.

In regard to the oscillations of shorter duration, more data are required before definite statements can be made. When our data are compared with those of Suess (54) and Damon (55), the other two laboratories that have been dating long series of sequoias and bristle-cone pines (a comparison of over 500 dates in all), the agreement on the average is excellent. However, we do not agree with respect to many of the short-term wriggles that one sees in Fig. 1.1. Naturally, some of the smaller wriggles are due to chance, that is to statistical uncertainty, but some of the more pronounced ones may be shown eventually to correspond with short-term oscillations with periods of hundreds of years or less.

Support for the veracity of the changes in $C^{14}$ inventory as determined from the tree-ring-dated samples has been shown by correlations with varve chronologies, with deep ice cores, and by other more comparative methods of dating, many of which were discussed at Uppsala in August 1969 (40).

If we therefore accept these $C^{14}$ variations in past times as real, we can use the data to obtain correction factors for $C^{14}$ dates. In order to apply them in some meaningful way to the radiocarbon dates obtained from archaeological samples, we have constructed a table that indicates the amount of deviation of $C^{14}$ dates and dendrodates for each sequential 250-year period (except for the first and last two periods which span longer intervals of years), as shown in Table 1.5. An alternative means of presentation is in the form of a calibration curve as advocated by Suess (54). In the table, the $C^{14}$ dates are based on the 5730 half-life. On the basis of deviations shown in column 2, we have adjusted the chronological positions of the radiocarbon dates (in our work sheets) and placed them opposite the spans of dendrodated samples with which they should be correlated in order to obtain a "true" date. Since the increase in the deviations in the B.C. millennia over the more than 3500 years under discussion is not quite linear, the adjustments of the

on a cyclic solution of the equation proposed by Elsasser, Ney, and Winckler (53), the magnetic changes account for only about half of the magnitude of the $C^{14}$ deviations.

Table 1.5 MASCA Correction Factors. Suggested method of adjustment of radiocarbon dates to calendric dates based on the determination of average deviations for 250-year periods in the A.D. and B.C. eras except for the first and last two periods which span longer intervals of years. $C^{14}$ dates are calculated with the 5730 half-life.

| Time Period Represented by Radiocarbon Dates | Average Deviation of $C^{14}$ Dates (+ = younger, − = older) | Calendric Period Represented by Precisely Dated Tree-Ring Samples | Number of Samples |
|---|---|---|---|
| A.D. 1525 — 1879 | + 50 | A.D. 1500 — 1829 (329 years) | 12 |
| A.D. 1250 — 1524 | 0 | A.D. 1250 — 1499 | 7 |
| A.D. 975 — 1249 | 0 | A.D. 1000 — 1249 | 8 |
| A.D. 700 — 974 | − 50 | A.D. 750 — 999 | 4 |
| A.D. 450 — 699 | − 50 | A.D. 500 — 749 | 11 |
| A.D. 200 — 449 | − 50 | A.D. 250 — 499 | 9 |
| 25 B.C. to A.D. 200 | − 50 | A.D. 1 — 249 | 7 |
| 225 B.C. — 26 B.C. | 0 | 249 to 1 B.C. | 7 |
| 450 — 226 B.C. | + 50 | 499 to 250 B.C. | 7 |
| 675 — 451 B.C. | + 50 | 749 to 500 B.C. | 7 |
| 900 — 676 B.C. | +100 | 999 to 750 B.C. | 8 |
| 1125 — 901 B.C. | +100 | 1249 to 1000 B.C. | 10 |
| 1325 — 1126 B.C. | +150 | 1499 to 1250 B.C. | 4 |
| 1550 — 1326 B.C. | +200 | 1749 to 1500 B.C. | 9 |
| 1750 — 1551 B.C. | +200 | 1999 to 1750 B.C. | 6 |
| 1900 — 1751 B.C. | +300 | 2249 to 2000 B.C. | 12 |
| 2050 — 1900 B.C. | +400 | 2499 to 2250 B.C. | 4 |
| 2225 — 2051 B.C. | +500 | 2749 to 2500 B.C. | 6 |
| 2450 — 2226 B.C. | +550 | 2999 to 2750 B.C. | 6 |
| 2650 — 2451 B.C. | +550 | 3249 to 3000 B.C. | 7 |
| 2850 — 2651 B.C. | +650 | 3499 to 3250 B.C. | 5 |
| [3700 — 2951 B.C.] | +700 | [4395 to 3645 B.C.] (750 years) | 11 |
| [4366 — 4060 B.C.] | +750 | [5116 to 4810 B.C.] (306 years) | 9 |
| | | Total | 176 |

positions of the radiocarbon dates sometimes result in overlaps in the chronological sequence. For example, the average deviation from 749 to 500 B.C. is +50 years, and from 999 to 750 B.C. it is +100 years. This results in a 50-year overlap of these two age spans.

Because of the overlaps, further adjustments must be made in positioning the radiocarbon dates in relation to the "true" dates of the tree-ring samples. The distortion of the overlap is minimized when the span of the overlap is equally divided and the halves assigned to adjacent (contiguous) 250-year periods. This final adjustment is indicated in column 1 of Table 1.5. Thus, to determine the adjustment of a $C^{14}$ date for a sample of unknown age, one selects the range into which the radiocarbon date falls in column 1 and applies the correction factor given in column 2. For instance, an archaeological sample from which a radiocarbon date of 2200 B.C. has been obtained falls into the range 2225 to 2051 B.C. (column 1, Table 1.5). To this radiocarbon date the correction factor of 500 years is added to obtain the date of 2700 B.C., which corresponds, on the basis of our findings, to the best estimate for the archaeological date.

In order to test the applicability of our correction factors (which we shall call the MASCA correction factors), we have undertaken a comparative study of Egyptian samples and $C^{14}$ dates, some of the results of which were reported at Uppsala (56) while other tests are still in process. The important confirmation as of now is that when MASCA correction factors are applied to $C^{14}$ dates for short-lived materials such as cloth, reeds, and grains, the agreement between radiocarbon dates and the egyptologists' dating of the early Egyptian dynasties is excellent.

This is only one comparison—others could be and are being made. These indicate, however, that even though we now know that there are problems associated with the radiocarbon calendar, we know more about them, and we are finding precise ways to correct for the discrepancies.

## 1.12

### Laboratory Methods

In this section it is intended to present general descriptions of the various dating methods with adequate references to the specific techniques for those who wish to pursue the subject in more detail.

### 1.12.1
### Solid Carbon

The solid-carbon method, today of historical significance only, is described in detail by Libby (4). He and his co-workers pioneered in the development of this technique, and other laboratories followed it in the early 1950s.

The counting of solid carbon or of other solid carbon compounds has one inherent drawback: self-absorption. The beta disintegrations from $C^{14}$ do not have much energy (150 keV maximum and 50 keV average). Consequently with an infinitely thick layer (8 grams of carbon spread uniformly on the inside of a brass cylinder 7.6 cm in diameter and 20.3 cm long), only 5 percent of the disintegrations were detected. An infinitely thick layer, that is, one so thick that the beta rays from the bottom (the outside of the cylinder) cannot penetrate through the carbon, was at that time the only practical means of obtaining uniformly reproducible layers on a routine basis.

Another disadvantage of solid carbon is that carbon is an excellent absorber, especially when freshly obtained from the reduction of carbon dioxide with magnesium, for instance. In the mid-1950s when there was much fallout from "dirty" atomic bombs, samples frequently became contaminated while exposed to the air during some of the steps necessary in the handling. This contamination could be removed by treatment with concentrated HCl, but one was never sure that the sample had not picked up fallout again during the mounting onto the inner surface of the cylinder.

A minor worry associated with the making of solid carbon was that the rate of reaction of carbon dioxide with magnesium varied from time to time and that it was a reduction rather than an oxidation reaction, in which some samples may have been fractionated isotopically, that is, their original $C^{14}/C^{12}$ ratios altered. This could have been tested by the mass-spectrographic measurements of $C^{14}/C^{12}$ ratios, but it generally was not done at the time. In my opinion, this possible fractionation may account for a few erroneously old $C^{14}$ dates that were obtained with the solid-carbon method.

## 1.12.2

### Gas Counting

Because of these inherent drawbacks and the problem of fallout, several laboratories began to experiment with proportional-gas counting techniques. Success with these was reported at the radiocarbon dating conference in Cambridge, England, in 1955 and again in Andover, Massachusetts, in 1956, after which date most laboratories decided to change over to the proportional counting of carbon dioxide ($CO_2$), methane ($CH_4$), or acetylene ($C_2H_2$), while a few others went to scintillation counting.

The majority of laboratories now count samples as <u>pure</u> carbon dioxide. "Pure" is emphasized because $CO_2$ is a good counting gas only if it is free of electronegative impurities such as halogens, oxygen, oxides of nitrogen and sulphur, and water vapor. The techniques of purification and counting were worked out independently and almost simultaneously by deVries and Barendsen in the Netherlands (57) and by Rafter in New Zealand (58), and very shortly thereafter by Brannon et al. in the United States (59). More recently, Srdoč and Sliepcevič have also discussed the effects of electronegative impurities and means for their removal (60). For all methods, the samples are first converted to $CO_2$ by burning in the case of organic, and by acidification for inorganic materials.

Diagrams of the $CO_2$ combustion and purification system used in our laboratory are shown in Figs. 1.2 and 1.3, and a photograph of it, in Fig. 1.4. For the reader who is not concerned with the details, the essence of the system is that the sample is burned or acidified in the upper left-hand corner of Fig. 1.2, and all of the rest of the stages and traps are for removal of electronegative and radioactive impurities.

As for the details, let us proceed more or less from left to right in Fig. 1.2. Inorganic samples are placed in flask A and covered with distilled water. From the separatory funnel above (with sintered stick attached), a solution of 50 percent $H_3PO_4$ is added until all $CO_2$ is evolved. For samples that do not dissolve readily in $H_3PO_4$, 3N HCl may be substituted.

Organic samples are placed in a Vycor combustion tube, oxygen is passed through, and the sample is ignited with a torch. Burning then

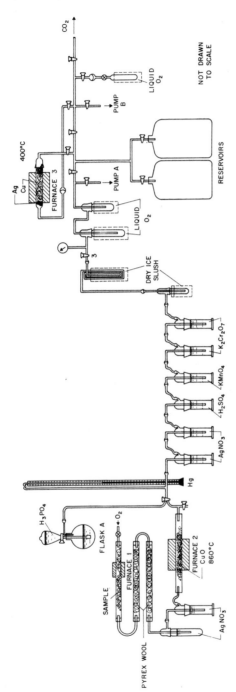

**Fig. 1.2** Block diagram of University of Pennsylvania carbon dioxide combustion and purification train. Section 1.

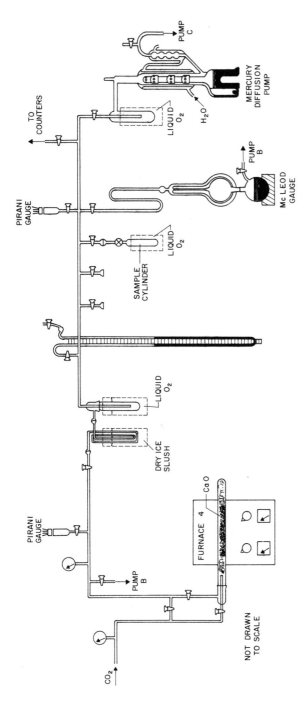

**Fig. 1.3** Block diagram of University of Pennsylvania carbon dioxide combustion and purification train. Section 2.

**Fig. 1.4** University of Pennsylvania carbon dioxide combustion and purification train.

proceeds with the aid of a small electric furnace (no. 1) which is moved from right to left as combustion proceeds. (For both types of samples the pressure is adjusted to approximately 1/2 atmosphere by means of a stopcock [no. 3] in the line between the reaction and rough pump A at the right-hand side of the figure.)

The $CO_2$ and other gases then go through the following stages, mostly for the removal of electronegative impurities:

1. Tubes filled with Pyrex wool for the trapping of tars.

2. Two traps filled with 0.1N $AgNO_3$ for the removal of chlorides and other halides. (Halides are strongly electronegative and must be reduced to less than one-tenth part per million.)

3. Vycor tube with CuO at 860° C to ensure the complete oxidation of carbon, sulphur, and other oxides.

4. Two additional traps with 0.1N $AgNO_3$ (250 ml Drechsel gas washing bottles).

5. Trap filled with 25-percent (by volume) $H_2SO_4$. The function of this solution is uncertain, but it seems to help in the purification process.

6. 250-ml trap filled to 2/3 capacity with 1 g $KMnO_4$ dissolved in 2-percent solution of $H_2SO_4$ for oxidization and removal of $SO_2$ and possible removal of other oxides.

7. Trap with solution consisting of 100 g $K_2Cr_2O_7$ in 2000 ml $H_2SO_4$ (this is prepared in advance and filtered) for removal of remaining sulphur oxides and possibly other electronegative impurities.

8. Standard trap and spiral trap surrounded with dewars containing a slurry of dry ice in equal parts of $CHCl_3$ and $CCl_4$.

9. Two traps surrounded with dewars containing liquid $O_2$ for the collection of $CO_2$. (Liquid air may be substituted for liquid $O_2$, but we have found that liquid $N_2$ is just enough colder to trap some $O_2$. The excess $O_2$, pulled through the traps by means of pump A, is also electronegative.)

10. When combustion or evolution of the $CO_2$ is completed, the stopcock to the left of the $CO_2$ traps is closed, and the remaining excess $O_2$, air, and other possible non-condensible gases are pumped off.

11. The liquid-$O_2$ dewars are then removed and the $CO_2$ passes through the Vycor tube surrounded by furnace no. 3. This tube contains thin strips of Cu foil at 400° C with Ag wool in the tube at each end of the furnace at a somewhat lower temperature. The function of the Cu is to reduce oxides of nitrogen so that when the $CO_2$ has again been frozen in the next trap (the last one on the right in Fig. 1.2) the $N_2$ and $O_2$ can be pumped off. The purpose of the Ag wool is to trap any $Cl_2$ that may have come this far.

12. At this stage (or before the Cu, if necessary), the $CO_2$ may be stored in one of the reservoirs (each of which is a wide-necked glass

bottle with a capacity of 5 gals). The pressure reading of the $CO_2$ in the reservoir serves also to give a measure of how much $CO_2$ has been collected.

After these steps, the $CO_2$ should be free of electronegative impurities. However, this is not always the case. Therefore, the next reaction is necessary both to remove the last traces of electronegative impurities and to remove radon. Radon is one of the decay products of uranium and thorium, traces of which may have been present in the soils or sediments mixed with the sample. We pass now from Fig. 1.2 to Fig. 1.3.

13. This final step, the slowest stage in the purification process, is the reaction of the $CO_2$ with 14- to 20-mesh CaO contained in a quartz tube and heated with furnace 4. At 725° to 750° C the $CO_2$ reacts with the CaO to form $CaCO_3$. The quartz tube is then cooled below the reaction temperature (400° C or less) and the impurities pumped off, first with rough pump B and finally with the mercury-diffusion pump (shown on right-hand side of Fig. 1.3) until a vacuum of 1 micron torr or less is attained. The quartz tube is then heated above the reaction temperature (825° to 850° C), the $CO_2$ is evolved, passes through another spiral trap surrounded with dry-ice slush for removal of water vapor, and is frozen once more in the adjacent glass trap. It is then pumped again, after which the $CO_2$ sublimes and is finally frozen into a stainless steel sample cylinder which has been evacuated previously.

An alternative procedure for radon removal, namely the slow condensation of $CO_2$ with stirring and pumping off a small amount of $CO_2$, has been described by deVries (61). This method is faster than the CaO reaction but requires more skill and does not help in removing the last traces of electronegative impurities.

In most laboratories it has been found that, no matter which system of radon removal has been employed, a small amount frequently remains. Fortunately, the half-life of radon is short (3.82 days) compared with $C^{14}$, so that if the samples are stored for two weeks before counting, this trace will have decayed below the limit of detection. This means, however, that at least three weeks and usually more in elapsed time are required to obtain a $C^{14}$ date from start to finish.

Some laboratories use methane as the counting gas, and a few others acetylene. Both of these are "better" gases than carbon dioxide; that is, they are much less sensitive to electronegative impurities, and counters have lower operating voltages in the proportional region. However, these gases are slightly more difficult and more hazardous to make. In the process, again, the sample is burned or acidified to make $CO_2$ which is then passed through traps surrounded with dry-ice mixtures for the removal of water vapor. Some laboratories purify the $CO_2$ additionally, using some of the preliminary steps of either the carbon dioxide or solid-carbon methods. The semipure $CO_2$ is then reacted with hydrogen over a heated ($375°$ C) ruthenium catalyst as follows (62, 63):

$$CO_2 + 4H_2 \overset{Ru}{\rightleftarrows} CH_4 + 2H_2O.$$

By trapping out the water as it is formed, the reaction goes in the right direction. Complete circulation is achieved either by pumping (62) or by rotation of the reaction flask (63). The methane is collected in a trap surrounded with liquid nitrogen. The last traces of methane are purified and separated from excess hydrogen in a charcoal trap.

Recently, some laboratories have experienced difficulty in obtaining hydrogen that is free of tritium and have had to manufacture their own from deep-well water (64).

The making of acetylene has been described by Suess (65) and by Barker (66). In the method of Suess, the following steps are involved:
1. Organic matter (wood, peat, etc.) $+ O_2 \rightarrow CO_2$.
$\qquad$ Carbonate (shells) $+ HCl \rightarrow CO_2$.
2. $CO_2 + 2NH_4OH \rightarrow CO_3(NH_4)_2 + H_2O$.
3. $CO_3(NH_4)_2 + SrCl_2 \rightarrow SrCO_3 + 2NH_4Cl$.
4. $2SrCO_3 + 5Mg \rightarrow SrC_2 + 5MgO + SrO$.
5. $SrC_2 + 2H_2O \rightarrow C_2H_2 + Sr(OH)_2$.
Steps 1 and 2 are carried out in essentially the manner described by Libby (5) but using one-third to one-half of the quantities. Instead of calcium chloride, strontium chloride is used in step 3 to precipitate the carbonate. Barium chloride can be used equally well, but preference was given to strontium chloride because of the possibility of a high radium content in commercial barium chloride.

Strontium carbonate after being washed and dried can be directly reduced with an excess of magnesium powder (80 mesh) to strontium carbide. If enough material is available, a mixture of 30 g of $SrCO_3$ to 35 g of magnesium is used, yielding about 2.2 liters STP of $C_2H_2$, corresponding to a yield of 90 to 100 percent. The reaction is carried out inside an evacuated stainless steel tube (2.8 by 38 cm) connected directly to a vacuum line through an O-ring seal. The mixture is ignited from the outside with a torch, and the reaction is completed in less than 5 minutes. The reaction product is then dumped into about 1 liter of water inside an evacuated system. The gases formed are dried by passing them through a trap cooled by an acetone mixture and a Drierite column. The acetylene is condensed in a liquid-nitrogen trap, and hydrogen, some of which also forms, is pumped off intermittently. After purification by passing over cooled charcoal, the acetylene is stored for 2 to 3 weeks to permit the decay of the few hundred radon atoms that are sometimes present in the gas sample.

The method of Barker (66) differs mainly in that it uses lithium instead of strontium.

The perfection of the chemical purification of carbon dioxide and the making of methane and acetylene on routine bases were interrelated with the development of better proportional-counting techniques. In most laboratories, chemists and physicists were collaborating closely to achieve this success. Especially notable was the joint work of Fergusson and Rafter in New Zealand. One of the most flexible and complete systems of electronic components was assembled by Fergusson (67), all or part of which has been copied by many other laboratories and commercial firms. The system in use at the University of Pennsylvania was modeled after his and is shown in the block diagram of Fig. 1.5.

Let us start with the $CO_2$ counter shown in Fig. 1.6. It can be made of uncontaminated metal such as copper, but even lower backgrounds have been obtained with quartz (68). The outline of one of the University of Pennsylvania counters, similar to Fergusson's, can be seen also in Fig. 1.5. It is a large copper cylinder with tapered ends into which large pyrex insulators with metallized bands are positioned by soldering. At each end, a 4-mil tungsten wire is attached to a 3-mm nickel rod which extends inside the counter about 2.5 cm beyond the Pyrex insulator in order to eliminate end effects. (All joints are sealed additionally with

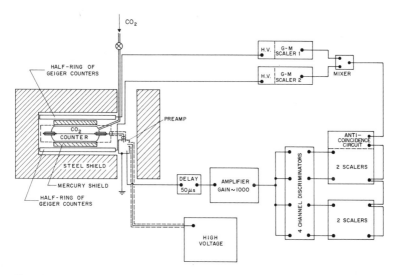

**Fig. 1.5** Block diagram of University of Pennsylvania carbon dioxide counting equipment.

**Fig. 1.6** University of Pennsylvania carbon dioxide counter and surrounding cosmic-ray counters. Steel bricks such as those painted black and white on right-hand side have been removed.

araldite.) Thus, the effective volume of the counter is considerably less than the total volume of 8 liters.

The $CO_2$ counter is surrounded with an annular ring of mercury contained between the double walls of a welded steel cylinder, which in turn is surrounded by the ring of cosmic-ray counters consisting of 30 counters 3 cm in diameter and 1 m long. These components plus a preamplifier are encased in a 20.3-cm shield of steel on all sides. (The addition of 15 cm of boron mixed with paraffin within the steel shield with additional steel on top around our second counter produced negligible reduction in background.)

The $CO_2$ counter is supplied with a well-regulated high-voltage supply. The preamplifier is actually just a cathode follower with a gain of slightly less than 1. Pulses are then delayed 50 microseconds by a series of coils with capacitors in parallel between each, to prevent their arrival prior to coincident pulses from the cosmic-ray geiger counters. The pulses are amplified, roughly X 1000, and are fed in parallel to the 4 channels of the discriminator unit. They are then counted on 4 separate scalers.

The anticoincidence geiger ring is divided in half (to reduce input capacitance), and each half is equipped with separate high-voltage supplies and scalers. Within the scalers, the pulses are inverted and slightly amplified. They are then mixed and fed to the anticoincidence circuit. The output of this is fed to three of the $CO_2$ scalers. Therefore, whenever one or more of the geigers is activated, the anticoincidence circuit blocks the input to the three $CO_2$ scalers; in this way most of the background due to mesons and other external sources of high energy is eliminated. This is the most effective part of the shielding. The fourth channel (without anticoincidence) is used to monitor all $CO_2$ counts. The $CO_2$ counter itself provides a very sensitive detector of possible external background variations. Background rates are determined with the $CO_2$ counter filled with anthracite coal and are roughly as follows:

|  | counts/minute |
|---|---|
| Unshielded counter (in basement with four stories above) | 1500 |
| Counter within Fe and Hg Shield | 400 |
| Counter within Fe and Hg Shield (with anticoincidence geigers activated) | 8 |

The 4-channel discriminator unit provides a flexible system of selection of pulse heights from the $CO_2$ counter. After various experiments, we now set channel 1 at 70 volts and therefore record on scaler 1 only the high-energy pulses with the thought that possible alpha-emitting contaminations, including radon, would be readily detected. For normal operation, channels 2, 3, and 4 are set at 5 volts. However, for each fresh sample introduced into the counter, channel 3 is set at 30 volts and counts versus increasing counter voltages (without anticoincidence) are recorded. The two curves shown in Fig. 1.7 provide a sensitive electronic check of possible electronegative impurities. If the crossover point moves up and the counting rates of pulses between 5 and 30 volts are low, the $CO_2$ is impure. Normally, high voltage changes of 10 volts or less can be tolerated. Depending upon the severity of the impurity, the $CO_2$ is either recycled through the whole purification train or through the copper and calcium oxide steps only.

In addition to the $CO_2$ scalers, many laboratories now use recorders. If readings are recorded every 100 minutes, any departure from normal counting statistics can be readily detected and discarded.

The over-all efficiency of any given counting system is frequently called its figure of merit and is equal to the ratio of the sample counting rate squared to the background counting rate B, that is, $S^2/B$, where S is the net zero-age counting rate. For our counters, S = 32 c/m, B = 8 c/m, and the figure of merit is 128. This corresponds to a limit of detection of 40,000 years. In comparison, the figure of merit for solid-carbon counting was 11, and the age limit less than 20,000 years.

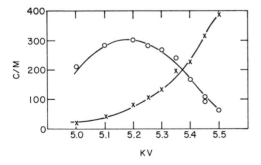

Fig. 1.7 Carbon dioxide counter curves. Curve with open circles represents pulses between 5 and 30 volts; with x's, pulses greater than 30 volts.

## 1.12.3

### Liquid Scintillation Techniques

A few laboratories have experimented also with liquid scintillation techniques. Scintillation counters, in a coincidence arrangement, allow the effective use of large samples and make it possible to achieve a figure of merit equal to or greater than gas-proportional counting. However, the chemistry is very much more complicated.

One of the earliest attempts was made by Arnold (69) with PPO and DPHT in toluene as the phosphor. He demonstrated with various proportions of natural $C^{14}$ in ethanol as a diluent to the phosphor that this technique could be used to a limit of 34,000 years (based on a limit in counting detection of 4 sigma).

Pringle, Turchinetz, and Funt (70) experimented with methanol as a diluent and also with incorporating the natural $C^{14}$ of the sample into the alkyl group of toluene. The latter had the advantage of not reducing the efficiency of the phosphor, but the chemistry was more involved. With this technique the age range could be extended to at least 45,000 years.

Later, it was found that methyl borate, a compound a bit more difficult to make than methanol, could be used as a diluent without seriously affecting the efficiency of fluorescence (71). This provided a slightly more practical system of liquid scintillation counting for routine dating.

Recently, significant advances have been made in the making of benzene (72-75), which has the advantage of having 6 carbon atoms per molecule, each of which with its complement of natural $C^{14}$, as well as being a good solvent for liquid scintillation counting. With the availability of improved catalysts for the conversion of acetylene to benzene, several laboratories have adopted this method, and it may soon become the choice of new laboratories. The technique of Kim et al. (75) employs a vanadium-alumina catalyst for the conversion of acetylene to benzene; they reported the achievement of purities exceeding 99.9 percent in the synthesis of benzene. The use of a catalyst that does not require activation in the $C^{14}$ laboratory was reported by Barker (76).

There are other advantages to liquid scintillation counting. One is that the counting equipment is readily available commercially and is usually semiautomated. For the counting, therefore, manpower requirements are much lower than with gases, and one can change from unknown sample to calibration or to background sample with a simple flip of a switch.

## References

1. Grosse, A. V.,
"An Unknown Radioactivity." Journal of the American Chemical Society 56 (1934): 1922-1923.
2. Anderson, E. C., Libby, W. F., Weinhouse, S., Reid, A. F., Kirshenbaum, A. D., and Grosse, A. V.,
"Natural Radiocarbon from Cosmic Radiation." The Physical Review 72 (1947): 931-936.
3. Libby, W. F.,
"Radioactivity of Neodymium and Samarium." The Physical Review 46 (1934): 196-204.
4. Libby, W. F.,
Radiocarbon Dating (The University of Chicago Press, 1955, 2nd ed.): pp. 43-75.
5. Arnold, J. R., and Libby, W. F.,
"Age Determinations by Radiocarbon Content: Checks with Samples of Known Age." Science 110 (1949): 678-680.
6. Anderson, E. C., and Libby, W. F.,
"World-wide Distribution of Natural Radiocarbon." The Physical Review 81 (1951): 64-69.
7. Karlén, I., Olsson, I. U., Kallberg, P., and Kilicci, S.,
"Absolute Determination of the Activity of Two $C^{14}$ Dating Standards." Arkiv Geofysik 6 (1966): 465-471.
8. Engelkemeir, A. G., Hamill, W. H., Inghram, M. G., and Libby, W. F.
"The Half-Life of Radiocarbon ($C^{14}$)." The Physical Review 12 (1949): 1825-1833.
9. Jones, W. M.,
"A Determination of the Half-Life of Carbon 14." The Physical Review 76 (1949): 885-889.
10. Miller, W. W., Ballentine, R., Bernstein, W., Friedman, L., Nier, A. O., and Evans, R. D.,
"The Half-Life of Carbon Fourteen and a Comparison of Gas Phase Counter Methods." The Physical Review 77 (1950): 714-175.
11. Engelkemeir, A. G., and Libby, W. F.,
"End and Wall Corrections for Absolute Beta-Counting in Gas Counters." The Review of Scientific Instruments 21 (1950): 550-554.

12. Hawkings, R. C., Hunter, R. F., Mann, W. B., and Stevens, W. H., "The Half-Life of $C^{14}$." The Physical Review 74 (1948): 696.

13. Godwin, H., "Half-Life of Radiocarbon," Nature 195 (1962): 984.

14. Ralph, E. K., "Review of Radiocarbon Dates from Tikal and the Maya Calendar Correlation Problem." American Antiquity 30 (1965): 421-427.

15. Stuckenrath, R., Jr., "University of Pennsylvania Radiocarbon Dates VI." Radiocarbon 5 (1963): 82.

16. Ralph, E. K., and Ackerman, R. E., "University of Pennsylvania Radiocarbon Dates IV." Radiocarbon 3 (1961): 11.

17. Ralph, E. K., "University of Pennsylvania Radiocarbon Dates III." American Journal of Science Radiocarbon Supplement 1 (1959): 54-56.

18. Olson, E. A., and Broecker, W. S., "Sample Contamination and Reliability of Radiocarbon Dates." Transactions of the New York Academy of Sciences Section of Geology and Mineralogy, Ser. 2 20 (1957-1958): 595, Table 1.

19. Berger, R., Horney, A. G., and Libby, W. F., "Radiocarbon Dating of Bone and Shell from Their Organic Components." Science 144 (1964): 999-1001.

20. Krueger, H. W., "The Preservation and Dating of Collagen in Ancient Bones." Proceedings of the Sixth International Conference Radiocarbon and Tritium Dating held at Washington State University, Pullman, Washington, June 7-11, 1965 [CONF-650652 Chemistry (TID-4500)] : 332-337.

21. Haynes, C. V., "Bone Organic Matter and Radiocarbon Dating." Radioactive Dating and Methods of Low-Level Counting (International Atomic Energy Agency, Vienna, 1967) pp. 163-168.

22. Rubin, M., Likins, R. C., and Berry, E. G., "On the Validity of Radiocarbon Dates from Snail Shells." The Journal of Geology 71 (1963): 84-89.

23. Rafter, T. A., "$^{14}$C Variations in Nature and the Effect on Radiocarbon Dating." New Zealand Journal of Science and Technology, Section B 37 (1955): 20-38.

24. Olson and Broecker (Reference 18): 596, Table 2.

25. Deevey, E. S., Gross, M. S., Hutchinson, G. E., and Kraybill, H. L. "The Natural $C^{14}$ Contents of Materials from Hard-Water Lakes." National Academy of Science Proceedings 40 (1954): 285-288.

26. Stuiver, M., "Long-Term $C^{14}$ Variations." (Reference 40)

27. Eriksson, K. G., and Olsson, I. U., "Some Problems in Connection with $C^{14}$ Dating of Tests of Foraminifera." Bulletin of the Geological Institutions of the University of Uppsala 42 (1963): 1-13.

28. Olsson, I. U., and Eriksson, K. G., "Remarks on $C^{14}$ Dating of Shell Material in Sea Sediments." Progress in Oceanography 3 (Pergamon Press, 1965): 253-266.

29. Olssòn, I. U., Göksu, Y., and Stenberg, A., "Further Investigations of Storing and Treatment of Foraminifera and Mollusks for $C^{14}$ Dating." Geologiska Föreningens: Stockholm Förhandlingar 90 (1968): 417-426.

30. Stuckenrath (Reference 15): 99-102.

31. Taylor, R. E., and Berger, R., "Radiocarbon Dating of the Organic Portion of Ceramic and Wattle-and-Daub House Construction Materials of Low Carbon Content." American Antiquity 33 (1968): 363-366.

32. Van der Merwe, N. J., The Carbon-14 Dating of Iron. (University of Chicago Press, 1969): pp. 3-137.

33. Haynes, C. V., Jr., "Radiocarbon Samples: Chemical Removal of Plant Contaminants." Science 151 (1966): 1391-1392.

34. Wilson, A. T., Personal Communication (October 18, 1968). Victoria University, Wellington, N.Z.

35. Satterthwaite, L., and Ralph, E. K., "New Radiocarbon Dates and the Maya Correlation Problem." American Antiquity 26 (1960): 165-184.

36. Segrè, E., Editor, Experimental Nuclear Physics 3 (John Wiley & Sons, New York, 1959): p. 32.

37. Craig, H., "Carbon 13 in Plants and the Relationships between Carbon 13 and Carbon 14 Variations in Nature." The Journal of Geology 62 (1954): 115-149.

**38. Craig, H.,**
"Mass-Spectrometer Analyses of Radiocarbon Standards." Radiocarbon 3 (1961): 1-3.

**39. Flint, R. F., and Deevey, E. S.,**
Editorial Statement, Radiocarbon 3 (1961): Preface.

**40. Olsson, I. U. (Editor),**
"Radiocarbon Variations and Absolute Chronology." Proceedings of the Twelfth Nobel Symposium, Uppsala, Sweden, August 11-15, 1969. Almquist and Wiksell, Stockholm (Wiley Interscience Division, John Wiley & Sons, New York, 1970).

**41. Ralph, E. K. and Michael, H. N.,**
"Problems of the Radiocarbon Calendar." Archaeometry 10 (1967): 3-11.

**42. Lal, D., and Rama,**
"Characteristics of Global Tropospheric Mixing Based on Man-Made $C^{14}$, $H^3$, and $Sr^{90}$." Journal of Geophysical Research 71 (1966): 2865-2874.

**43. Tauber, H.,**
"Copenhagen Radiocarbon Measurements VIII, Geographic Variations in Atmospheric $C^{14}$ Activity." Radiocarbon 9: (1967): 246-256.

**44. Haugen, R. K.,**
"Tree Ring Indices: A Circumpolar Comparison." Science 158 (1967): 773-775.

**45. Heymann, D., and Schaeffer, O. A.,**
"Constancy of Cosmic Rays in Time." Physica 28 (1962): 1318-1323.

**46. Crèvecoeur, E.,**
"Détermination de la constance du rayonnement cosmique et des âges terrestres et cosmiques des météorites ferreuses par la radioactivité de l'aluminium 26 et du béryllium 10." Bulletin Classe Science Académie Royale Belgique Ser. 5, 52 (1966): 261-275.

**47. Fireman, E. L., and Goebel, R.,**
"Argon 37 and Argon 39 in Recently Fallen Meteorites and Cosmic-Ray Variations." Journal of Geophysical Research 75 (1970): 2115-2124.

**48. Sullivan, W.,**
"Meteorite is Traced to Asteroid Belt." New York Times (January 21, 1970).

**49. Link, F.,**
Variation de l'activité solaire et de la production de C-14 par les rayons cosmiques." Bulletin Classe Science Académie Royale Belgique, Ser. 5, 52 (1966): 486-489.

50. Bray, J. R.,
"Variation in Atmospheric Carbon-14 Activity Relative to a Sunspot-Auroral Solar Index," Science 156 (1967): 640-642.

51. Stuiver, M.,
"Variations in Radiocarbon Concentration and Sunspot Activity."
Journal of Geophysical Research 66 (1961): 273-276.

52. Houtermans, J., Suess, H. E., and Munk, W.,
"Effect of Industrial Fuel Combustion on the Carbon-14 Level of Atmospheric $CO_2$." Radioactive Dating and Method of Low-Level Counting. (International Atomic Energy Agency, Vienna, 1967): 57-68.

53. Elsasser, W., Ney, E. P., and Winckler, J. R.,
"Cosmic-Ray Intensity and Geomagnetism." Nature 178 (1956): 1226-1227.

54. Suess, H. E.,
"Bristlecone Pine Calibration of the Radiocarbon Time Scale 5200 B.C. to the Present." (Reference 40).

55. Damon, P. E.,
"Climatic versus Magnetic Perturbation of the Atmospheric Carbon-14 Reservoir." (Reference 40).

56. Michael, H. N., and Ralph, E. K.,
"Correction Factors Applied to Egyptian Radiocarbon Dates from the B.C. Era." (Reference 40).

57. DeVries, Hl., and Barendsen, G. W.,
"Radio-Carbon Dating by a Proportional Counter Filled with Carbon Dioxide." Physica 19 (1953): 987-1003.

58. Rafter, T. A.,
"Carbon Dioxide as a Substitute for Solid Carbon in $^{14}$C Age Measurements." New Zealand Journal of Science and Technology, Section B, 36 (1955): 363-370.

59. Brannon, H. R., Taggart, M. S., Jr., and Williams, M.,
"Proportional Counting of Carbon Dioxide for Radiocarbon Dating."
Review of Scientific Instruments 26 (1955): 269-273.

60. Srdoc, D., and Sliepcevic, A.,
"Carbon Dioxide Proportional Counters: Effects of Gaseous Impurities and Gas Purification Methods." International Journal of Applied Radiation and Isotopes 14 (1963): 481-488.

61. DeVries, Hl.,
"The Removal of Radon from $CO_2$ for Use in $^{14}$C Age Measurements."
Applied Science Research, Section B, 6 (1957): 461-470.

62. Burke, W. H., Jr., and Meinschein, W. G.,
"$C^{14}$ Dating with a Methane Proportional Counter." The Review of Scientific Instruments 26 (1955): 1137-1140.

**63. Fairhall, A. W., Schell, W. R., and Takashima, Y.,**
"Apparatus for Methane Synthesis for Radiocarbon Dating." The Review of Scientific Instruments 32 (1961): 323-325.
**64. Stuckenrath, R., Jr.**
Personal Communication.
**65. Suess, H. E.,**
"Natural Radiocarbon Measurements by Acetylene Counting." Science 120 (1954): 5-7.
**66. Barker, H.,**
"Radiocarbon Dating: Large-scale Preparation of Acetylene from Organic Material." Nature 172 (1953): 361-362.
**67. Fergusson, G. J.,**
"Radiocarbon Dating System." Nucleonics 13 (1955): 18-23.
**68. DeVries, Hl., Stuiver, M., and Olsson, I.,**
"A Proportional Counter for Low Level Counting with High Efficiency," Nuclear Instruments and Methods 5 (1959): 111-114.
**69. Arnold, J. R.,**
"Scintillation Counting of Natural Radiocarbon: I. The Counting Method." Science 119 (1954): 155-157.
**70. Pringle, R. W., Turchinetz, W., and Funt, B. L.,**
"Liquid Scintillation Techniques for Radiocarbon Dating." The Review of Scientific Instruments 26 (1955): 859-865.
**71. Pringle, R. W., Turchinetz, W., Funt, B. L., and Danyluk, S. S.,**
"Radiocarbon Age Estimates Obtained by an Improved Liquid Scintillation Technique." Science 125 (1957): 69-70.
**72. Polach, H. A., and Stipp, J. J.,**
"Improved Synthesis Techniques for Methane and Benzene Radiocarbon Dating." International Journal of Applied Radiation and Isotopes 18 (1967): 359-364.
**73. Noakes, J. E., Kim, S. M., and Stipp, J. J.,**
"Chemical and Counting Advances in Liquid Scintillation Age Dating." 6th International Conference on Radiocarbon and Tritium Dating Proceedings, U.S. Atomic Energy Commission CONF-650652 (1965): 68-92.
**74. Noakes, J. E., Kim, S. M., and Akers, L. K.,**
"Recent Improvement in Benzene Chemistry for Radiocarbon Dating." Geochim. et Cosmochim. Acta 31 (1967): 1094-1096.
**75. Kim, S. M., Ruch, R. R., and Kempton, J. P.,**
"Radiocarbon Dating at the Illinois State Geological Survey." Environmental Geology Notes (Illinois State Geological Survey) no. 28 (October 1969): 1-19.
**76. Barker, H.**
Personal communication.

**Climates, Tree Rings,**    Henry N. Michael
**and Archaeology**

## 2.1

### Introduction

The history of dendrochronology is well known to field workers who
are interested in dating methods; it will therefore suffice to review the
pertinent points but very briefly.

Douglass (1, 2) studied tree rings initially with the hope of correlating
sunspots and climatic behavior with tree-ring growth. Almost naturally
this led to a precise dating process that was eventually extended by
him, his collaborators and successors to the present-day limit of approximately 7400 years (3, 4). One of the major applications of dendrochronology has been the dating of structures containing the appropriate
kinds of wood (not all lend themselves to tree-ring dating), particularly
in the pueblos in the Southwest of the United States (5). Indian claims
based on the age of fence posts have been resolved through dendrochronology (6). In all cases the resolution is brought about by the cross-
indexing, that is, the correlation of plotted (measured) tree rings present in a cross-section of a piece of structural lumber (in the case of the
pueblos) with other such pieces and also with plotted sections of trees
that contain corresponding tree rings.

In order to provide reliable data, the series of tree rings must contain
a signature, that is, sequential arrangements of wide and narrow rings
forming patterns that are readily recognizable in all the series to be
correlated.

In this manner, through a series of overlapping plottings of tree rings,
one may carry the dating through to the present (Fig. 2.1). Of course, if
the rings are "complacent," that is, if there is little or no variation in
the widths of individual rings in the entire series, then no correlation
can be effected.

Both of the conditions—signatures and complacent runs—occur in
certain ecological settings. A sensitive run of rings, that is, one with
signatures, is more likely to develop if the tree grows on a well-drained
slope, in relatively shallow soil (with underlying rock). Such conditions
will readily reflect in the growth of annual rings: if soil moisture is
plentiful, a wide ring will grow; if it is deficient, a narrow one will form.
In years of extreme dryness a ring may not form at all. Obversely, if the
ecology is such that the tree is supplied with constant amounts of water

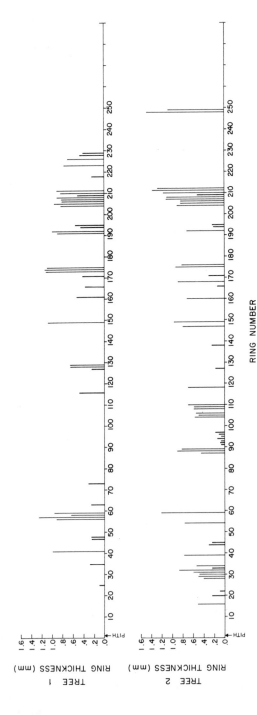

**Fig. 2.1** A comparison of skeleton graphs of two trees. While not all rings or signatures match, the significantly positioned ones do. For better visual comparison, rings that are relatively narrow in a run of complacent or wide ones, are drawn with a thick line. Rings that are comparatively wide among complacent or narrow rings are drawn with a thin line. The lengths of the lines are proportional to the widths of the tree rings.

throughout its growing seasons, then ring after ring will grow to approximately the same width—a result which we have called "complacent."

## 2.2
### Long-Lived Trees

It is an interesting fact that the major roles in the formulation of tree-ring chronology were played by two thoroughly different types of trees—the giant sequoia (Sequoia gigantea), one of the two surviving species of the family Taxodiaceae which flourished during the Tertiary period, and several trees of the genus Pinus, among them most prominently the bristlecone pine (Pinus aristata).

The west-facing or windward slopes of the southern Sierra Nevada of California receive considerable precipitation, thus creating conditions favorable to the survival of the giant mountain sequoia. This tree will be found in fairly extensive groves at elevations of 5000 to 7000 feet (1520 to 2130 m), although smaller groves and individual trees are encountered at much higher elevations. Among these trees are some that have withstood the assaults of age, fire, and insects for more than 3000 years and at the same time, because of an ecological environment more severe than that for the average tree (on ridges or well-drained slopes) have grown a sensitive sequence of rings thus forming many signatures through which they may be correlated so that a precise chronology can be determined.

Despite its long life, the sequoia could not be used for archaeological dating simply because it was not associated with archaeological sites. Aside from being a guide to local climatological events, it only came into its own as a dating medium a few years ago when it was used to check on the accuracy of radiocarbon dates (see chapter 1).

In standard encyclopedias there is no mention of the bristlecone pine as being one of the 33 major species of pines in the United States. And, from a commercial point of view, this tree is indeed of little significance. Yet, in the early 1950s, the very great age of the bristlecone pine was recognized, and a chronology that spanned more than seven millennia has now been established.

The reason for the long survival of some of the bristlecone pines is tied to its ecological setting, as in the case of the giant sequoias. The oldest bristlecone pines are found to be surviving in extremes of natural conditions, at elevations of 9000 to 11,000 feet (2740 to 3350 m) and even higher. The oldest trees appear to grow in the Inyo Range of southeastern California. The very short growing season of only a few weeks, the continual danger of frost even during this short period, the severe winters with high winds, the thinness of the mountain soils, all contribute to the extinction of all but the hardiest specimens. Only about 100 trees older than 4000 years are known. Even after death, these scraggly trees continue to favor the dendrochronologist. Because of their high resinous content (about 30 percent), they do not rot easily, and even after having fallen to the forest floor (after standing for perhaps several hundreds of years as snags) they remain there for many thousands of years until they are eroded by the blasting effect of wind-driven, frozen snow. It is from cross-indexing these "dead and down" snags that we get the oldest segments of the 7400-year chronology; samples of these have been used to test the inconsistencies of radio-carbon dates and to establish correction factors for the inconsistencies.

## 2.3
### Application

Some of the less-known achievements of the dendrochronological method are the 800-year "floating" chronology established by analysis of the rings in cross sections of beams reinforcing the tomb of King Midas' father near Gordion in Turkey (7), and by the work of Kolchin in dating the successive stages in the development of the ancient city of Novgorod in northern European Russia (8). In the latter, it was the succession of corduroy streets buried in the boggy soil—up to twenty-eight layers of streets—that enabled the establishment of a precise chronology spanning approximately 1200 years (Fig. 2.2).

## 2.4
### Development of Chronology

As mentioned before, a series of tree rings was examined and cross-indexed and eventually extended into a run of several hundred years in the form of a "master log" by Douglass. Apparently he was also first to average tree-ring growth of several trees found over a wide area and to suceed in correlating several such areas in the United States South-

**Fig. 2.2** Sectional view of 28 corduroy street levels in the ancient Russian city of Novgorod. The street levels were preserved as they slowly sank into the boggy soil several years after they were laid down. (After Kolchin.)

west (9). Eventually the record of the giant mountain sequoias was resolved through tree-ring growth standardization and was extended to 1306 B.C. (10). Parenthetically, this achievement was important in initiating the subsequent comparative studies of dendrochronological and radiocarbon dates.

After Douglass' retirement, Edmund Schulman continued the work and by 1956 became aware of a species of pine which exceeded the giant sequoias in age (11). This was of course the bristlecone pine.

Before his untimely death in 1958, Schulman succeeded in extending the precise chronology of the bristlecone pine to only 700 B.C. It was at about this time that several laboratories became interested in comparative studies of dendrochronological and radiocarbon dates, spurred on by the initial study of deVries, who, after analyzing North American tree-ring samples, noted significant oscillations between tree-ring dates and radiocarbon dates (12). It was logical to start with sequoias, since Schulman's death caused a delay in the analyses of bristlecone pines. However, since 1960 the collecting and analyses of the latter have been vigorously pursued by C. W. Ferguson and his associates, and precisely dated samples were made available to the three laboratories (Arizona, La Jolla, and Pennsylvania) interested in the comparative studies described in chapter 1.

As of August 1970 the dendrochronology of bristlecone pines has been extended to 5450 B.C. Samples reaching to 5116 B.C. have been made available to the radiocarbon laboratory of the University of Pennsylvania. Further studies of appropriate trees, most likely bristlecone pines, may eventually reach a point in time that will enable us to confirm or deny the "postglacial" theory as a causal factor for oscillations between radiocarbon and dendrochronological dates, the latter representing secular dates. Some support for this postglacial theory is seen in the behavior of radiocarbon dates during the so-called Little Ice Age prevailing both in Europe (13) and in North America (14). With the decreased atmospheric temperatures of this period and the consequent lower $C^{14}$ content in the air, the radiocarbon dates are slightly older than the dendro-dates. With the reversal of these conditions during the altithermal, the dates become progressively younger and should continue to be so until the warmest period of the altithermal is reached. After the warmest period, they should show progressively less deviation from dendro-dates as the terminal period of the last glaciation is approached.

## 2.5
### Collecting Samples

In view of present-day developments, wood samples from archaeological sites may be collected with a double purpose in mind: dendrochronological correlation with other samples from the same or other sites; and radiocarbon analysis (if the dendrochronological date is a relative, "floating" one). In the latter case, the application of correction factors should place the chronology of the sample within fairly precise bounds.

In collecting wood samples for dendrochronological analyses, the collector should have the following points in mind:
1. The tree must be of a genus and species able to formulate (at least in most years) a well-defined ring.

2. The record of the tree rings must not be a complacent one, that is, it has to contain both relatively narrow and wide rings so as to form a "signature" that can be recognized in a run of tree rings from a related sample and thus lend itself to cross-dating for a chronological extension of the tree-ring series.

3. Whenever possible, a cross section of a tree is preferable to a "pie" section or a mere coring.

4. If the tree-ring sample is to be used for radiocarbon analysis eventually (and thus destroyed completely or in part), no preservatives should be used that might infiltrate the wood. Conditions pertaining to the collection of wood and charcoal samples have been described in chapter 1.

## References

1. Douglass, A. E.,
Climatic Cycles and Tree Growth. Vol. 1, no. 289. Washington, D.C.: Carnegie Institution of Washington (1919).

2. Douglass, A. E.,
Climatic Cycles and Tree Growth. Vol. 2. Washington, D.C.: Carnegie Institution of Washington (1928).

3. Schulman, E.,
Dendroclimatic Changes in Semiarid America. Tucson: The University of Arizona Press (1956).

4. Agerter, S. R., and Glock, W.,
An Annotated Bibliography of Tree Growth and Growth Rings, 1950-1962. Tucson: The University of Arizona Press (1965).

5. Douglass, A. E.,
"Dating Pueblo Bonito and other ruins of the Southwest." Contributed Technical Papers, Pueblo Bonito Series No. 1. Washington, D.C.: National Geographic Society (1935).

6. Stokes, M. A., and Smiley, T. L.,
"Dates from the Navaho Land Claim. I. Northern Sector." Tree-Ring Bulletin 25 (1963), nos. 3-4: 8-18.

7. Bannister, B.,
"Dendrochronology in the Near East: Current Research and Future Potentialities." Paper read at the VIIth International Congress of Anthropological and Ethnological Sciences, Moscow, August 3-10, 1964.

8. Kolchin, B. A.,
"Dendrokhronologiya Novgoroda" (The Dendrochronology of
Novgorod). Materialy i issledovaniya po arkheologii SSSR, 117 (1963):
5-103.
9. Douglass
(Reference 1): 111.
10. Douglass
(Reference 1): 49; 117.
11. Schulman
(Reference 3): 136.
12. DeVries, Hl.,
"Variation in Concentration of Radiocarbon with Time and Location
on Earth." Koninkl. Nederl. Akademie van Wetenschappen, Amsterdam: Proceedings, Series B, 61 (1958); 2: 1-9.
13. Lamb, H. H.,
The Changing Climate. London: Methuen & Co. Ltd. (1966).
14. Denton, G. H., and Porter, S. C.,
"Neoglaciation." Scientific American 222; no. 6 (June 1970): 101-110.

# 3  Archaeomagnetic        Václav Bucha
Dating

## 3.1
## Introduction

Archaeomagnetism, a branch of geophysics, deals with the study of the
earth's magnetic field and its changes during several tens of thousands
of years. The aim of archaeomagnetic research is to examine, on the
basis of indirect magnetic methods, that is, by measurement of the
remanent magnetization of baked clay materials in an archaeological
context, changes in the magnetic declination, inclination, and the
earth's magnetic intensity and to contribute in this way to the knowledge of the geomagnetic secular variations. The resulting data characterize the behavior of the earth's magnetic field and provide a basis for a
method of dating baked clay objects. Archaeomagnetic data may be
derived from the direction and strength of remanent magnetization in
samples taken from such sources as ancient kilns, fire pits, wattle-and-
daub remains, as well as from pottery, sherds, bricks, tiles, and so on.
The thermoremanent magnetization (TRM) of baked clay which was
generated as a result of the temperature effect (provided the clay has
been mineralogically stabilized) is proportional to the intensity of the
earth's magnetic field that acted on the clay as it cooled. As long as we
can accurately determine the sample's position during the primary
heating, all three magnetic components—declination, inclination, and
total field intensity—may be derived. The vertical position of bricks and
pottery during baking is usually known, so that besides the intensity,
the inclination can also be examined. Wattle-and-daub, which normally
is easily obtainable among Neolithic archaeological materials, and other
unoriented baked objects are suitable for geomagnetic intensity determinations by means of the double-heating method. Neither ancient iron
tools nor slag from iron furnaces constitute appropriate materials because they contain ferrimagnetic minerals (mainly magnetite and
titanomagnetite) which undergo mineralogical changes when successively heated in the laboratory. Unlike palaeomagnetic investigations
where the averaged directions of the geomagnetic field are studied (i.e.,
without their short-term secular variations), only relatively short
changes with periods of several hundreds or thousands of years are the
object of the archaeomagnetic research reported here. The latter results

in greater accuracy since it involves a greater number of samples of approximately the same age. In connection with this type of research, special attention must therefore be given to the collection of samples.

Archaeomagnetic analyses may provide a basis for confirmation of "direct" (i.e., stratigraphic or typological, and other) dating methods in archaeology and moreover make possible a calculation of correction factors for radiocarbon dates, since the production rate of $C^{14}$ depends in an indirect way on the intensity of the geomagnetic field. Thus, a knowledge of changes in the earth's magnetic intensity during the several tens of thousands of years of the immediate past contributes greatly to a more precise calibration of archaeological chronologies.

## 3.2
### The Earth's Magnetic Field and its Changes

The planet earth may be considered as a large magnet; its magnetic field is usually expressed as a field of a magnetic dipole at the earth's center aligned along the axis of rotation (Fig. 3.1) (1, 2). The results of investigations of the sources of the geomagnetic field, apart from having many applications in other scientific disciplines, may help to clarify the origin and evolution of the earth.

Direct monitoring of magnetic changes on the surface of continents and oceans, which has been carried out for several centuries by means of increasingly precise instruments, provides a relatively exact picture of the geomagnetic field and its changes during this period. Indirect dates of geomagnetic changes in the historical past (several thousands of years) are provided by archaeomagnetic measurements of fired archaeological clay objects. The character of long-term geomagnetic changes

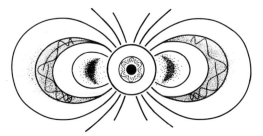

Fig. 3.1 The field of the magnetic dipole placed at the earth's center. (Author's modification of J.A. Van Allen and D. Inglis) (1,2).

in the remote geological past can be established on the basis of palaeomagnetic investigations. It is possible to say that the dynamic behavior of the earth's magnetic field and its prevailing magnetic component are most probably created by physical processes in the earth's core and in the boundary layers between the core and mantle.

Magnetic charts of the earth reveal that additional components are superimposed on a homogeneous (dipole) field (Fig. 3.2) (3). Subtraction of the homogeneous field enables us to observe the nondipole field, which is composed of six continental (terrestrial) anomalies. In addition to these so-called permanent components, other dynamic effects of the earth's field manifested as secular variations can be discerned. By means of palaeomagnetic measurments, reversals of the geomagnetic field's polarity and extensive polar wanderings have been identified as a specific form of secular variations in previous eras. All these main components are included in the expression for the inner field representing the major part of the earth's magnetic field (about 95 percent). In the outer field the daily and annual variations, pulsations and geomagnetic storms are manifested, with solar activity their principal source. The distribution, components, and characteristics of the earth's magnetic field are described in section 3.8.

## 3.3
### Remanent Magnetization of Baked Clays and Types of Samples

The thermoremanent magnetization of baked clay generated by the effect of temperature, provided it had been mineralogically stabilized, is proportional to the intensity of the earth's magnetic field acting on the clay as it cools. Because of this phenomenon it is possible to redetermine the original magnetic intensity at a later time period. However, the properties of the magnetization are further influenced by the conditions under which ferrimagnetic minerals were originally created in the rocks and which could have acted on them during their existence as rocks. Therefore, a process must be pursued with which unambiguous results can be verifiedly obtained.

### 3.3.1
### Archaeomagnetic Samples

The measurement of remanent magnetization in archaeological samples is rapidly becoming one of the significant methods of determining the

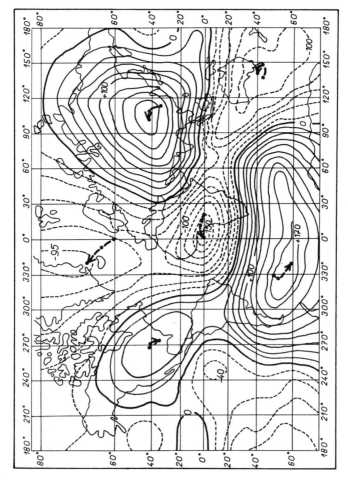

**Fig. 3.2** Nondipole magnetic field of Z component for A.D. 1945.0. The isolines are in units of $10^{-3}$ Oe. Heavy dashed lines mark the migration of the centers of terrestrial (continental) anomalies for A.D. 1885.0 and 1907.5 to their positions in A.D. 1945.0. (Author's modification of E. H. Vestine, et al.) (3).

relative age of objects. At the same time it is very important for geophysics: so far it is the only method by which information may be obtained about the changes of the geomagnetic field in the past. However, successful results can be obtained only when a sufficient number of samples of good quality are available. Any baked object that contains at least a small amount of iron compounds sensitive to magnetization is suitable. Successful measurements have so far been carried out with baked soils in situ (fire-pits and kilns), wattle-and-daub structures, clay weights, bricks and tiles, and potsherds of various kinds. The degree of magnetization of baked soils is dependent, apart from the mineralogical content, primarily on the degree of baking. The most suitable are those which have been baked to a red color at temperatures between $500°$ and $900°$ C. Gray and black samples undergo mineralogical changes during laboratory heating that cause nonlinearities and thus are unreliable. The magnetic properties of minerals inherent in clays are described in section 3.9.

### 3.3.2
### Types of Remanent Magnetization
The presence of ferrimagnetic minerals in rocks (the sources of magnetization in clays) is considered the main factor determining the value of their remanent magnetization and its properties. Palaeomagnetic stability, that is, the ability of rock to retain direction and strength of primary magnetization acquired during its genesis, is the most important characteristic for analysis. Not much less significant are the physical and chemical processes that took place at genesis (mainly the temperature, stresses, and phase changes), the shape and size of grains of the individual minerals, and their mixing, creating compactness or porosity. It often happens that rocks containing a specific mineral are appropriate in all respects for archaeomagnetic analyses while others experience a total disappearance of the primary magnetization, either because of a difference in grain size or because of greater porosity.

When rocks are analyzed after they are collected, the intensity of their remanent magnetization may be determined. The ascertained value usually includes several types of magnetization which frequently have differing magnetic characteristics because of differing conditions of the magnetic field attending their genesis. Depending on the circumstances of their origin, the following basic types of magnetizations are recognized: thermoremanent, partially thermoremanent, chemical, inverse, dynamic, and cyclic. To these we can add normal and ideal magnetizations, the characteristics of which have been studied in detail.

(a) Thermoremanent magnetization (TRM) of rocks originates during the cooling of ferrimagnetic minerals from the Curie point to room temperature, specifically in the presence of the earth's magnetic field. It represents the most important type both in extent and in unique characteristics. During the process of thermomagnetization a new distribution of magnetostrictive tensions as well as significant changes of elastic tensions occur. At high temperatures the energy barriers of the domains are released so that the influence of the magnetic field on the domain arrangement becomes very intensive and, in fact, operates without obstacles. The thermoremanent magnetization increases nonlinearly. Experimentation revealed that only 15 percent of the total magnetization was created when the sample was heated from $0°$ C to one-half of its Curie point temperature $T_c$. The main increase occurred at temperatures representing the segment of 0.9 $T_c$ to 1.0 $T_c$ and accounted for 75 percent of the total magnetization. For instance, a sample with hematite achieves its major magnetization between $600°$ and $675°$ C. The results suggest that thermomagnetization acquired by the cooling of the sample in a geomagnetic field usually represents the main component even when later secondary magnetization takes place. This is true unless the rock has undergone considerable interference or chemical changes in its ferrimagnetic minerals. In the case of a highly coercive force, the direction of the primary TRM is prevented from changing. If a rock sample was exposed to another heating during its existence, a change of direction or intensity of magnetization can occur. In such a case the interfering effect depends largely on the temperature. The primary magnetization can be entirely eliminated if the new temperature exceeds the Curie point; the sample then acquires a new thermoremanent magnetization which is parallel in direction and proportional in intensity to the field in existence at the moment. If the temperature is lower than 1.0 $T_c$, the sample acquires a partial thermoremanent magnetization in addition to its primary magnetization.

(b) As has been shown, partial TRM originates when the acting temperature is lower than the Curie point of the ferrimagnetic minerals in the sample. The portion of the partial magnetization as well as the temperature at which it was acquired can be examined in the laboratory by heating the sample successively to higher temperatures, making it possible to determine whether or not the sample was exposed to several heatings.

(c) Chemical remanent magnetization is acquired when the grains of ferrimagnetic minerals had a chemical origin, again in the presence of the earth's magnetic field. It occurs mainly in red-colored sedimentary rocks in which the red pigment originated by precipitation of $Fe_2O_3$ under arid climatic conditions or by dehydration of $Fe_2O_3 \cdot H_2O$ suspended in saltwater. A yet different process takes place when magnetite, after the weathering of rocks, is changed to hematite. The mechanism of chemical magnetization is connected with the growth of individual ferromagnetic grains. Its stability undergoes constant change depending upon the different ferromagnetic minerals and the size of their grains. Fine-grained hematite pigment on flint grains provides relatively high magnetic stability, while the magnetization due to weathering of rocks usually is less stable.

(d) Viscous remanent magnetization is acquired as a result of the action of the magnetic field over a long period. The increase in the normal magnetization during this action is dependent on the length of exposure, and it decreases logarithmically as the field is removed. The residuum of this type of magnetization remaining in the rock is called viscous magnetization. It can change both the direction and intensity of the primary magnetization considerably. However, because of its low stability it can be removed easily by magnetic cleaning either during heating or by demagnetization in an ac field.

(e) Inverse remanent magnetization is said to be present when the rock sample shows magnetization directly opposite $(180°)$ to rocks underlying it. One of the explanations of this phenomenon assumes at least two different ferromagnetics bound to compact grains which acquire opposite magnetic orientations as they are exposed to the appropriate fields at different times. In many cases, however, inverse magnetization may be due to the reversal of the earth's magnetic field during the time of the rock's genesis.

(f) Dynamic remanent magnetization is caused by the changing stresses in rocks. It originates as a consequence of tectonic processes, tilting, and metamorphism while under the influence of the earth's magnetic field.

(g) Cyclic remanent magnetization includes repeated physical processes that influenced the rock during its existence. These consisted mostly of several successive heatings and coolings or repeated metamorphic processes.

(h) Ideal remanent magnetization may be created in the laboratory by the sample being simultaneously exposed to both direct and alternating fields with changing amplitudes. Because of the lack of strong alternating fields in nature it does not occur spontaneously. The magnetic stability of ideal magnetization is relatively high.

## 3.4
### Archaeomagnetic Measurements

Archaeomagnetic methods can achieve full significance in archaeology only after a sufficient number of basic measurements have been made and only after the course of the earth's magnetic field changes become known in as accurate a way as possible.

Techniques used for archaeomagnetic determination include the use of either an astatic or a spinner magnetometer, the double-heating method, magnetic cleaning, demagnetizations, and formulas to calculate the results. These are described in detail in section 3.10.

## 3.5
### Archaeomagnetic Curves

The dependence of changes in the earth's magnetic field on time is usually expressed by means of curves for individual geomagnetic elements which represent a very distinct picture of the over-all course.

### 3.5.1
### Archaeomagnetic Changes in Declination and Inclination

The values of magnetic declination D have been examined by direct magnetic measurements ever since the sixteenth century and the inclination I since the eighteenth century. To our advantage, the measurements of the direction of remanent magnetization in oriented archaeological samples make it possible to extend our knowledge by several thousand years. The presently determined curves of the geomagnetic elements D, I are shown in Figs. 3.3 and 3.4. Through analyses of samples from ancient kilns and fire-pits in Japan, their course in Japan has been determined for the period from A.D. 200 to the present (4, 5, 6). The results have been correlated with data obtained by measurements of lava flows and more recently with direct measurements. Both curves are cyclic in character, one cycle for declination being 400 to 500 years and having an amplitude of 30°, whereas the length of the inclination cycle is roughly 1000 years.

The Thelliers' investigation (7) of the remanet magnetization in old vases resulted in data characterizing the inclination in Rome for nearly 3000 years. At around 800 B.C. it approached zero; then a rapid increase took place, reaching values of approximately 70°. Later, cycles with a periodicity of only ~400 years and an amplitude of ~15° were ascertained.

In Sicily, measurements of Mt. Etna's lava flows afforded data for the changes in declination and inclination from A.D. 800 to the present. The course of inclination in Tbilisi in the Transcaucasus was examined

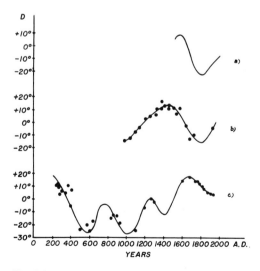

**Fig. 3.3** Variation in magnetic declination at (a) London, (b) Mount Etna, and (c) Japan for the years indicated.

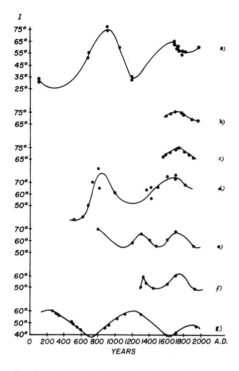

**Fig. 3.4** Variation in magnetic inclination at various localities for the years indicated. (a) Tbilisi; (b) London; (c) Paris, direct measurements; (d) Paris, archaeomagnetic measurements; (e) Rome; (f) Sicily; (g) Japan.

by Burlatskaya (8) by measuring the remanent magnetization of bricks, spanning a period of 2000 years (Fig. 3.4). The curve has a sinusoidal shape in the first approximation with decreasing period and amplitude.

Significant results for changes of D and I have been obtained with samples from burnt clay floors in Indian pueblos in the U.S. Southwest for the past 2000 years by R. L. DuBois (9). The curve in Fig. 3.5 represents changes of the magnetic pole determined on the basis of D and I; the interval between points is approximately 100 years. Because the samples collected so far are located within a relatively small area of the earth's surface, the curve represents changes of the pole relative to this limited area only.

The first attempt to express the changes in the location of an averaged magnetic pole covering the period of the past 1300 years was made by Japanese geophysicists (4). They exploited the curves of

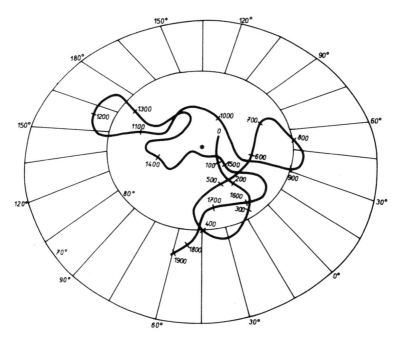

Fig. 3.5 Temporal changes in the location of the North magnetic pole determined on the basis of D and I within the territory of the U.S.A. over the past 2000 years. The numbers on the curves indicate years A.D. (After K. F. Weaver) (9).

changes of the apparent pole for England, Iceland, Japan, and the United States. As is evident from Fig. 3.6, the axis of the magnetic dipole turned counterclockwise, the whole rotation taking approximately 1400 years.

### 3.5.2

### Archaeomagnetic Changes of the Earth's Magnetic Intensity

Initially, investigators of archaeomagnetism concentrated their efforts on the study of directions of the earth's magnetic field on the basis of angles D and I. Shortly after E. and O. Thellier suggested the double-heating method (7), studies of the earth's total magnetic intensity were undertaken. Despite the ready availability of archaeological materials, not too many data on the earth's magnetic intensity in antiquity have been determined, perhaps because of the complexity of the procedure. This type of research is being done at ten laboratories distributed in various parts of the world and provides important data for the study of the dynamics of the earth's magnetic changes and of hydromagnetic

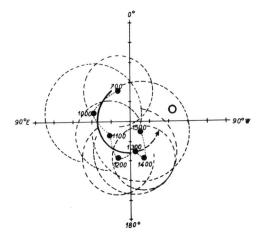

Fig. 3.6 Locational changes of the averaged North magnetic pole over the past 1800 years. The numbers on the curves indicate years A.D. (After N. Kawai and K. Hirooka) (4).

dynamo theories. An even geographic distribution of the sites of collection is needed to make the data more reliable. The known results, especially from those countries where archaeomagnetic curves were investigated over a relatively long period of time, are here reviewed:

In France, samples were obtained from bricks, tiles, and kilns that spanned a period of 2500 years. There were 10 to 15 samples from each object. These were subjected to temperature tests, their magnetic cleaning was carried out, and inclination as well as total intensity was determined by means of the double-heating method. The results are shown in Fig. 3.7.

In the U.S.S.R. (8) a large number of samples collected in the city of Tbilisi from bricks of various ages were analyzed, covering a period from about 1000 B.C. to the present. Additionally one brick dating to 2600 B.C. was examined. Magnetic cleaning and the double-heating method were used. The results shown in Fig. 3.8 represent the approximate changes of intensity for the past 4600 years. From it we may discern that at about the A.D.-B.C. juncture the magnetic intensity in the Caucasus was 1.6 times greater than at the present and that during the 3rd millennium B.C. it dropped to 0.8 times the present.

Archaeomagnetic investigations in Japan were carried out on basaltic

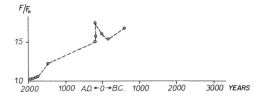

Fig. 3.7 Archaeomagnetic curve for the ratio of the changes in the earth's magnetic field of intensity in France. (After E. and O. Thellier) (7).

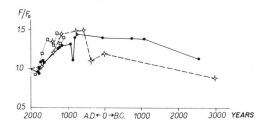

Fig. 3.8 Archaeomagnetic curves for the ratio of the changes in the earth's magnetic intensity for three localities in the Transcaucasus, U.S.S.R. (After S. P. Burlatskaya) (8).

and archaeological samples, the age of which is known for the time interval of the 5000 years of the immediate past (4, 5, 6). The results do not show a linear decrease during the past 2000 years but two small minima before and after A.D. 1000 (Fig. 3.9). Starting with the earliest years of the period we see an increase of values from 0.78 times the present-day intensity (around 3000 B.C.) to 1.54 at 150 B.C. Although the difference between the geographical position of Japan and Central Europe is considerable, the averaged course of curves for both areas show the same maxima around the beginning of our era. Archaeomagnetic studies were also carried out in India (10) (Fig. 3.10A), in Canada (11) (Fig. 3.10B), and in South America (12, 13) (Fig. 3.10C). The low-intensity values for Indian samples are most probably due to the inadequacies of the method used. Our measurements on some Indian samples dating to approximately 1000 B.C. and older showed higher values of the earth's magnetic intensity (1.2-1.4 times that of the present).

The archaeomagnetic intensity investigations in Central Europe (14) (mainly Czechoslovakia), and Mexico and Arizona (15) were carried out in the laboratory of the Geophysical Institute in Prague. Most of the samples were obtained from burnt clay of soils, kilns, and fire-pits. Bricks, pottery, waste, and slag were also analyzed. The best results were obtained for the first group, especially the burnt clay from wattle-and-daub structures and kilns. In the selection of samples, color plays an important role. The red-brown and red-colored baked clays showed uniformly unambiguous results. Their primary baking apparently occurred at temperatures ranging from 500° to 900° C. Nonlinearity between demagnetization and remagnetization resulted when some pottery samples with a red-brown surface but a gray-to-black interior were processed. After the samples were heated in the laboratory, the gray color changed to red, indicating a transition of magnetite into oxides of the $Fe_2O_3$ series. Thus, gray or black samples are not satisfactory.

The homogeneity of the original heating throughout the sample is also a very important factor. It is better to use smaller specimens but baked to the same temperature throughout rather than larger samples that were heated inhomogeneously.

With the double-heating method in a laboratory-produced field equal to the earth's present magnetic field, the coefficient k, characterizing the past intensity, was obtained for many localities in Czechoslovakia and other parts of Central Europe (Fig. 3.11). For the majority of the samples included in Table 3.1 we have adopted archaeological dating and for some, radiocarbon dating.

Until we had more detailed results of short-term intensity changes (say on the basis of 50 to 100 years), we could not know whether the

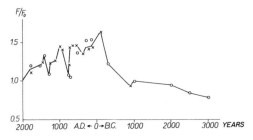

Fig. 3.9 Archaeomagnetic curve for the ratio of the changes in the earth's magnetic intensity for Japan. (After T. Nagata and S. Sasayima) (5, 6).

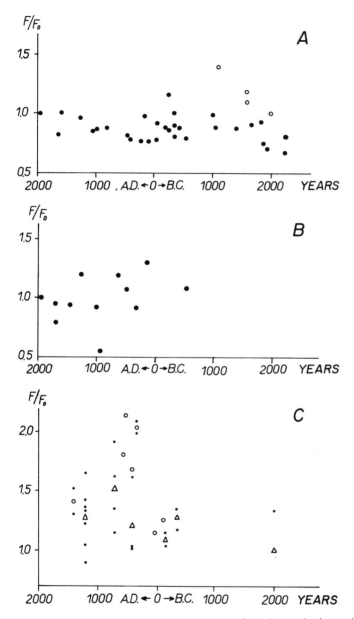

**Fig. 3.10** Archaeomagnetic results for the ratio of the changes in the earth's magnetic intensity for (A) India (after R. N. Athavale) (10), (B) Canada (after E. J. Schwarz and K. W. Christie) (11), (C) South America (after T. Nagata et al.) (12). In (A), solid dots represent Athavale's measurements, circles Bucha's; in (C) solid dots are discrete values after Nagata, triangles represent mean values, and circles are values after Kitazawa and Kobayashi (13).

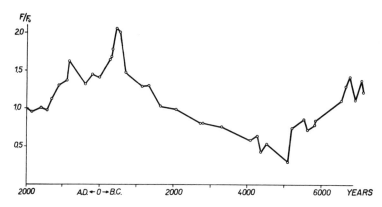

**Fig. 3.11** Archaeomagnetic curve of the ratio of the earth's magnetic intensity in Czechoslovakia and other parts of Central Europe.

deviations of the k value for a given locality were due to inaccuracies in the dating or to real fluctuations in intensity; the latter is more probable. Results published previously showed the individual k value for each sample graphically, whereas for Fig. 3.11 mean values for each site were calculated.

Also shown in Fig. 3.11 are results for Çatal Hüyük in Turkey for the period 5700 to 6500 B.C., with k values computed on the basis of the present-day field at the site, which is 2500 gamma less than the field in Czechoslovakia. The k values simply express the ratio of the ancient field as determined for a locality to the present-day one. The curve indicating the earth's magnetic field intensity shows a maximum around 400 B.C. when it reaches 1.6 times the present intensity. (The exceptional value of 2.045 for Želénky in western Czechoslovakia may be due to a short-period deviation from the smoothed basic curve.) The minimum occurs between 5000 and 4500 B.C., at which time the field drops to around 0.6 times its present intensity. For more ancient periods the field was more intense again, as evidenced by results from Çatal Hüyük.

As already mentioned, earlier results of investigations in Czechoslovakia have indicated fluctuations of intensity. At the same time, some significant deviations from the smoothed curve were found (for instance, the peak around 400 B.C. in Fig. 3.11, which was based on 13 specimens). As these deviations are much greater than the standard statistical error, the only explanation seems to be that there exist intensity changes of short duration. Thus, it becomes apparent that a complete examination of the short-term fluctuations would require more detailed archaeomagnetic data spaced at intervals not longer than 100 years.

Investigations of samples from Mexico and Arizona (15) resulted in rather interesting additional data: two maxima of intensity were established (Fig. 3.12), but their positions were shifted compared to the maxima of the European curve. Similar differences can also be seen in the Japanese curve (Fig. 3.9) which shows small minima at the times when European peaks occurred.

Between the ninth and fifteenth centuries A.D. as well as during a period centered around the fifth century B.C. increases in values are apparent. The latter, based on values from several localities, shows an intensity twice that of the present-day. The difference in time between the two maxima is approximately 1000 to 1500 years. Changes in magnetic inclination with shorter intervening periods have been discussed (see Fig. 3.4). It becomes evident that the smoothed curve for Czechoslovakia, which was calculated earlier, has superimposed on it changes of shorter periods. Because precise dating of several contemporaneous samples for each era is not always possible, some inaccuracies may be present. Yet despite this possibility the results enable us to draw new conclusions concerning the westward drift of the earth's nondipole magnetic field.

### 3.5.2
**Westward Drift and the Earth's Magnetic Moment During the Past**
Numerous archaeomagnetic measurements of inclination on samples from different places on the earth's surface have made it possible to verify the westward drift of the nondipole field. The direct magnetic monitoring of the earth carried out over the past 300 years already has shown some evidence of this, but the conclusions are ambiguous, especially with respect to the westward shift of the centers of terrestrial anomalies (Fig. 3.2).

The archaeomagnetic data span a much longer time period. Between $0°$ and $140°$ E. longitude, the course of inclination changes was investi-

**Table 3.1** Results of Archaeomagnetic Analyses

| Site | Code Letter | Lat. North | Long. East | Archaeo-logical Age | Type of Structure | No. of Field Samples |
|------|-------------|-----------|-----------|---------------------|-------------------|---------------------|
| Věstonice | V | 48.9° | 16.7° | 22800 B.C. | burnt earth (b.e.) | 8 |
| Bylany | By 1/64 12/64 16/64 | 49.9° | 15.3° | 4400 B.C. | b.e. | 4 |
| Bylany | By 2,3 4/64 | | | 3900 B.C. | b.e. | 3 |
| Bylany | By 5A,5B 6/64 | | | 3600 B.C. | kiln b.e. | 3 |
| Bylany | By 7,8 9/64 4/60 | | | 3300 B.C. | kiln | 4 |
| Bylany | By 10 11/64 | | | 3100 B.C. | b.e. | 3 |
| Most | 39,40 | 50.5° | 13.3° | 3000 to 3500 B.C. | pottery | 2 |
| Močovice | MČ | 49.9° | 15.1° | 4000 to 3500 B.C. | b.e. | 10 |
| Uhřetice | ÚHŘ | 50.0° | 15.0° | 3200 to 2800 B.C. | b.e. | 3 |

| No. of Measured Samples | No. of Measured Samples Accepted | $F/F_o$ for All Samples Accepted | $F/F_o$ Average | Standard Error of The Mean | Aver. No. of Temp. Intervals Accepted for Each Sample |
|---|---|---|---|---|---|
| 11 | 7 | 0.497 | 0.553 | ±0.040 | 3.6 |
|  |  | 0.643 |  |  |  |
|  |  | 0.631 |  |  |  |
|  |  | 0.686 |  |  |  |
|  |  | 0.385 |  |  |  |
|  |  | 0.483 |  |  |  |
|  |  | 0.546 |  |  |  |
| 8 | 6 | 0.561 | 0.755 | ±0.059 | 4.2 |
|  |  | 0.777 |  |  |  |
|  |  | 0.631 |  |  |  |
|  |  | 0.739 |  |  |  |
|  |  | 0.920 |  |  |  |
|  |  | 0.905 |  |  |  |
| 4 | 4 | 0.940 | 0.940 | ±0.049 | 4.2 |
|  |  | 0.820 |  |  |  |
|  |  | 1.060 |  |  |  |
|  |  | 0.940 |  |  |  |
| 7 | 6 | 0.485 | 0.544 | ±0.041 | 4.0 |
|  |  | 0.500 |  |  |  |
|  |  | 0.630 |  |  |  |
|  |  | 0.581 |  |  |  |
|  |  | 0.670 |  |  |  |
|  |  | 0.400 |  |  |  |
| 5 | 5 | 0.720 | 0.696 | ±0.067 | 4.0 |
|  |  | 0.600 |  |  |  |
|  |  | 0.878 |  |  |  |
|  |  | 0.783 |  |  |  |
|  |  | 0.500 |  |  |  |
| 5 | 4 | 0.840 | 0.912 | ±0.038 | 4.5 |
|  |  | 0.890 |  |  |  |
|  |  | 0.900 |  |  |  |
|  |  | 1.020 |  |  |  |
| 3 | 2 | 0.609 | 0.655 | ±0.047 | 4.0 |
|  |  | 0.702 |  |  |  |
| 13 | 10 | 0.683 | 0.741 | ±0.033 | 4.1 |
|  |  | 0.786 |  |  |  |
|  |  | 0.774 |  |  |  |
|  |  | 0.767 |  |  |  |
|  |  | 0.634 |  |  |  |
|  |  | 0.690 |  |  |  |
|  |  | 0.600 |  |  |  |
|  |  | 0.735 |  |  |  |
|  |  | 0.988 |  |  |  |
|  |  | 0.752 |  |  |  |
| 5 | 3 | 0.850 | 0.876 | ±0.033 | 3.7 |
|  |  | 0.836 |  |  |  |
|  |  | 0.942 |  |  |  |

**Table 3.1** continued

| Site | Code Letter | Lat. North | Long. East | Archaeo-logical Age | Type of Structure | No. of Field Samples |
|------|-------------|------------|------------|---------------------|-------------------|----------------------|
| Kamenná Voda | 11, 12 | 50.4° | 13.7° | 2500 to 3000 B.C. | pit | 2 |
| Želénky | 14 | 50.6° | 13.8° | 1400 B.C. | dwelling | 1 |
| Radonice | 16-19 | 50.4° | 13.9° | 1150 B.C. | pit | 4 |
| Kamenná Voda | 73,74 | 50.4° | 13.7° | 1000 B.C. | pit | 2 |
| Jinonice | PJ 75,76 | 50.1° | 14.3° | 550 B.C. | pit | 4 |
| Želénky | 21.72 | 50.6° | 13.8° | 450 B.C. | b.e. | 5 |
| Tuchomě-řice | TCHM | 50.2° | 14.2° | 300 B.C. | b.e. | 6 |
| Klecany | KL | 50.3° | 14.5° | A.D. 400 | kiln | 3 |
| Srbsko | S | 49.9° | 14.1° | A.D. 700 | bricks | 3 |
| Mikulčice | M | 48.8° | 17.0° | A.D. 900 | fire places | 2 |

| No. of Measured Samples | No. of Measured Samples Accepted | F/F$_o$ for All Samples Accepted | F/F$_o$ Average | Standard Error of The Mean | Aver. No. of Temp. Intervals Accepted for Each Sample |
|---|---|---|---|---|---|
| 2 | 2 | 0.762<br>0.781 | 0.771 | ±0.009 | 3.0 |
| 3 | 2 | 1.037 | 1.034 | ±1.001 | 4.0 |
| 5 | 4 | 1.367<br>1.151<br>1.360<br>1.350 | 1.307 | ±0.052 | 4.0 |
| 3 | 3 | 1.240<br>1.220<br>1.420 | 1.293 | ±0.063 | 3.5 |
| 6 | 6 | 1.360<br>1.530<br>1.580<br>1.570<br>1.470<br>1.300 | 1.468 | ±0.047 | 3.0 |
| 13 | 13 | 1.940<br>2.020<br>2.050<br>2.110<br>2.030<br>2.030<br>2.000<br>2.170<br>2.310<br>1.970<br>2.110<br>2.010<br>1.840 | 2.045 | ±0.032 | 4.5 |
| 9 | 6 | 1.770<br>1.923<br>1.632<br>1.703<br>1.481<br>1.593 | 1.684 | ±0.062 | 3.8 |
| 5 | 5 | 1.329<br>1.391<br>1.425<br>1.291<br>1.246 | 1.336 | ±0.032 | 4.2 |
| 3 | 3 | 1.375<br>1.220<br>1.413 | 1.336 | ±0.059 | 3.3 |
| 5 | 4 | 1.200<br>1.520<br>1.350<br>1.440 | 1.377 | ±0.068 | 3.8 |

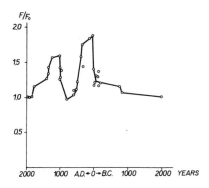

**Fig. 3.12** Archaeomagnetic curve of the ratio of the changes in the earth's magnetic intensity in Arizona and Mexico.

gated for eleven places located within approximately 20° of geographical latitude; this made it possible to compare the times during which the maxima and minima occurred. Figure 3.13 (16) shows a practically linear dependence and shift of the maxima for eleven localities (London, Rome, Paris, Sicily, Hungary, Bulgaria, Leningrad, Novgorod, the Caucasus, Central Asia, and Japan). The evidence for the westward drift in inclination during the past 700 years seems to indicate an average velocity of 0.23° per year, the shift being practically the same in the whole sector described. The mean error caused by inaccuracies in the dating of some of the objects used for archaeomagnetic investigation is ± 0.06° per year. The velocity of the westward drift approaches the values found by direct magnetic measurements, so that an important conclusion concerning the linearity of the westward drift may be drawn.

The three curves of the earth's magnetic intensity in the past for Europe (Fig. 3.11) for Mexico and Arizona (Fig. 3.12) and for Japan (Fig. 3.9) are based on data that can be further analyzed (17) for study of the westward drift (Fig. 3.14). The areas from which the samples were taken are longitudinally roughly equidistant: in Europe at 15° E., in Mexico at 115° W., and in Japan at 135° E. Both archaeological and radiocarbon dating underlie the values shown in the three curves. The westward shift between maxima is approximately 120° in 500 years, or 0.24° per year. When examining the geographical distribution of the present nondipole magnetic field along the continuum joining Central

Europe, Mexico, Arizona, and Japan (Fig. 3.15), we note two maxima: the first due to a positive terrestrial magnetic anomaly in North America (A), and the second, the Siberian positive anomaly (B). There are two minima: the North Pacific (C) and the Icelandic (D), both negative anomalies. A study of the westward drift (i.e., relative movement of terrestrial anomalies and secular isoporic foci to the west as shown in Fig. 3.16), shows good correlation between the maximum and minimum values.

Recently analyzed archaeomagnetic data revealed changes in the earth's magnetic field during the historical past. It appears that these changes are of periodic character, both for inclination and declination, the length of the periods being 1000 to 1500 years. Moreover, a long period of approximately 9000 years occurs for the earth's average change in magnetic intensity.

In conclusion, archaeomagnetic results from approximately equidistant areas (Fig. 3.14) were used for determining the earth's magnetic moment and its changes during the past, the calculated values being based on intensity measurements (Fig. 3.17). The averaged curve a represents changes of both magnetic dipole moment and nondipole

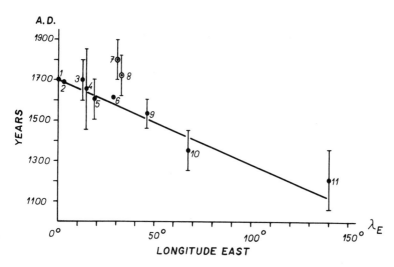

Fig. 3.13 Westward drift in inclination during the past 700 years, as determined for eleven localities between 8° and 140° of longitude East. The interpolated line expresses the relationship of the occurrence of the last maximum value of inclination and geographic longitude.

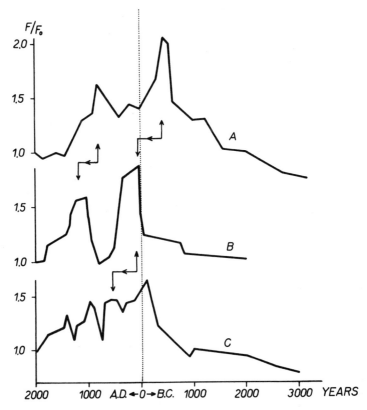

Fig. 3.14 Archaeomagnetic curves for Czechoslovakia (A), Mexico and Arizona (B), and Japan (C), showing westward drift of maximum and minimum values. Note maximum in Central Europe at 400 B.C., while in Mexico it occurs around A.D. 100.

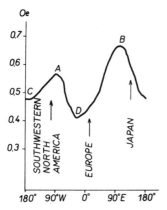

Fig. 3.15 Course of the present-day nondipole magnetic field along the continuum joining southwestern North America, Europe, and Japan.

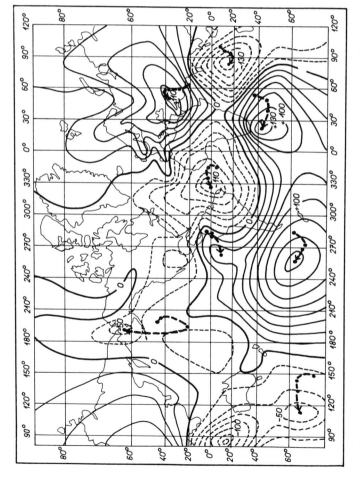

Fig. 3.16 Secular variation of the Z component of the geomagnetic field for A.D. 1942.5. The isolines represent anomalous changes in units of gammas ($10^{-5}$ Oe). Westward drift of the focal centers is indicated for A.D. 1912.5, 1922.5, 1932.5, and 1942.5, in heavy dashed lines. (Author's modification of E.H. Vestine, et al.) (3).

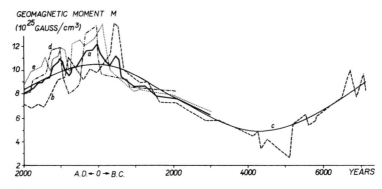

**Fig. 3.17** Changes of the averaged reduced earth's magnetic moment (solid line a) determined from European (dashed line b), southwestern North American (dash-dotted line d), and Japanese (dotted line e) results. The smoothed curve c expresses the average.

moment. The smoothed curve c represents the main changes of the earth's magnetic moment during the past 8500 years and may be expressed as a sinusoidal in the first approximation:

$$M(t) = \left[ 2.8\sin \frac{2\pi}{8900} (t+405) + 7.7 \right] 10^{25} \text{ gauss/cm}^3.$$

The reason for the fluctuations of the magnetic moment should be traced to the sources of the earth's magnetic field, i.e., to hydromagnetic processes in the boundary layers between the earth's liquid core and mantle.

## 3.6
### The Archaeomagnetic Dating Method
The radiocarbon dating method is finding increasing application. Its general validity rests mainly on the assumption that the rate of $C^{14}$ production is constant (see chapter 1). This assumption, however, is not fulfilled, mainly because of secular changes in geomagnetic intensity, on which the $C^{14}$ production rate is dependent. These show deviations of more than 40 percent from the mean value. Therefore, new methods are needed to verify the validity of the results and moreover to be used for age determinations themselves.

The measurement of remanent magnetization in archaeological samples has become one of the significant methods for determining the relative and, eventually, also the absolute age of archaeological objects.

The course of changes for one or more magnetic components (magnetic declination, inclination, and intensity) has to be known for the entire era in which age determinations of unknown objects are to be considered.

In order to obtain basic geomagnetic curves, an investigation into the representative values of magnetic components is necessary; this has to be done by using archaeological samples of known age. The values are found by measuring the direction and intensity of remanent magnetization which originated in the object after its heating and cooling in the presence of the earth's magnetic field. If the natural remanence in pottery is magnetically stable, the ancient field that acted on a sample when it originally cooled may be found by reheating the sample and cooling it in a known field. The ancient field intensity $F_p$ is then expressed as

$$F_p = F_0 \times \frac{J_p}{J_0},$$

where $F_0$ is the known field applied which produces the new thermoremanent magnetization $J_0$, and $J_p$ is the natural thermoremanent magnetization.

It was already pointed out that changes of a certain geomagnetic component can be expressed by curves representing time-dependent values (Figs. 3.9, 3.11, and 3.12). These curves were obtained from archaeomagnetic determinations made with samples of known age. Their accuracy depends on the number of samples and the reliability of dating. Also, it is necessary to determine all cycles of magnetic changes that occurred during the period investigated.

Because the amplitudes of the curves vary only to 40° for D, and 20° for I (at the most), the highest possible accuracy of sample measurement is needed. Thus, it is important to collect samples carefully and to keep in mind the following possible sources of error: inhomogeneous heating of the clay in the fire-pits and kilns; magnetic influence of iron objects that might have been placed close to the archaeological object during its original heating; not quite vertical positioning of bricks or pottery in the process of firing (this does not apply to the samples on which intensity only is measured); mistakes in marking the orientation in the process of collection. Samples subject to other possible errors can be eliminated by statistical methods. Obviously, numerous samples are necessary for this procedure.

According to the results hitherto obtained, the rate at which the direction of the earth's magnetic field has changed is not the same at all places and varies during different periods of time; the method therefore has to be applied with differing accuracy ranging from 25 to 50 years if the determinations of D and I are to be carried out with an accuracy of 1° and if the curve for the earth's magnetic intensity is known.

When the curves for D, I, and F for a certain area are known, each can be used directly for archaeomagnetic dating. Because the course of geomagnetic changes for all components is of a cyclic character, some values may be repeated for several eras. Therefore, the curves for at least two of the three components are preferred for precise dating. At present, the course of the earth's field is known for these geomagnetic components for several areas in the world. The results obtained in France, Italy, England, and Czechoslovakia can be taken as being representative for Europe. The data from Tbilisi are valid for the Near East, while the Japanese results provide sufficient accuracy for an area of an approximately 1000-km radius centered on Japan.

The application of the archaeomagnetic method is still restricted to those areas for which the archaeomagnetic curves have been determined, but it has been extended to Mexico and Arizona on the basis of fundamental geomagnetic characteristics in D (Fig. 3.5) and in F (Fig. 3.12) covering the past 3000 years. In this area, the method can improve the dating of the sherds of unknown age and substantially facilitate their classification.

### 3.6.1
### Selection of Archaeological Samples

All baked objects that contain at least a small amount of iron compounds, sensitive to magnetization, and which are red or brown in color are suitable for archaeomagnetic analyses. Various kinds of baked soils and certain kinds of rocks also come under consideration. So far, successful measurements have been made with the following archaeological materials: baked soils in situ (fire-pits and kilns), clay floors, weights, crockery, bricks, tiles, and various other ceramic objects.

As pointed out earlier, the degree of magnetization of baked clayey soils is dependent, apart from the mineralogical content, on the degree of baking. The most suitable are objects baked to a red color at a temperature of over 670° C; exceptionally, it is possible to measure the magnetization when the object was baked at a lower temperature.

There are no fast auxiliary methods for determining the baking temperature. In objects of red-brown or brick color, cohesiveness is usually quite suitable for archaeomagnetic analyses. The resulting color is dependent on the amount of oxidation during baking. Objects baked in the presence of sufficient air display various shades of brown and red, while those denied plentiful air turn to shades of gray and black. In the latter, changes in magnetization may occur as a result of chemical changes during laboratory heating. For this reason not all samples containing a larger amount of organic admixture are suitable.

In rare cases samples that were baked several times in succession may prove suitable. However, the remanent magnetizations from the various bakings add up and their differentiation is very difficult if not impossible. Finally, samples that contain large fragments of rocks or large cavities and samples strongly overbaked are unsuitable.

### 3.6.2
### Collection of Samples

In collecting, it is possible to work with simple tools without endangering the quality of the sample. The objects are rarely so hard that cutting them with a steel knife leaves traces of iron on them.

Since the sample is magnetized during cooling, a process that continues even at comparatively low temperatures, it is necessary to take care that it is not subjected to higher temperature variations after collection, so as to avoid partial magnetization which would influence the results of the analysis. Objects, such as tablets with cuneiform inscriptions, that have been subject to a heating process in archaeological laboratories are altogether unsuitable.

Samples may be classified into three groups according to the characteristics of the earth's magnetic field that can be determined from them:

1. Oriented samples—those in their original position with respect to the local meridian as well as in their original horizontal plane. With few

exceptions, they yield declination, inclination, and magnetic intensity.
2. Partially oriented samples—those in their original horizontal plane.
Inclination and magnetic intensity may be deduced.
3. Unoriented samples whose original position cannot be determined.
Nevertheless, they can be used for determination of magnetic intensity.

Examples of oriented samples are kilns or fire-pits. Even in these,
however, one must consider the possibility of disturbance of the original position, e.g., by solifluction, local tectonic activity, and so on.
Such changes of position may occur in most locations without disturbing the object itself. The horizontal plane and the direction of the local
meridian must be marked on the samples while they are in situ. The
horizontal plane can best be established by cutting away the upper part
of the sample until a plane horizontal surface is achieved. The determination of the meridian is more complicated. One can proceed by
either establishing magnetic North or geographic North by geodetic
methods. The first consists of placing the compass on the horizontal
surface of the sample, zeroing the magnetic needle, engraving or marking a straight line parallel to the needle along the edge of the compass.
For the time being, declination is neglected—its value will be determined at the laboratory. When using the compass, all iron objects must
be removed from the vicinity of the sample. The accuracy of the results
depends on the accuracy of the initial orientation. Errors tend to multiply and if the orientation is not accurate it can influence the applicability of results considerably.

One must bear in mind the advantage of cutting 2-cm or 1-cm cubes
(only in exceptional cases smaller ones) and of obtaining several cubes
from the same object. With samples so large that they may fracture due
to their own weight during transport, it is important to mark the
horizontal surface with several lines indicating the direction of magnetic
or geographic North. In partly oriented samples it may be possible to
determine, or at least to assume, their position with respect to the
horizontal plane during firing. Bricks are a classical example where one
can credibly assume that they were fired while resting on one of their
long, narrow sides. Bricks usually provide two inclination values, but by
comparison it is easy to decide which one is the right one.

While there is a relative paucity of oriented or partly oriented samples, unoriented samples are plentiful. With the latter, it is always necessary to collect a large number of samples so that deviant analyses may be rejected.

Markings should appear not only on the horizontal sample surface but also on the covers of the boxes in which they are enclosed; samples should be accompanied by a description of the circumstances of the find, a description of the object, its archaeological dating, and so on. Additionally, the following data are needed: geographic coordinates of the site, nearest locality, country, collector's name, field number, type of the sample (e.g., clay floor, bottom of kiln, and so forth), color of surface, color of cross-section, consistency, estimate of absolute age, archaeological culture or cultural phase.

### 3.6.3
**Preparation of Samples in the Laboratory**

In the laboratory, the archaeological objects are cut into cubes. If the sample is sufficiently magnetized, the cubes can be small, with a minimum edge length of about 0.5 cm. Such samples have the advantage of the likelihood of even firing, but the disadvantage of accruing larger errors in the measurements of remanent magnetization.

If the cohesiveness of the object is low, it may be difficult to cut it into cubes. In such cases it is necessary to reinforce the sample with a plaster cast or to impregnate it with water glass (sodium silicate).

### 3.6.4
**Effects that Disturb Magnetic Properties of Samples**

Different properties of baked archaeological samples, differences in temperatures to which the samples were originally heated, the presence of secondary magnetizations, as well as phase changes in ferrimagnetic minerals—all these often influence the linear dependence characterizing the coefficient k. For example, the effects of mineralogical phase changes are expressed in Fig. 3.18 where the demagnetization and magnetization of baked clay from Želénky are plotted. Also shown in Fig. 3.18 is a plot (c) of the demagnetization values at given temperatures versus the remagnetization values. Ideally the small circles indicating temperature values should lie on a straight line, the slope of which indicates the value k. In Fig. 3.18A we see that the circle at 20° C does not lie on the line; this is due to the presence of small viscous magne-

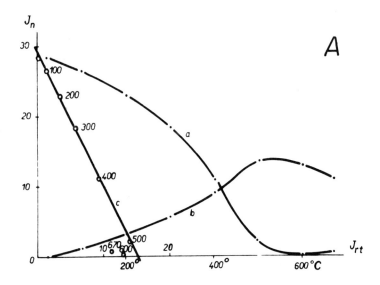

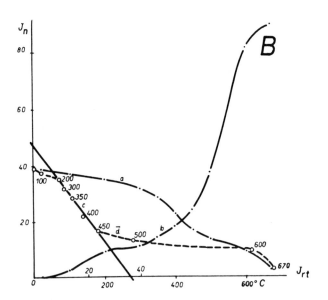

**Fig. 3.18** Demagnetization curves (a) and remagnetization curves (b) for samples from various sites. The straight line (c) shows the relationship between demagnetization and remagnetization for various fixed temperatures in °C. A: Želénky; k = 2.02. B: Vrchnice. Note the nonlinear relationship (d) between 20° and 200° C and between 500° and 670° C. C: Bylany; k = 0.63. D- Štěti; k = 1.55. $J_n$ = natural magnetization; $J_{rt}$ = thermoremanent magnetization.

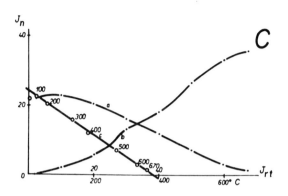

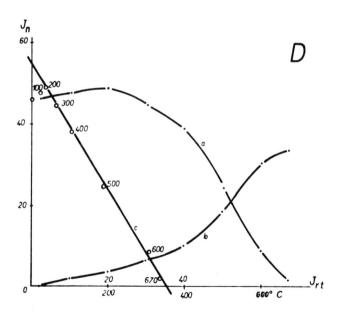

tization. From 100° to 500° C the circles lie quite accurately, but between 600° and 670° C they are considerably off, presumably because of mineralogical phase changes. An important factor that may influence the accuracy of the method is the lack of replicability of the temperature to which the sample is exposed in the normal and reverse positions, as well as sufficiently homogeneous heating throughout the sample. Even with a small-sized sample (cube edge less than 2 cm), it is necessary to heat the sample at least 15 minutes.

When there is secondary (viscous) magnetization present, linear relationship is not obtained at low temperatures (up to 200° C as, for instance, in Fig. 3.18 B). In samples that had been insufficiently or disproportionately baked in the past, a successive diminution of the coefficient k takes place with increasing temperature. This phenomenon starts at the temperature to which the sample was originally baked and is caused by the phase transitions of iron-containing minerals.

Two examples of a reliable determination of k for the different temperatures are shown in Figs. 3.18 C and 3.18 D. Further verification of the method may be obtained by analyses of samples of clay, either porcelanite or fired clay, that acquired thermoremanent magnetization in the known present-day field. Such a sample was used in each of the 60 series investigated. In this way the value of the laboratory field is established and can serve as a check on any significant changes of field during the time of investigation (approximately one month); also, it monitors the accuracy of the temperature settings at which the field samples are heated.

In some cases it is possible to analyze samples that had been fired at temperatures lower than 600° C. However, for temperatures below 350° C there are not sufficient temperature intervals for the construction of the line. Such specimens manifest a sharp increase of magnetization at higher temperatures, and the values cannot be used for determination of the intensity. This can be avoided by measuring the values at lower temperatures at shorter increments, say, every 50° C.

Experimental samples, heated at various temperatures, were analyzed for purposes of verification. Parallelism was found between experimental and archaeological samples. Figure 3.19 shows results gained by heating an experimental sample first to the temperature of 670° C and

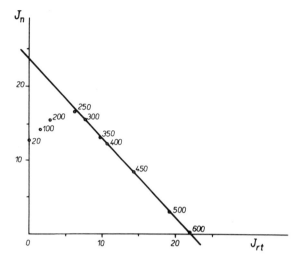

**Fig. 3.19** Temperature relationship for an experimental baked clay sample. The sample was first baked at 670° C and then at 350° C in a 180° reverse position. The temperature segment between 350° and 670° C can be utilized for the determination of intensity.

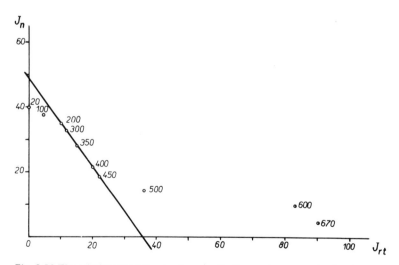

**Fig. 3.20** The relationship between demagnetization and remagnetization for an archaeological sample which was heated twice in the past.

then, while in a $180°$ opposite position, to $350°$ C. Figure 3.20 depicts the essential parallelism of an archaeological sample.

Only a very small percentage of samples manifested consistent values of the coefficient k for the entire temperature range from $20°$ to $670°$ C. The majority of samples provided good results only between $100°$ and $500°$ C.

Most samples baked in ancient times within the range $500°$ to $900°$ C, gave unambiguous results. For bricks, some irregularities appeared, probably due to the bricks having been heated above $1000°$ C with the resultant partial formation of magnetite. When this happens the results are upset by oxidation, and a nonlinear relationship between the demagnetization and the remagnetization processes is obtained.

Homogeneity of the original heating throughout the sample is very important. It is better to use specimens of small size but baked to the same temperature than to use a large sample that may have been heated differentially.

Results of some archaeomagnetic analyses, expressing the basic dates, are listed in Table 3.1. The error is the standard statistical error of the mean:

$$m = \left( \frac{\Delta_i^2}{N(N-1)} \right)^{1/2} ,$$

where $\Delta_i = k_i - k_{AV}$, the deviation from the average of the k value for the $i$th sample, and N is the numer of acceptable samples for the locality.

### 3.6.5
### Archaeomagnetic Dating

Curves of declination D, inclination I, and the earth's magnetic intensity F obtained from a given area may be used directly for archaeological dating in other areas. The existence of a westward drift of the earth's magnetic field is the principal reason for the shape of archaeomagnetic curves being different at various locations on the earth's surface, especially in relation to geographical longitude. For example, Fig. 3.4 reveals that about A.D. 1700 an inclination maximum for Europe corresponds to a minimum for Japan. The shifts in maximum values of intensity become obvious from the graphs for Europe, America, and

Japan (see Figs. 3.11, 3.12, and 3.9). Moreover, because of the cyclic character of D and I, most values appear to be the same at different time periods. Therefore a single curve for D or I is not sufficient for dating, even in an area for which the basic archaeomagnetic curve was determined.

The shape of F, which differs considerably from both D and I curves, is very significant for dating purposes. Even though the same values may appear on it at different times, the time segments for such duplication are very long (of the order of 9000 years). With magnetic intensity determined, the dating is more accurate, especially when the curve for I is additionally available. In such a case, the archaeomagnetic dating can be applied with an accuracy of ± 50 years. When only F is known, the age of an unknown archaeological sample can be determined with an accuracy of ± 100 to 400 years, depending upon the period to which it belongs and on the distance from the area from which the basic data were obtained. Thus, when basic archaeomagnetic data are known for Central Europe they can be utilized for dating in all of Europe, but for North America data derived from American archaeological materials are necessary.

## 3.7
## Correlations Between $C^{14}$ Deviations and Changes
## in the Earth's Magnetic Moment

Elsasser, Ney, and Winckler (18) observed that a decrease of the magnetic moment is followed by an increase in the cosmic-ray flux and thus by an increase in the production rate of $C^{14}$. Higher values of the field have the opposite effect. Radiocarbon analyses of dendrochronologically and historically dated samples by Ralph and Michael (19), Suess (20), and Berger and Libby (21) have revealed deviations of the radiocarbon contents when calculated either with a half-life of 5568 or 5730 years. Figure 3.21 offers an interesting comparison of radiocarbon deviations and changes in the earth's magnetic moment. A close correlation of both events is apparent.

The increase of the magnetic moment around A.D. 900 is immediately followed by the decrease of $C^{14}$ deviations to negative values. This is valid for older periods also. The differences in the trend of the

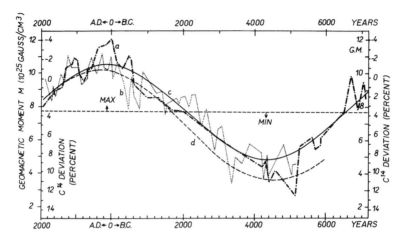

**Fig. 3.21** Comparison of deviations of radiocarbon dates (half-life 5730 years) according to Suess (20) (curve b), with changes in the geomagnetic moment (curve a). The smoothed sinusoidal curve for changes of the magnetic moment is represented by c, and for the radiocarbon deviations by d. In the latter, the 5568-year half-life was used.

curves (a and b) between A.D. 1600 and 1900 could be the result of the paucity of archaeomagnetic data for the North American continent. In the nineteenth century, combustion of fossil fuels (Suess effect) could be the cause of $C^{14}$ irregularities. It may be said that all changes of the magnetic moment seem to have caused changes in the cosmic-ray flux at approximately the same time (maximally with the lag of 100 years). Changes within short periods are probably due to the nondipole magnetic field. In turn, the increase of the earth's magnetic moment may be caused by an intensification of the turbulent processes in the earth's interior.

If we apply the sinusoidal curve shown in Fig. 3.17 to Fig. 3.21, we see a very good coincidence not only for the main changes of the earth's magnetic moment but also for radiocarbon deviations. This is especially true if we apply a slightly different value for the $C^{14}$ content of biological materials and use the half-life of 5730 years. (The dashed sinusoidal curve d in Fig. 3.21 with the half-life of 5568 years shows values that are too low, particularly between 3000 and 4000 B.C.). We may then conclude that the fluctuations in the radiocarbon production rate seem to correlate inversely with the changes in the earth's magnetic

moment. Some of the differences between the trends of both curves a̲
and b̲ in Fig. 3.21 appear to be due to imprecise archaeological dating
of samples used for the analyses. The deviation of 1 percent in $C^{14}$
production corresponds to the change of $0.645 \times 10^{25}$ gauss/cm$^3$ of
the earth's magnetic moment.

From what was here presented, it may be deduced that the earth's
magnetic field has shown significant changes not only during the last
centuries (as determined by direct geomagnetic measurements) but also
in the prehistoric and geologic past. These changes included reversals of
geomagnetic polarity.

The solution of an important problem—examination of the geomagnetic field for the past 40,000 years—so important for dating in archaeology and geology will require additional, more detailed archaeomagnetic and palaeomagnetic investigations of both archaeological objects
and rocks as well as more accurate dating of basic samples. The archaeomagnetic results so far achieved warrant the continuation of these
studies.

## 3.8
### Distribution and Characteristics of the Earth's Magnetic Field

### 3.8.1
### The Geographical Distribution of the Magnetic Field
The earth's magnetic field has been studied by direct measurements
over the past 400 years. The oldest magnetic charts, even though based
on relatively scarce measurements, provide a good basis mainly for the
study of secular variation (22).

The total intensity of the geomagnetic field F̲ is a vector, the direction and strength of which is constantly changing. For example, in
southern Europe at the present, its value is about 46,000 γ (i.e., 0.46
Oe) and in northern Europe about 50,000 γ. In the North the intensity
vector subtends the angle of 65° (inclination) from the horizontal. It
may be subdivided into six geomagnetic components D̲, H̲, Z̲, I̲, X̲, Y̲,
as follows from Fig. 3.22. The geomagnetic field is usually described in
terms of three measured components D̲, H̲, Z̲ which unambiguously
define its direction and value at different places of the earth's surface.
Conventional instruments are used for measurement of these magnetic

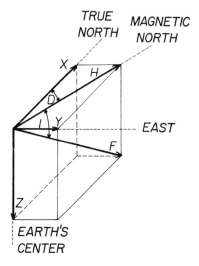

**Fig. 3.22** Division of the earth's magnetic field F into six geomagnetic components D, H, Z, I, X, and Y.

values. As the chart of geomagnetic intensities (Fig. 3.23) shows, the highest values are in the polar regions (around 0.6 Oe), the lowest (around 0.3 Oe) near the equator (23). The location of the magnetic poles was determined on the basis of measurements in Canada ($\varphi$ = 72.5° N. Lat., $\lambda$ = 100° W. Long.) and in Antarctica ($\varphi$ = 70° S. Lat., $\lambda$ = 140° E. Long.) From the same chart it is evident that besides the main dipolar fields other smaller fields, i.e., anomalies, are present.

**3.8.2**

**Temporal Distribution of the Field**

Secular variation of the geomagnetic field is usually defined as a change between average values of certain geomagnetic components at any point of the earth's surface for two points of time divided by the number of years between them. The secular variation is variable in dependence on geographical latitude and longitude. Its continuous course at magnetic observatories is given by the curves of average annual geomagnetic values for the time period during which the registration of magnetic values took place. The surface distribution of the secular variation is charted with isopors (lines passing through points of equal annual changes of any geomagnetic component).

Chronological series of the average annual geomagnetic values show a

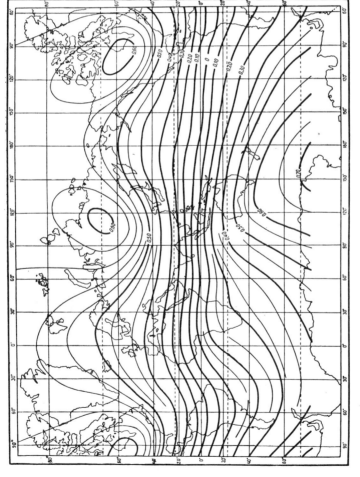

**Fig. 3.23** Chart of the vertical geomagnetic intensity for A.D. 1950.0. Units of intensity are oersteds. (After B. M. Yanovskiy) (23).

relatively complicated course of changes. In studying graphs of the changes during the past 50 years for observatories at specified longitudes (Fig. 3.24) we observe, for instance, a decrease of 4,000 $\gamma$, or 7 percent, in Baldwin, Mississippi, U.S.A., while an increase of only 5 percent took place at Dehra Dun, India. This is strong evidence for wide changes of the earth's field. When proceeding westward from Asiatic to European observatories we observe at first an increase of the field, which is then followed in Europe by a minimum in A.D. 1915. This minimum shifts with time. It had appeared in eastern Europe before it did in western Europe. The steady and continuing decrease of the geomagnetic values (7 percent) over the entire North American continent during the last 50 years is remarkable.

When expressing the main features of the magnetic field by means of the eccentric dipole, we see that at present its position is some 400 km off the earth's center and is steadily moving toward China at the speed of 3 km/year (24). Also, as numerous geomagnetic measurements since 1700 show, the surface positions of the magnetic poles have changed. Apart from their daily variations, as the poles transfer along a circle with a 50-km radius, the secular changes for the past 250 years total about 20° of geographical longitude and 10° of latitude. The curves representing the progression of changes in the magnetic poles' positions in chronological order express essentially a spiral movement, which is most probably influenced by the nondipole magnetic field as well as by the rotation of the not wholly homogeneous earth. Even though the direct magnetic measurements do not allow determination of the exact change during a long time period, the conclusions of several geomagnetologists show the velocity of the westward drift to be approximately 5° in 120 years. This means that the time necessary for a complete cycle of the secular variations is about 9000 years.

The changes of the earth's magnetic moment have been investigated on the basis of spherical harmonic analyses of the world's magnetic charts since A.D. 1550. It increased from 0.324 gauss (in 1550) to 0.329 gauss about 1850. Then a considerable decrease took place until in 1945 its value amounted to only 0.310 gauss. It thus is evident that the magnitude of the earth's magnetic moment also depends on the secular variation.

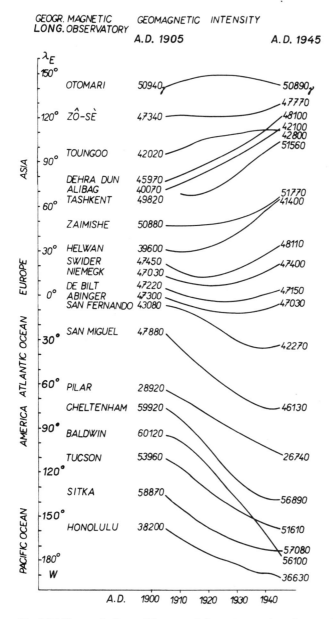

Fig. 3.24 Changes in the earth's magnetic intensity at selected magnetic observatories arranged longitudinally. Intensities are given in gammas.

### 3.8.3

### Characteristics of the Earth's Magnetic Field

The shape of the field on the earth's surface indicates a complicated character that points to the fact that on a homogeneous (dipole) field further components are superimposed. Their sources are also rather complicated. On the basis of different effects, it is possible to identify the following main components:

1. homogeneous (dipole) magnetic field;
2. nondipole field of continental (terrestrial) anomalies;
3. isoporic foci of the earth's magnetic field;
4. westward drift of the nondipole field and of isoporic foci;
5. changes in direction of earth's magnetic field vectors;
6. reversals of the earth's magnetic field polarity;
7. polar wandering.

Of these components, the homogeneous (dipole) field represents the slowly varying main part of the whole earth's field. The nondipole field is composed of six continental (terrestrial) magnetic anomalies. The chart of the $Z$-component (Fig. 3.2) shows three positive anomalies (the Asiatic, Antarctic, American) and three negative ones (African, Icelandic, Australian). The nondipole field and foci of the secular variations can be regarded as specific stages of a regenerative cycle; however, processes that create the earth's magnetic field are so complicated that an unambiguous explanation is very difficult. Isoporic foci and westward drift of the geomagnetic field are shown in Fig. 3.16 for the period 1912-1942; it represents magnetic isopors characterizing the equal annual changes of the magnetic field; the shift of isoporic foci (centers of positive or negative changes) during the past 40 years is indicated with heavy dashed lines.

The drift of terrestrial anomalies and isoporic foci in a westward direction is important as a manifestation that part of the earth's core is liquid. This can be explained on the basis of the assumption that the angular velocity of rotation of the earth's mantle and that of the upper core are different. In recent models, the earth is composed of three concentric shells rotating at different speeds; the inner two are in the core, and it is here that the dynamomechanism regenerating the earth's magnetic field arises as a consequence of different velocities. Such a system, which can maintain a magnetic field in an electrically conducting field, is designated as a hydromagnetic dynamo. The reason for this activity in the earth's interior is convection, probably caused by radioactively generated heat and by simultaneous rotational or Coriolis forces. Further studies of changes of the geomagnetic field over longer time intervals in the past are sorely needed to clarify the dynamic processes inside the earth. Reversals of the earth's magnetic polarity were found to have taken place not only during past geological periods (i.e., several hundreds of millions of years ago) but also within the past one million years. A typical example of the course of the total geomagnetic reversal about 900,000 years ago is shown in Fig. 3.25. The magnetic declination changed from $180°$ to near $0°$; magnetic inclination determined from the remanent magnetization of older layers of sedimentary rocks had values that were changing to positive ones as they approached the present. Even in more recent periods, geomagnetic reversals of short duration took place. Finally, long-term palaeomagnetic polar wandering has occurred during the past billion years; it is explainable either by slow but extensive movements of the magnetic (and probably geo-

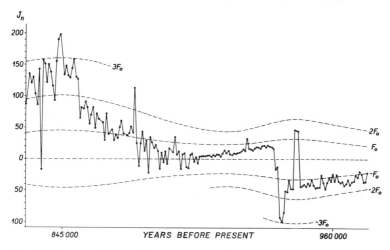

**Fig. 3.25** Changes of the earth's magnetic intensity F calculated on the basis of the curve for stable remanent magnetization and of curves which characterize the values of the geomagnetic field in terms of the present-day field (curves marked $F_0$ and $-F_0$), its double values (curves $2F_0$ and $-2F_0$), and its triple values (curves $3F_0$ and $-3F_0$). The minus values, below the 0-axis, represent reversed polarity. The horizontal axis expresses years, the vertical axis represents natural remanent magnetization ($J_n$).

graphical) axes of the earth or by continental drift. Both these phenomena as well as the changes of the total geomagnetic intensity in the
interval of the past 9000 years were investigated by means of indirect
magnetic methods based on measurements of remanent magnetization
of baked clay and of rock samples.

## 3.9
### Properties of Minerals Inherent in Clays

Rocks containing minerals with magnetic properties can be classified
into four basic groups: diamagnetic, paramagnetic, antiferromagnetic,
and ferrimagnetic. We are mainly interested in the ferrimagnetic and
partially antiferromagnetic minerals. Despite their scarcity (only several
percent of the total volume), they are the main carriers of rock magnetism. Ferrimagnetics are known to be spontaneously magnetized at
temperatures far lower than their Curie point temperature. Individual
grains are further divided into magnetic areas, the so-called domains.
Within each domain they possess spin magnetic moments with the same
direction; the direction, however, differs in neighboring domains. Individual domains are surrounded by domain walls that separate successive changes in the direction of the magnetic moment of atoms. The
grains of the ferrimagnetic minerals are composed of one or more domains, depending on the grain size. During the magnetization process,
the spin moments are aligned in one direction. The most important
group of minerals is found in the $FeO-Fe_2O3-TiO_2$ system. Hematite,
goethite, lepidocrocite, and magnetite occur most frequently in the
archaeological clay samples used for archaeomagnetic analyses.

Hematite ($\alpha$-$Fe_2O_3$), a carrier of stable remanent magnetization and
from which reliable results are obtained, has a rhombohedral or hexa-
hedral lattice. It is paramagnetic when heated to more than 675° C, but
below this temperature it is antiferromagnetic. The antiferromagnetic
display is not perfect because of certain differences in the sublattices
that cause the ferromagnetic properties. This asymmetry may be due to
the presence of elementary domains in which the sublattices were not
equivalent either geometrically or because of changes in their composition; hence, each domain will experience spontaneous magnetization,
but without perfect compensation among domains. When heated in air,
dissociation of hematite to magnetite takes place at 1400° C.

Goethite ($\alpha$-FeO·OH) and lepidocrocite ($\gamma$-FeO·OH) display remanent magnetization which is relatively low. They usually occur in clays and red-brown sedimentary rocks. The dehydration process created hematite and incidentally maghemite; these were chemically formed for the most part after the sedimentation of materials containing hematite in the oxidized environment took place. The remanent magnetization of samples containing goethite and lepidocrocite amounts to less than $10^{-5}$ to $10^{-8}$ CGSM units; their palaeomagnetic investigation was possible only after the highly sensitive astatic and spinner magnetometers had been developed. These two minerals often build very complicated solid solutions with hematite and have stable magnetization; therefore samples in which they occur, especially when heated to higher temperatures, are frequently suitable for archaeomagnetic and palaeomagnetic investigations. The elimination of unstable components in the remanent magnetization which sometimes occur in such samples may be effected by means of appropriate magnetic cleaning methods.

Magnetite ($Fe_3O_4 Fe^{++}Fe_2^{+++}O_4$) has a cubic lattice and belongs to the spinel group, its lattice constant $\underline{a}$ being 8.396 Å (for natural magnetite). The elementary cell contains 32 ions of oxygen and 24 cations. The magnetic moments of cations for tetrahedral and octahedral positions are antiparallel and differing, thus giving the ferrimagnetic properties of magnetite. When cooled to about $-160°$ C, the structure of magnetite deforms into a rhombohedral shape.

Other ferrimagnetic minerals, such as maghemite ($\gamma$-$Fe_2O_3$), ilmenite ($FeTiO_3$), and pyrrhotite ($FeS_{1+x}$), do not usually occur in baked clays; their presence can cause inhomogeneities of results obtained after the laboratory heating because they display mineralogical and chemical phase changes and their remanent magnetization usually is not stable.

## 3.10
### Techniques of Archaeomagnetic Measurements
## 3.10.1
### The Astatic and Spinner Magnetometers

Among the devices used for the measurement of remanent magnetization, the astatic and spinner magnetometers have proved to be the most convenient.

The basic element of the astatic magnetometer is the astatic system, usually composed of two magnets of approximately equal magnetic moment, installed with opposite polarity on a bar at a distance of several millimeters, and the system is suspended on a fine thread. The suspension compensates for the prevailing portion of the earth's magnetic field. The achievable sensitivity is maximally $10^{-8}$ Oe/division and depends on the properties of the magnets used and on the degree of resulting astatization. It may be expressed by the equation

$$\epsilon = \frac{t_k^2 \, \Delta M}{4\pi^2 \, \alpha R} \, ,$$

where $t_k$ is the period of oscillation, $\Delta M$ is the difference in the magnetic moments of the magnets used, and $\alpha R$ represents moments of inertia of the whole system around its vertical axis. The Dolginov magnetometer is a simple astatic magnetometer with lower sensitivity. It is used for strongly magnetic samples (sensitivity of $10^{-4}$ Oe/division) (Fig. 3.26). For measurements of weakly magnetic samples, Pešina's magnetometer, with a sensitivity of $10^{-7}$ Oe/division, is used in Czechoslovakia. Samples of regular shape, mostly cubes, are used to determine the magnetic field and to calculate its magnetic moment M. The use of cubic samples enables determinations of the remanent magnetization for three perpendicular axes x, y, and z, where x trends to the North, y to the East, and z to the earth's center. The samples are measured in a side (first gauss) position at a fixed distance from the lower magnet. Altogether the sample is measured in twelve positions, i.e., four for each axis, in order to eliminate any errors due to inhomogeneities in samples and to negate the influence of the upper magnet. Average values of measurements for individual axes provide the remanent magnetization in components $J_x$, $J_y$, $J_z$. When the oriented samples are measured, the values of declination (D) and inclination (I) also can be calculated by the equations

$$\tan D = \frac{J_y}{J_x}$$

and

**Fig. 3.26** The Dolginov astatic magnetometer.

$$\tan I = \frac{J_z}{\sqrt{J_x^2 + J_y^2}} \cdot$$

The magnetic moment is then calculated by use of the equation

$$M = (\chi H + J_r)v = v \sqrt{(J_x)^2 + (J_y)^2 + (J_z)^2}$$

where $\chi$ is the magnetic susceptibility, H the intensity of the magnetic field, $J_r$ the remanent magnetization, and v the volume of the sample. This equation may also serve for the calculation of magnetic susceptibility, principally in strongly magnetic rocks.

The spinner magnetometer, as developed by V. Jelinek of the Institute of Applied Geophysics in Brno (25) is composed of two parts, a demagnetization coil and a detecting coil (Fig. 3.27). The cubiform sample (2-cm edge) is positioned in the holder and rotated at a given velocity, inducing an alternating field whose amplitude and phase are proportional to the vector of the remanent magnetization of the sample. At the same time there is a rotating magnet that induces a calibration voltage in the reference coil. Either amplitude or phase of the voltage is then measured. By means of the Jelinek spinner, measurements can be carried out at five amplifications, its maximum sensitivity being $4 \times 10^{-9}$ CGSM units. The samples are tested in six positions; thus, each component of remanent magnetization is measured four times. The resulting values provide the remanent magnetization for the

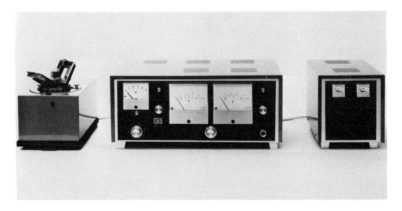

**Fig. 3.27** Spinner magnetometer developed by Jelinek.

three axes x, y, z. The spinner magnetometer of Jelinek currently represents an instrument of peak performance so that samples of all rock types and all types of materials can be examined with high reliability.

### 3.10.2
### The Successive Double-Heating Method

The technique used in archaeomagnetism is based on the fact that thermoremanent magnetization (TRM) of baked clay is proportional to the intensity of the magnetic field acting on the clay as it cools (7). By comparing the strength of the TRM found in an archaeological sample of baked clay with the value acquired after reheating in the earth's field of the present, a ratio of the ancient nature and the present-day field in the laboratory is obtained, and the ancient intensity can thus be determined. In order to get reliable results, a step-by-step technique of heating to successively higher temperatures must be used. The TRM is proportional, in fields of low intensity, to the intensity of the field in which it originated. A partial magnetic moment of the sample having a volume v corresponds to the partial thermoremanent magnetization $J_p(t_2, F_p, t_i)$ originating in the temperature interval $(t_2, t_1)$ and in the known field $F_p$; it follows that

$$M_p(t_2, F_p, t_1) = v\, I_p(t_2, F_p t_1).$$

In an analogous way temperatures are increased to $675°$ C, the Curie point of hematite. As long as a given field $F_0$ affected the rock or archaeological sample at the time when it was originally heated to a high temperature, the value of the magnetic moment $M_p(t_{i+1}, F_0, t_i)$ also increases for successive intervals $(t_{i+1}, t_i)$. According to the law of addition the ratio of the ancient geomagnetic field $F_0$ and the laboratory field $F_p$ corresponds to the ratio of their partial moments and hence to the partial TRMs in the samples of equal volumes, that is,

$$\frac{F_0}{F_p} = \frac{M_p(t_{i+1}, F_0, t_i)}{M_p(t_{i+1}, F_p, t_i)} = \frac{J_p(t_{i+1}, F_0, t_i)}{J_p(t_{i+1}, F_p, t_i)}.$$

For instance, in applying this equation to hematite samples for the entire range of temperatures up to the Curie point, we obtain

$$\frac{F_0}{F_p} = \frac{J_p(t_{675°}, F_0, t_{20°})}{J_p(t_{675°}, F_p, t_{20°})}.$$

After having examined several hundreds of samples, it has been our experience that temperatures above 600° C engender mineralogical phase changes in the majority of rocks and baked clays. On the other hand, weathering brings about certain changes in remanent magnetization at low temperatures; in this case the application of the above equation would result in inaccurate and often incorrect values of the strength of the geomagnetic field. Therefore, particularly in the range of 100° to 500° C the increment of increase should be 50° or 100° C. This will give us more values of the ratio $F_0/F_p$, the average of which will express more accurate data and moreover serve as a check of the linearity of the heating process. If a successive increase or drop of the coefficient k occurs, certain phase changes of ferrimagnetic minerals are to be anticipated.

Measurements of TRM are done with an astatic magnetometer. Owing to the relatively high value of the TRM in archaeological objects, a magnetometer of the Dolginov or Pešina type is adequate.

A nonmagnetic furnace is used (Fig. 3.28) for heating. Its capacity allows simultaneous heating of from 30 to 150 specimens, depending on their size. The wiring of the furnace was designed to provide a uniform temperature throughout, without disturbing fields. The samples

**Fig. 3.28** Nonmagnetic oven for the archaeomagnetic double-heating method.

are heated successively to temperatures of 100°, 150°, 200°, 300°, 350°, 400°, 450°, and 500° C (first in one position and then in a position reversed 180° for each temperature). The influence of the laboratory field is most pronounced in the z-component, while in the y-component (perpendicular to the laboratory field) it is much smaller and always regular. Because of this we choose the axes of the cube in such a way that the z-component of the magnetization is the greatest and the y-component the least (26).

The demagnetization curve is then plotted from the measurements obtained for the direct and reversed positions and the remagnetization curve from the difference between these measurements. In most cases a temperature of 500° C was sufficient to eliminate the primary TRM. Only in special cases was it necessary to go to 600° and sometimes 670° C. This procedure, compared with the method of first measuring the demagnetization curve in zero field and then the magnetization curve in the laboratory field, has certain advantages and provides more reliable results.

Although the TRM of archaeological objects is relatively stable, approximately half of the samples manifested enough viscous magnetization at low temperatures to change the primary TRM significantly. In these cases it was not possible to calculate results in the range of 20° to 100° C and in exceptional cases, up to 300° C. Whether or not it is still possible to utilize the sample then depends on the number of results obtainable from the remaining temperature ranges. An important criterion for sample acceptability is that at last three adjacent increments provide values of k within the limits of the acceptable error of ± 10 percent.

In cases where archaeological objects were heated to temperatures higher than 500° C in ancient times, the increments from 100° to 500° C usually prove suitable for magnetic-field determinations. At 600° to 670° C, changes of the coefficient k often take place, probably because of phase changes of ferrimagnetic minerals in the sample. In baked archaeological objects these minerals are mostly composed of different oxides of the $Fe_2O_3$ series; hematite is not necessarily the predominant mineral. This tends to confirm the hypothesis that the Curie point of archaeological samples often lies between 500° and 600° C.

### 3.10.3

### Magnetic Cleaning

To eliminate the secondary, disturbing magnetizations that may have arisen in archaeological samples because of chemical changes or of long-term continued action of the earth's magnetic field, it is necessary to carry out "magnetic cleaning" of the remanent magnetization of oriented samples when declination and inclination are to be determined. One of two methods may be used.

(a) When a sample is subjected to an alternating magnetic field, the weak coercive forces in domains of ferrimagnetic minerals are successively overcome and the remanent magnetization is demagnetized step by step. While this process is being carried out in zero direct field, less stable components of the remanent magnetization are removed first; after the application of more intense alternating fields, the stable component of remanent magnetization also begins to drop. Thus, this method provides both accurate separation of unstable and stable magnetizations, and the determination of the direction of the stable primary magnetization. The absence of all direct magnetic fields that could cause a new magnetization is essential.

The device for demagnetization by means of an alternating field, with the sample rotating around three mutually perpendicular axes (Fig. 3.29), was developed in the Geophysical Institute in Prague. It contains a rotating head in which the sample is placed in the center of a system of Helmholtz coils. The earth's magnetic field is compensated for by means of these coils. A solenoid in which an alternating field up to 1600 Oe (peak value) can be generated is positioned on a track and can be moved from the center of the Helmholtz coils to a distance of 3 m, allowing a gradual increase and decrease of the field during the demagnetization process. A step-by-step technique of successively increasing values of the ac field is applied in the procedure of magnetic cleaning, until the direction of the remanent magnetization remains constant. This procedure removes all unstable magnetic components and the direction of the remanent magnetization will then correspond to the earth's ancient magnetic field. The declination and inclination of the past era can then be determined.

(b) It has been our experience that samples with large hematite con-

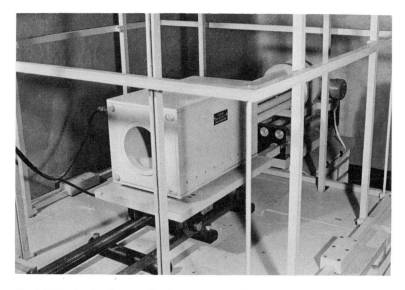

**Fig. 3.29** Device for demagnetization by means of an alternating field up to 2000 Oe, with sample rotating.

tents have very stable disturbing magnetic components of remanent magnetization which cannot be removed by an ac field of even as large as 1000 Oe. On the other hand, thermal demagnetization is very efficient in such cases because it eliminates secondary components at temperatures as low as 100° or 200° C. A nonmagnetic oven is again used for this method. To assure zero magnetic field in the oven, a device with Helmholtz coils is utilized. Because the sample must not be moved during heating, perfect alignment for compensation of the field with an accuracy of several $\gamma$ is required since otherwise new disturbing magnetizations could originate even in small magnetic fields. When the direction of the field remains the same after several successive heatings, the procedure of cleaning is finished.

**3.10.4**

**Evaluation of Results**

Magnetic measurements of a series of archaeological samples represent basic material for evaluating the changes of the earth's magnetic field and constructing the archaeomagnetic curve for a period of a length determined by archaeological objects of known age. If oriented samples are available, magnetic intensity, declination, and inclination can be established. With unoriented samples only the ancient magnetic intensity and its changes are determinable.

A reliable course of changes in the earth's magnetic field can be found by measuring samples from artifacts covering the span of time to be studied and datable to points within that span which are 50 to 100 years apart.

(a) In order to determine the direction of the earth's magnetic field in the past reliably, a relatively large number of samples, at least five of the same age, are needed. Additionally, any change in position of the fire-pits or other sources of samples that occurred since their original heating must be verified. Average values of D and I, the direction of the field and magnetic poles are calculated from the measured values. Fisher's statistical method (27), which was developed for palaeomagnetic purposes, is very convenient.

By examining the archaeomagnetic declination and inclination for all samples from a given locality, we obtain a set of values for the determination of average dates.

Let us assume that N samples have been collected at a locality and their declination $D_n$ and inclination $I_n$ have been determined; then the cosines $L_n$, $m_n$, $n_n$ of the vector of magnetization are expressed as

$$L_n = \cos D_n \cos I_n,$$

$$m_n = \sin D_n \cos I_n,$$

$$n_n = \sin I_n .$$

The direction of an average vector for a certain group of samples can be found by calculating average values of cosines, that is,

$$L = \sum_{n=1}^{N} \frac{L_n}{R} \, , \; m = \sum_{n=1}^{N} \frac{m_n}{R} \, , \; n = \sum_{n=1}^{N} \frac{n_n}{R} \, ,$$

where

$$R = \sqrt{\left( \sum_{n=1}^{N} L_n \right)^2 + \left( \sum_{n=1}^{N} m_n \right)^2 + \left( \sum_{n=1}^{N} n_n \right)^2} .$$

On this basis the average values of D and I can be determined.

Both in palaeomagnetism and archaeomagnetism the coordinates are usually applied to define a geocentric dipole; this would indicate that the direction of the earth's magnetic field is examined by means of geomagnetic elements D and I. Hence, by determining the mean vector of magnetization for a group of samples we can calculate the position of the magnetic dipole axis that corresponds to the field which had acted on the sample at the time of its origin. The declination indicates the direction in which the magnetic pole is to be found. The inclination is related to the geomagnetic latitude $\underline{p}$ of the site where the samples were collected, as expressed by

$$\cotan p = \frac{1}{2}\tan I.$$

Supplementary geographic latitude $\Theta_0$ and the length $\lambda_0$ of the pole can be found from equations for the spherical triangle

$$\cos \Theta_0 = \cos \Theta_s \cos p + \sin \Theta_s \sin p \cos D,$$

$$\sin (\lambda_0 - \lambda_s) = \frac{\sin p \sin D}{\sin \Theta}$$

$$\cos (\lambda_0 - \lambda_s) = \frac{\cos p - \sin \varphi_s \sin \varphi_0}{\cos \varphi_s \cos \varphi_0} = \frac{\cos p - \cos \varphi_s \cos \varphi_0}{\sin \varphi_s \sin \varphi_0},$$

where $\Theta_s = 90°$ and $\varphi_s$, $\lambda_s$ are the geographic coordinates of the locality. These formulas simultaneously define the circle of probability around the determined poles. If $\alpha$ is a semivertical angle of the circle of probability, then

$$\alpha = dI = dD \cos I,$$

where dI and dD define changes in declination and inclination. The semi-axes of an oval of probability around the mean palaeomagnetic pole are determined by applying the equations

$$\delta p = \frac{1}{2}(1 + 3\cos^2 p)dI,$$

$$\delta m = \frac{\sin p}{\cos I}.$$

The semi-axis δp connects the center of the site of collection with the calculated palaeomagnetic pole; the semi-axis δm is perpendicular to δp. The calculated average values of D and I for groups of samples of different ages can be used directly to construct basic archaeomagnetic curves of D and I or the path of changes in the archaeomagnetic pole. Archaeomagnetic curves are discussed below.

(b) By applying the successive double-heating method we obtain values characterizing a correlation between the demagnetization and the magnetization process. We prefer to determine the coefficient k on the basis of the graphic construction using the straight line mentioned in subsection (a), rather than from the individual temperatures increments. The graphic method enables us to decide reliably which points are to be taken into consideration and which must be excluded. If it is possible to draw a straight line through at least four successive points, and if this line is defined for at least two thirds of its length between the y- and x-axes, the results should be valid (as long as the spread of k computed from each two values for neighboring temperatures is not greater than ± 10 percent). It is desirable, of course, to verify the results by measuring additional samples from the same archaeological feature.

It is not always possible to carry out the investigation of total intensity with a sufficient number of samples. The minimum number should be five. To learn what the standard error might be for fewer samples, we undertook the investigation of thirteen samples of burnt clay (baked to red color) acquired from one locality. The resulting k values showed a standard error of the mean of only 0.032 (i.e., 1.6 percent) thereby justifying the method even with as few as five samples. As long as the archaeological material provides a reliable linear dependence of demagnetization and remagnetization values (the number of temperature increments should not be smaller than three), the ratio so obtained provides a valid measure of the intensity of the earth's magnetic field in the period studied.

## References

1. Van Allen, J. A.,
"The Geomagnetically Trapped Corpuscular Radiation." Journal of Geophysical Research 64 (1959): 1683.

2. Inglis, D.,
"Theories of the Earth's Magnetism." Reviews of Modern Physics 27
(1955): 212.
3. Vestine, E. H., Laporte, L., Lange, I., Cooper, C., and Hendrix,
W. C.,
"Description of the Earth's Main Magnetic Field and Its Secular
Change, 1905-1945." Carnegie Institute of Washington Publication 578
(1948).
4. Kawai, N., and Hirooka, K.,
"Wobbling Motion of the Geomagnetic Dipole Field in Historic Time
During These 2000 Years." Journal of Geomagnetism and Geoelectricity 19 (1967): 217-227.
5. Nagata, T., Arai, Y., and Momose, K.,
"Secular Variation of the Geomagnetic Total Force during the Last
5000 Years." Journal of Geophysical Research 68 (1963): 5277-5281.
6. Sasayima, S.,
"Geomagnetic Secular Variation Revealed in the Baked Earths in West
Japan. Part 2: Change of the Field Intensity. Journal of Geomagnetism and Geoelectricity 17 (1965): 413-416.
7. Thellier, E., and Thellier, O.,
"Sur l'intensité du champ magnétique terrestre dans le passé historique
et géologique." Annales de Géophysique 15 (1959): 285-376.
8. Burlatskaya, S. P.,
Arkheomagnetizm: Issledovaniye polya zemli v proshliye epochi
(Archaeomagnetism: A study of the Earth's Field in Former Epochs).
Izdatelstvo Nauka, Moscow (1965): 65-94.
9. Weaver, K. F.,
"Magnetic Clues Help Date the Past." National Geographic Magazine
131 (May 1967): 696-701.
10. Athavale, R. N.,
"Intensity of the Geomagnetic Field in India over the Past 4000
Years." Nature 210 (1966): 1310-1312.
11. Schwarz, E. J., and Christie, K. W.,
"Original Remanent Magnetization of Ontario Potsherds." Journal of
Geophysical Research 72 (1967): 3263-3269.
12. Nagata, T., Kobayashi, K., and Schwarz, E. J.,
"Archaeomagnetic Intensity Studies of South and Central America."
Journal of Geomagnetism and Geoelectricity 17 (1965): 399-405.
13. Kitazawa, K., and Kobayashi, K.,
"Intensity Variation of the Geomagnetic Field during the Past 4000
Years in South America." Journal of Geomagnetism and Geoelectricity
20 (1968): 1, 7.

14. Bucha, V.,
"Changes of the Earth's Magnetic Moment and Radiocarbon Dating."
Nature 224 (1969): 681-683.
15. Bucha, V., Taylor, R. E., Berger, R., and Haury, E. W.,
"Geomagnetic Intensity: Changes during the Past 3000 Years in the
Western Hemisphere." Science 168 (1970): 111-114.
16. Burlatskaya, S. P., Nechayeva, T. B., and Petrova, G. N.,
"Otsenka zapadnogo dreyfa vekovogo khoda nakloneniya i izmeneniya
magnitnogo momenta zemli po arkheomagnitnym dannym (An Appraisal
of the Westward Drift of the Secular Variations of the Earth's Magnetic
Inclination and Moment on the Basis of Archaeomagnetic Data)."
Izvestiya AN SSSR: Fizika Zemli 6 (1965): 31-42.
17. Bucha, V.,
"Influence of the Earth's Magnetic Field on Radiocarbon Dating." In
Olsson, I. U. (Editor), Radiocarbon Variations and Absolute Chronol-
ogy, Proceedings of the Twelfth Nobel Symposium, Uppsala, Sweden,
August 11-15, 1969, 501-512. Almquist and Wiksell, Stockholm (Wiley
Interscience Division, John Wiley & Sons, New York, 1970).
18. Elsasser, W., Ney, E. P., and Winckler, J. R.,
"Cosmic-Ray Intensity and Geo-Magnetism." Nature 178 (1956):
1226-1227.
19. Ralph, E. K., and Michael, H. N.,
"University of Pennsylvania Radiocarbon Dates XII." Radiocarbon 11
(1969): 469-481.
20. Suess, H. E.,
"Die Eichung der Radiokarbonuhr." Bild der Wissenschaft 6 (1969):
121-127.
21. Berger, R., and Libby, W. F.,
"UCLA Radiocarbon Dates VI." Radiocarbon 9 (1967): 477-504.
22. Bock, R.,
Katalog der Jahresmittel der magnetischen Elemente der Observatorien
und der Stationen, an denen eine Zeitlang erdmagnetische Beobach-
tungen stattfanden, Band I-IV. Geophysikalisches Institut Potsdam,
Abhandlungen. Edited by R. Bock, Nr. 8, 1948.
Akademie-Verlag Berlin.
23. Yanovskiy, B. M.,
Zemnoy magnetizm. Moscow (1953).
24. Malin, S. R. C.,
"Geomagnetic Secular Variation and its Changes, 1942.5 to 1962.5."
The Geophysical Journal, Royal Astronomical Society 17 (1969): 415-
441.

**25. Jelinek, V.,**
"A High Sensitivity Spinner Magnetometer." Studia Geophysica et Geodaetica (Prague), 10 (1966): 58-78.

**26. Bucha, V.,**
"Intensity of the Earth's Magnetic Field during Archaeological Times in Czechoslovakia." Archaeometry 10 (1967): 12-22.

**27. Fisher, Arne,**
Mathematical Theory of Probabilities and Its Application to Frequency Curves and Statistical Methods, Vol. 1, Second Edition Greatly Enlarged. Macmillan Co., New York (1922).

# 4

### Thermoluminescent Dating of Pottery

John Winter

## 4.1
## Introduction

Archaeologists will scarcely need to be tcld of the potential value of a dating method that can be applied directly to pottery and similar wares. The fact that ceramics are themselves prime study materials assures great interest in any method of dating them that does not assume any association with something else (e.g., carbonaceous remains). Thermoluminescent dating is one such technique; more precisely, it sets out to measure the time elapsed since a piece of pottery was last heated to more than about 500° C—normally the time elapsed since firing.

This chapter will try to describe the principles of the method and the various factors that may affect the calculation of a date, and hence to give some idea of the breadth of its application and reliability. Experimental techniques will only be touched on insofar as they are involved in the foregoing questions.

## 4.2
## Thermoluminescence

Any piece of matter emits visible light if heated to a high enough temperature; it becomes incandescent or "red hot." Some materials, in certain circumstances, can emit light additional to the incandescent glow when heated. This additional emission is not repeatable on reheating; it represents a discharge of stored energy during the heating process. The phenomenon is known as thermoluminescence, or TL; the extra light emission is the thermoluminescent glow. It is usually rather weak—often too weak to be visible to the human eye. A substance exhibiting the phenomenon is called a luminophor or a phosphor.

Thermoluminescence occurs with electrical nonconductors in the solid state and is induced by the action of ionizing radiation on many such materials. The radiation may originate from radioactive isotopes (e.g., $\alpha$, $\beta$, or $\gamma$-radiation) or from other sources (e.g., X rays or cosmic radiation). A small proportion of the energy of the ionizing radiation is stored in the solid material, by virtue of the properties of the rigid array of atoms, and later reappears as light. The proportion of energy that is stored varies a good deal among different luminophors, but the amount of light emitted may as a rule give a measure of the total radiation dose the material has received since it was last heated. In a favorable case, the light output will be linearly proportional to the radiation dose over a wide range. Thermoluminescence can therefore be used to measure radiation doses, for example in the medical field (1). Another application is in dating ceramics.

## 4.3
## Basic Dating Method

Some of the common constituents of pottery, such as quartz, are capable of showing thermoluminescence. When the artifact is fired, it reaches a temperature high enough to discharge any previously stored thermoluminescent energy—a process that may be compared to setting a dial to zero. Subsequently the pottery material is subjected to a small amount of ionizing radiation year by year (Fig. 4.1). Much of this comes from traces of radioactive isotopes in the ceramic itself, some derives from similar isotopes in the burial medium, and a minor proportion from cosmic radiation. When a sample of the ceramic is heated in suitable apparatus, the thermoluminescent glow can be measured; this "natural" glow is assumed to be proportional to the total radiation dose received and also to the sensitivity of the particular ceramic to a given dose. The latter can be measured by giving the material a known, "artificial" dose of suitable radiation and measuring the glow induced as a result. The ratio of "natural" and "artificial" light emission, multiplied by the artificial dose given, should then equal the radiation dose received during burial, that is, the product of the average dose received per year and the number of years elapsed. One must also estimate, therefore, the rate at which the pottery has received its "natural" radiation dose. Assuming this can be done, we sum up the whole process in the basic age equation:

$$\text{Age} = \frac{\text{Natural TL}}{\text{Artificial TL}} \times \frac{\text{Artificial Dose}}{\text{Natural Dose Rate}}$$

There are many complications inherent in these measurements, and the age equation may be modified in the process of dealing with them.

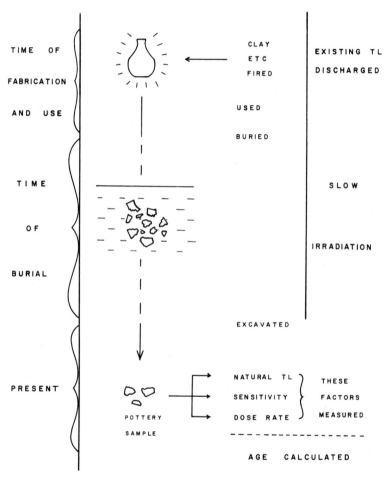

**Fig. 4.1** Schematic diagram showing the principle of the thermoluminescent dating of ceramics.

For example, the amount of thermoluminescence induced can depend on the type of ionizing radiation, so that certain dating techniques involve splitting the "artificial" terms of the equation. However, it is the basis on which TL dating rests. Broadly speaking, the difficulties and complexities of the method fall into two groups: those that arise from the TL phenomenon itself, and those that, external to the phenomenon, arise from the peculiarities of pottery and the circumstances in which it exists. The following section will deal with those points that pertain to the TL phenomenon as such.

## 4.4

### The Mechanism of Thermoluminescence

The origin of TL is both complex and in many ways poorly understood. However, the general features of the physics involved may be indicated in a qualitative and simplified way. For more detailed discussions, see references (1, 2, 3, 4).

When ionizing radiation impinges on a luminophor, energy is transferred to the material in various ways. Some of it excites electrons to higher energy states; many of the excited electrons will rapidly fall back to their original energy states, but a small proportion are able to migrate through the lattice, leaving behind a positively charged vacancy, and may then be trapped at a higher energy than they possessed initially. These trapped electrons are said to be in "metastable" states. For one of them to leave such a state, a certain amount of energy must be supplied to eject it from the trap in which it is situated. Most often, this energy is supplied by thermal vibration—that is, by bringing the material to a high enough temperature. Thus, when a mestastable electron is ejected from its trap, it can recombine with a positive vacancy and thereby drop to the ground state. The energy thus lost by the electron appears as a quantum of electromagnetic radiation, usually in or near the visible region of the spectrum. The sum of these light quanta, taken as the temperature is raised, constitutes the thermoluminescent glow. Once all of the "ejectable" metastable electrons have left their traps— i.e., once the temperature has gone high enough—all of the glow will have been discharged. A graph of the intensity of TL against temperature forms a glow curve; usually it will have one or more peaks as the

TL rises to a maximum. The temperatures at which these occur depend on the energy needed for ejection, that is, on the depth of the traps, and are to some extent characteristic of the material. This has a direct bearing on the dating measurements.

The foregoing accounts for thermoluminescence in terms of the trapping of electrons excited by the radiation. In fact, electron traps themselves can be created by some kinds of ionizing radiation (5, 6, 7) so that at least two physical processes (trap filling and trap creation) are present in practice. Present dating methods are usually interpreted in terms of trap filling, as indicated. The traps themselves are believed often to be associated with defects in the crystal lattice, and their concentration can depend on the chemical nature of the substance, on impurities, and on the thermal and radiation history of the specimen. The sensitivity of luminophors is therefore apt to vary a good deal, even among chemically similar samples.

Some factors inherent in the TL phenomenon that affect the dating process may now be discussed. The first is the question of trap depth (3). Shallow-trapped electrons may be displaced by the thermal energy present at ordinary temperatures; consequently, any TL that appears at relatively low temperatures will decay with time and will not show up in the glow curve from archaeological pottery. A typical pottery glow curve might look like Fig. 4.2 (lower). There is no emission below about 150° C, all TL from this region having decayed to zero. The thermoluminescent emission reaches a maximum at 300° to 350°C; the curve obtained by reheating the sample after all the TL has been discharged is also shown. A necessary assumption is that the metastable electrons responsible for glow at such temperatures are sufficiently deeply entrapped for any decay over archaeological periods to be negligible. This appears to be justified; for example, Tite and Waine (7) made measurements of the half-life for decay from these traps and found it to be in the region $10^5$ to $10^7$ years for peaks around 300° C in the pottery samples they used (it varies somewhat among samples). This is much longer than the age of any archaeological pottery, so that it appears reasonable to accept this assumption, though it might conceivably be questioned, for example, with samples of unusual composition.

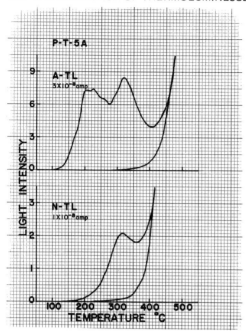

**Fig. 4.2** Typical pottery glow curves. Lower curve: natural glow in a sample of archaeological pottery; upper curve: more intense artificial glow induced by 1000 rads of X radiation. Note change of vertical scale from an amplification of 1 x $10^{-8}$ to 3 x $10^{-8}$ amp.

If a pottery sample, after being heated to drain the natural TL, is given a dose of artificial radiation, it may yield a glow curve like that of Fig. 4.2 (upper). The low-temperature emission will gradually decay with time, a higher-temperature peak remaining. If necessary, a simple test (the "ordinate ratio test") can be used to determine where the nondecaying portion of the artificial curve begins (8). Of course, any electrons in especially deep traps will only be displaced at temperatures where the resulting glow is confused with incandescent emission; such high-temperature TL is therefore of little use for dating. Fortunately, most pottery exhibits glow peaks in the 300-350° C range, and this emission is quite suitable for dating purposes.

So far we have only considered the ejection of metastable electrons from their traps by thermal vibrations. But ejection can also be achieved by other means, e.g., by ultrasonic energy (perhaps as a result of concomitant heating) (9) and by ultraviolet radiation or possibly visible light (5, 10). This latter effect is called optical drainage or optical bleaching and must be avoided during sample processing; for this reason powdered or crushed samples should not be exposed to bright light, particularly if it contains ultraviolet radiation. Because of their opacity, this effect is not a problem with massive pieces of pottery (sherds, etc.).

Next there is the question of how nearly the thermoluminescent emission is directly proportional to the radiation dose. Such a linear relationship is clearly convenient, if not strictly essential. In a plot of TL output against dose (Fig. 4.3) it would look like curve A. In practice it is more usual for such a plot to flatten out at high doses, as with curve B. This is called saturation (7) and may be visualized as being caused by all the existing traps in the material getting filled by electrons. It turns out, however, that this limit is usually well above the doses normally received by archaeological materials. Potentially more worrying is the situation where the plot bends slightly upward, as with curve C. This is known as supralinearity, and its origin is not yet entirely clear. According to Aitken et al. this can sometimes be observed with pottery, though usually in a minor degree, and means of checking for it have been proposed (11, 12). Other workers (13) have not reported such departures from strict proportionality.

A point to mention briefly is the question of non-radiation-induced, or "spurious," TL (10, 14). It was early discovered that a pulverized

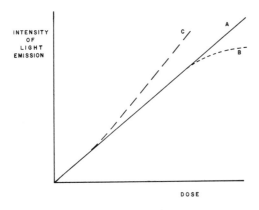

Fig. 4.3 Ways in which TL intensity may vary with absorbed dose. A: ideal result; B: showing saturation; C: showing supralinearity.

sample of pottery would show a light emission quite independent of any radiation it may have absorbed. This additional luminescence seemed to be a surface phenomenon and somehow associated with the pulverizing process. Its origin is still obscure, but fortunately it was found to be suppressed by excluding oxygen from the sample, either by heating the sample in an inert gas atmosphere (14) or by immersing it in a silicone oil (15, 16). Spurious TL is not generally considered a serious problem.

Although the physics of the TL phenomenon remains incompletely understood, the complexities directly associated with it are of a type that can be investigated empirically without too much difficulty. The following sections will outline what is involved in measuring the parameters necessary to obtain a TL age, and in doing so will cover some of the complications deriving from the idiosyncrasies of archaeological pottery.

## 4.5
### Natural Thermoluminescent Glow

The measurement of natural TL glow falls into three stages: sampling the pottery, preparation of the sample, and performing the measurement itself. The latter two are of interest chiefly to the person actually doing the dating.

A distinction should be drawn between techniques that use a piece of pottery material in toto (16) and those that segregate different fractions, usually of different grain size, and treat them separately (11, 17, 18, 19). The reasons for doing the latter arise from the subtleties of dose rate estimation and will be dealt with under that head. The literature may be consulted for methods employed in fractionation (20, 21, 22, 23). Where a whole sample of pottery is used, the sherd is pulverized under carefully controlled conditions. In any case certain precautions are necessary. One is to avoid optical drainage of TL from the powdered sample and another is to avoid any heating, even very local heating, during sampling. The latter is also important where it is necessary to sample a complete artifact rather than fragments. The sampling process will obviously depend on the specific case, but in general it is better to drill out material than to scrape or grind it from a surface, and

better still to detach whole pieces. The last method allows comminu-
tion and/or fractionation to be performed by the dating laboratory as
desired. Drilling produces a sample already in powdered form and needs
to be done carefully if local heating is to be avoided. For this reason,
power tools are better avoided both here and with any form of scraping
or grinding away of material. Sampling from an old surface is undesira-
ble in any event, since the sample may be anomalous: the composition
may have altered by contamination or leaching during burial, and a
surface is more subject to soil radioactivity.

Once the pottery sample is obtained in suitable form, portions of it
need to be mounted so as to allow the TL to be measured, or "read
out"; the mounting must be in a highly reproducible form that permits
rapid and uniform heating of the material. The literature may be consulted for details (15, 16, 21, 22, 23), and also for information on
apparatus (13, 24, 25, 26, 27). The main features of the latter are:
1. A photomultiplier tube which "views" the sample in a light-tight
enclosure, detects the very weak emission and produces a signal that
may be amplified and recorded.
2. Means of heating the sample rapidly and at a reproducible rate. The
reason for rapid heating is mainly to improve the signal-to-noise ratio
by compressing the light emission into as short a time as possible. The
limits on heating rate are placed by one's ability to control and reproduce it accurately and by the limited thermal conductivity of the
sample itself. For reasons dealt with in section 4.3, an inert atmosphere
and/or an admixture of the sample with silicone oil are also employed.
3. The results are generally displayed on some form of chart recorder
producing a plot of light emission vs. temperature.

The result will be a glow curve such as that shown in Fig. 4.2. Although it may be possible for more than one maximum to be present, a
fast heating rate tends to smooth them into one, rather than leaving
them resolved. This, however, is not usually a drawback for dating
purposes.

Strictly speaking, the total thermoluminescent emission is measured
by the area between the glow curve and the background curve. In practice, the peak height is also a good measure (13) and is easier to determine, provided the heating rate is sufficiently well controlled. The two

parameters do not measure exactly the same thing. Integrated area represents the total TL emitted over the temperature range chosen, whereas peak height is proportional to the area under the highest peak in the curve (assuming there is more than one, even if not resolved). Using the latter, therefore, makes it easier to avoid emission belonging to a lower-temperature "fading" peak during the sensitivity measurement involving artificial dosage.

## 4.6

### Sensitivity Measurement

The sensitivity of a given ceramic is always measured in basically the same way: samples of the material are given a known, calibrated radiation dose and the resulting TL is then read out. The artificial dose will also give rise to much low-temperature TL (Fig. 4.2, upper), which is unstable and therefore irrelevant to a comparison with the natural curve. It is usual to allow a week or more for this to decay far enough so that it does not interfere with the part of the curve used for comparison.

A possible objection to the comparison of artificial with natural TL is that the dosages are given at enormously different rates. However, investigations with various luminophors in the medical dosimetry field have failed to show any measurable dependence of TL on the dosage rate (1).

An important point to consider is whether the same luminescent sensitivity is found with the different kinds of radiation involved. Virtually the same response is found for a given energy dose of $\beta$, $\gamma$, or X radiation (the last is sometimes used for sensitivity measurement) (13) but $\alpha$-particles are found to be much less efficient at inducing TL on an energy-absorbed basis (11, 28). The ratio of efficiencies for different pottery samples is reported as varying from 0.05 to 0.3 (11). It will be seen later that this is an important matter with certain dating techniques; one approach (11) makes it necessary to do two separate evaluations of the sensitivity of each sample, using standard $\alpha$ and either $\beta$ or $\gamma$-radiation sources. An appropriate modification to the age equation (section 4.3), involving separate estimations of the $\alpha$ and the $(\beta + \gamma)$ dose rates, will then also be necessary.

## 4.7

### The Radiation-Dose Rate

It is in connection with this factor that some of the more difficult and subtle complications of TL dating are to be found. The unit of radiation dose usually used in this work is the rad, one rad representing an energy absorption from the radiation of 100 ergs per gram of material.

A piece of buried pottery will be subject in general to the following sources of ionizing radiation:

(a) Cosmic radiation. There is general agreement that this is not of great importance, and it will not be considered in detail here.

(b) Radiation from traces of radioactive material in the immediate environment: the environmental dosage. The sum of this and (a) is often called the external, or extrinsic, dosage.

(c) Radiation from traces of radioactive material in the pottery itself: the internal, or intrinsic, dosage.

In the case of (b) and (c) one has to consider $\alpha$, $\beta$, and $\gamma$-radiation. Their relative penetrating powers are of some importance, and may be illustrated by typical ranges listed in Table 4.1. Ranges are to some extent a function of the particular radioactive isotope involved; those for $\beta$ and $\gamma$-radiation, in particular, are maximum values, most of the energy being absorbed within much smaller distances.

Alpha particles have very short ranges, comparable in some cases to the "grain size" in pottery; $\beta$-particles penetrate as much as a few millimeters but not to ranges comparable to the size of average sherds; $\gamma$-radiation typically penetrates to ranges greater than the sizes of sherds.

Two consequences follow at once from these properties: the first is that the environmental radiation contribution is effectively due to

Table 4.1 Penetration of $\alpha$, $\beta$, and $\gamma$-radiation through pertinent media.

| Radiation and Medium | Approximate Range | Refs. |
|---|---|---|
| $\alpha$-Particles in quartz | 0.016 to 0.05 mm | (29) |
| $\beta$-Particles in ceramic, specific gravity about 2.0 | Up to ca. 8 mm | (29) |
| $\gamma$-Radiation in typical soil (95% absorption) | Up to ca. 30 cm | (12) |

$\gamma$-emission from the burial medium, since the other types cannot affect more than a superficial layer of the sherd. The second is that since most $\gamma$-radiation has a range greater than the dimensions of typical sherds, only a fraction of the internal $\gamma$-radiation energy will be dissipated within the sherd, and therefore only a fraction of the total $\gamma$-emission from within the pottery will be responsible for generating TL. In practice, it is usually a better approximation to regard the $\gamma$-radiation contribution as entirely external rather than internal (11).

The main radioactive sources present both in pottery and in soil are isotopes of potassium, thorium, and uranium—specifically $K^{40}$, $Th^{232}$ and $U^{238}$. $K^{40}$ disintegrates to give mostly $\beta$, with a small proportion of $\gamma$-radiation. The thorium and uranium isotopes each give rise to a lengthy decay chain (30, 31) from which all three types of radiation emerge. Here it is found that most of the energy is associated with $\alpha$-particles, but we must recall the lower efficiency of $\alpha$-radiation (on an energy-absorbed basis) in inducing TL. As mentioned in section 4.6, it is reported as from 0.05 to 0.3 times as efficient as the others in pottery constituents; therefore in practice the predominance of $\alpha$-radiation is less overwhelming in thermoluminescent terms. Aitken (8, 11) has computed the relative energies associated with the $\alpha$, $\beta$, and $\gamma$-radiation from these three isotopes, and hence their relative effect, for a typical pottery (Table 4.2). The total effective dose rate (corrected for the $\alpha$-factor) may be around 0.5 rad per year (12).

Before turning to the practical means of estimating dose rate, a distinction must be drawn between absolute and relative estimations. An absolute estimation will aim to find the energy absorbed from each of the radiation sources by the ceramic (or some fraction of it) and hence permit a date to be calculated from the physical measurements alone. A relative estimation gives some value assumed to be proportional to the dose rate, making it possible to compute a factor proportional to the age. To get chronometric ages, one then has recourse to pottery dated by other means.

The parameter measured for a relative estimation has been a count of the $\alpha$-disintegrations in the pottery (13, 32). This can readily be done by using a zinc sulphide scintillation screen (7). Table 4.2 shows that one is estimating the single most important factor in the total dose rate.

Table 4.2 Relative importance of $\alpha$, $\beta$, and $\gamma$-radiation in hypothetical buried pottery. Pottery and soil assumed to have $U^{238}$, 3 ppm; $Th^{232}$, 12 ppm; $K^{40}$, 1 percent. Relative effectiveness of $\alpha$-radiation taken as 0.2. (From Aitken, references 8, 11.)

| Radiation | Proportion of Total Energy | Relative Effect on TL |
|---|---|---|
| $\alpha$ | 86% | 57% |
| $\beta$ | 8% | 24% |
| $\gamma$ | 6% | 19% |

This process may require up to 3 grams of sample material, depending on the particular laboratory, and it may impose the minimum sample requirement.* In addition, since the amounts of radioactive isotopes are small, several days of counting time are usually needed. It will be seen in section 4.8 how this has yielded age correlations via the age equation.

For an absolute dose rate estimation, the following measurements appear to be required (7, 11, 12):

(a) An $\alpha$-disintegration count, as described. This enables the (uranium + thorium) concentration to be inferred; from this the $\beta$ (and the $\gamma$) dose rate from these sources will follow. Usually a few parts per million (ppm) of $U^{238}$ and $Th^{232}$ are present.

(b) A determination of the $K^{40}$. This is usually done by determining the total potassium concentration in the ceramic (typically 1 to 5 percent) and using the known isotope ratio for this element.

(c) Some estimate of the external dose rate. There are two ways of approaching this problem: One is to obtain a sample of the surrounding soil and perform measurements of types (a) and (b) on it. This will enable a value for the $\gamma$-emission of the soil to be inferred, and will therefore give the environmental dose rate. However, such an estimate will be reliable only if the burial medium is reasonably homogeneous to a distance of about 30 cm from the position from which the sherd was recovered (Table 4.2). Heterogeneous burial contexts, such as tombs or destruction layers, are less reliably evaluated in this way. The other approach (22, 34, 35) is that of utilizing thermoluminescent dosimetry itself to measure external dose rates. A capsule containing a highly

*Authenticity testing can sometimes be done on as little as 25 milligrams (33), but at some cost in precision, a cost usually not important in authentication work.

sensitive luminophor (such as fluorite or calcium sulfate) is placed in a burial situation on the site as similar as possible to that from which the dated sherd has been removed. Over a period of time the luminophor will build up TL as a result of the external (including the cosmic) radiation which can later be read out. For preference, the capsule is left in place for a whole year, though as far as luminophor sensitivity is concerned, a few weeks are sufficient (35). A point to note is the possible difficulty of finding a "similar" burial situation for the capsule on some sites, especially for contexts such as tombs.

It is also possible to measure internal dose rates by thermoluminescent dosimetry. Mejdahl (18, 22) has published a technique for placing a suitable luminophor on the outside of a complete sherd to obtain the dose rate other than that due to $\alpha$-particles. Other experiments have appeared using the same principles (36). The approach is an attractive one in that the phenomenon being investigated is also used to measure certain of the factors involved, and it is possible that more will be seen of it in the future.

The picture painted so far is a much simplified one as far as pottery in practical circumstances is concerned. We may now consider some of the complications likely to be present.

In many cases the most important difficulty is a lack of homogeneity in the ceramic material (19, 20, 28, 37). Where large grains of "inclusions" form part of the ceramic, these frequently have dimensions greater than the $\alpha$-particle range in the mineral present (usually quartz). Since the $\alpha$-radiation sources (thorium and uranium) are mostly distributed outside these inclusions (20), it follows that the interior of a large grain will receive little or no $\alpha$-irradiation. For this reason some workers have adopted the policy of fractionating the material to give different grain sizes (see section 4.5). Coarse-grained material may have its surface layer etched away and is then treated as if the $\alpha$-dosage were not present, while the $\beta$ and $\gamma$-dose rates remain unchanged (18, 20, 23). These dose rates are estimated as before, but the external dose becomes much more important. Another consequence of this technique is that the sample requirement may be larger, and suitable inclusions (in size about 100 microns or greater) have to be present. Where dating is performed on a fine-grained sample (sizes about 1 to 5 microns), it is treated as if uniformly affected by each of $\alpha$, $\beta$, and $\gamma$-radiations (remembering that the $\alpha$-dose rate has to be "weighted" by the factor described in section 4.6) (11, 21, 38, 39).

Further complications concerning the dose rate have also been pointed out (8, 12, 39). One is the fact that the decay chains of $Th^{232}$ and $U^{238}$ both contain isotopes of radon, a gaseous element. There is therefore the possibility that some of the radon may diffuse out of the pottery or the soil during the $\alpha$ counting process before it has had a chance to decay into an involatile element, leading to an apparently reduced activity from the later parts of the decay chains. Results from $\alpha$ counts on sealed and unsealed samples suggest that such an effect may be present at least in some cases (12). The exact importance of this is not clear at the moment; it may be noted that the "dosimetry capsule" method of external dose-rate estimation should, if carried out properly, compensate for the effect in the burial medium (22, 34, 35).

Another possible difficulty concerns the effect of groundwater on the dose rate. Since such water has little radioactivity, its presence will tend to attenuate the dosage (both internal and external) in comparison with any estimate on dry material. The best way of correcting for this seems to be to measure the water content of the sherd "as dug" and assume that the dose rate is attenuated in direct proportion. Again, the capsule method of measuring external dose rates will automatically correct for groundwater present at the time of measurement. The fact that this may have varied with changes in climatic and geological conditions since the pottery was buried represents a potentially considerable difficulty, since information for estimating water contents of both the sherd and its immediate surroundings is unlikely to be available for the whole of the sherd's lifetime. However, it has been argued (39) that, where both the radon-loss effect and the groundwater effect exist, the errors they generate will be in opposite senses and tend to cancel.

There are still certain possible complications that have been little investigated. One is the gradual washing in or leaching out of radioactive traces during the sherd's burial time (11) (this being applicable both to the sherd and the surrounding soil), or a slow change of the thermoluminescent sensitivity of the material. Another is the variation in relevant properties over the cross section of a sherd, for example as a result of the ceramic having been more highly oxidized near the outside than in the interior (6). The relative lack (and indeed the difficulty) of practical investigation makes points such as these hard to evaluate, but the existence of good age correlations (see next section) suggests that such effects are probably not of great importance.

## 4.8
### Current Dating Techniques

In this section are summarized the salient features of several of the more recently published pottery dating techniques, especially as regards the precision and accuracy claimed. Doubtless work in the field is also in progress at other places and, in any case, the situation here indicated may quickly be superseded. It may be taken as the "literature" position in mid-1970. In what follows, the customary scientific usage is employed: "precision" means the ability to reproduce a result on a given sample; "accuracy" means the ability to achieve a result agreeing with the correct one. Precisions are indicated where possible by estimated standard deviations (as percentages). The estimation of accuracies is more speculative, partly because of possible systematic errors in the results and partly also because of uncertainties in many of the archaeological ages. An estimated "standard deviation," based on individual proportional deviations of TL age from "true" age, has been quoted for each case, but it should be regarded with caution.

The distinction drawn in section 4.7 between "relative" dose-rate estimations (i.e., estimations of a parameter assumed to be proportional to the dose-rate) and "absolute" estimations (i.e., those of the entire dose-rate from various sources) has led to age determinations themselves being dubbed "relative" and "absolute," respectively. Since these terms are already in use by archaeologists in other senses, their employment in the present way is perhaps unfortunate. On the other hand, since the replacement here of "relative" and "absolute" by other terms would probably only add confusion, the author adopts, with some misgivings, the usage found in the thermoluminescence literature: all methods attempt to measure chronometric dates; "relative" dating is that which computes from the measurements a factor putatively proportional to the age and then calibrates the technique with known-age samples; "absolute" dating is that which derives an age from the physical measurements alone and is therefore independent of other chronological scales.

The first suggestion of using T L for dating seems to have originated with Daniels (40). The literature may be consulted for the earlier attempts at pottery dating (6, 7, 10, 15, 41, 42, 43, 44) as well as for the widespread work on geological dating (i.e., of rocks and minerals) (45). Recent work has appeared from four locations: The University Museum, Philadelphia; The Research Laboratory for Archaeology, Oxford; Nara University, Japan; and the Danish Atomic Energy Commission, Roskilde, Denmark.

"Relative" dating has generally been based on the following assumption:

$$\text{Age} = K \left[ \frac{\text{Natural TL}}{\text{Artificial TL} \times R(\alpha)} \right]$$

The factor in square brackets is often called the "specific glow" or "specific TL," $R(\alpha)$ is the $\alpha$-particle count rate on a sample of the pottery, and K an empirical constant that may be determined by measuring the specific TL for a number of samples of known age and then plotting a graph. This serves to calibrate the technique. The equation derives from the basic age equation (section 4.3) if one assumes that $R(\alpha)$ is proportional to the annual dose rate received by that part of the ceramic being used, and also that its sensitivity to $\alpha$-particles is a constant fraction of the sensitivity to other kinds of radiation. This approach has been used by Ichikawa and by Ralph and Han.

Ichikawa (32) has dated coarse colorless grains (probably quartz) separated from known-age samples of Japanese pottery (age range: A.D. 600 to 7300 B.C.). The quoted precisions range from 11 to 19 percent. A plot of the mean specific-glow factor against the archaeological age for thirteen results enabled a "best fit" straight line to be drawn. Measurements made by the present author on the published diagram to give an approximate idea of the accuracy suggest a scatter from the line over all thirteen results of more than ± 40 percent. However, this included four especially deviant results, each (interestingly enough) having a particularly high $\alpha$-count. If these samples are dropped as "undatable" by this technique, the scatter for the rest is only about ± 16 percent.

Ralph and Han (13, 24) have dated whole (unfractionated) samples of pottery from several parts of the world, including Iran, Turkey, and southern Italy. The precision on individual results is about 5 percent. The specific-thermoluminescence factor for 23 samples (age range: A.D. 1350 to 7000 B.C.) was plotted against archaeological age (Fig. 4.4), and the straight line fitted to the more reliably dated samples (actually numbers 6, 7, 12, 13, and 30). The post-2000 B.C. samples are historically dated, the "known ages" thus probably being more reliable than those pre-2000 B.C., which were radiocarbon dated* from associated carbonaceous material. In the post-2000 B.C. range, the scatter from the calibration line is about ± 10 percent. For earlier periods the association is less good, and for the whole range this measure of the accuracy becomes about ± 20 percent. This, however, includes one particularly poor result: No. 1; if this is dropped as "undatable," the accuracy for the whole is ± 17 percent.

These two techniques give some idea of the present accuracy of a "relative" dating approach. A big weakness is the difficulty of identify-

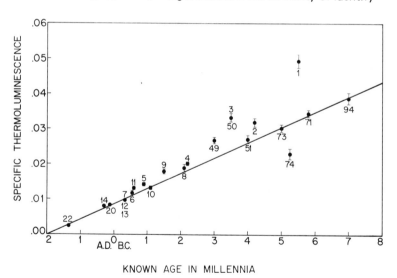

Fig. 4.4 "Relative" dating plot from University Museum, University of Pennsylvania (13). Sources: 71, 73, 74, 94 from Turkey; 1, 2, 3, 4, 5, 9, 10, 11, 49, 50, 51 from Iran; 8 from Baluchistan; 6, 7, 12, 13, 14, 20 from southern Italy; 22 from southwest U.S.A.

*Correction factors (see chapter 1) not applied.

ing a sample that will turn out to be poorly datable. For this reason, relative dating is likely to be most reliable when several samples, differing in relevant properties, are tested from the same context. However, since the external dose rate is assumed to be a constant fraction of the total, the possibility of a "context error" cannot be ruled out.

The "absolute" dating approach has been attempted by Mejdahl and by a group under Aitken at Oxford. Mejdahl has dated coarse-grained inclusions separated from samples of pottery found in Denmark. The method of estimating the internal dose rate is unusual: the radiation emanating from an intact sherd was measured by means of a sensitive thermoluminescent dosimetry powder, and the internal radiation flux taken to be twice this (see section 4.7). The short range of $\alpha$-radiation (which should be irrelevant to a coarse-grain technique) means that its contribution will be ignored by this method. In an initial survey (22) of 26 samples (A.D. 475 to 3830 B.C.), a constant value was assumed for the external dose rate. The accuracy, based on deviations from the middle of the archaeological age span, then came to about ± 30 percent, including three very deviant results. Removing the latter left a scatter of about ± 20 percent. In later work Mejdahl (18) has redated ten of the same samples (A.D. 475 to 400 B.C.), incorporating dosimetry-capsule measurements of the external radiation. An improvement has resulted: in the initial work those ten results showed an accuracy of ± 17 percent; the redating gave an accuracy of ± 13 percent. There is little evidence of an over-all systematic error: the redated results had a mean systematic deviation of + 1.5 percent (i.e., TL ages too old). More recent work by Mejdahl has included detailed measurements of environmental dose rates, to be incorporated into dating results in due course (34).

Intensive investigations by the group at Oxford have resulted in two different dating techniques, one using fine and the other coarse grains (section 4.5). Both are characterized by extremely painstaking attempts to correct for as many as possible of the various perturbing factors and are consequently more complex than the approaches here described. In both cases, internal and external dose rates were estimated by methods described in section 4.7; for the external dosage, soil analysis was used with the fine-grain dating, and the dosimetry-capsule method for the coarse grains (where the external dose becomes more important). Results have been published (11, 21) on the fine-grain dating of 51 samples from 17 different contexts (A.D. 1370 to 1530 B.C., all but two being in the range A.D. 320 to A.D. 20), two, three, or four samples being drawn from each dated context. The precision was 5 percent; the accuracy of context dates (after averaging the 2, 3, or 4 results for each) was about ± 10 percent. Since the accuracy for individual sample results was ± 15 percent, evidently "sherd errors" as well as "context errors" are present. The mean systematic deviation was about −1 percent. It should also be noted that samples were chosen for having known and accessible burial circumstances.

Initial work applying the coarse-grain technique (19, 20) to eight samples suggested an agreement with archaeological ages to within roughly 20 percent. Results from a more recent test program on twenty samples have been quoted (12) as showing an accuracy of ± 8.6 percent, with a mean systematic deviation of −2 percent. Since completion of the manuscript, more detailed results have been published and discussed (46).

It has been pointed out that the coarse-grain and fine-grain approaches differ in the physical information utilized (12), the $\alpha$-radiation contribution being missing in the coarse-grain technique. Therefore, the fact that "absolute" estimates of the ages agree reasonably well in the two cases lends encouraging support to the fundamental assumptions of the thermoluminescent dating method.

The maximum age that can be determined by TL dating is set, in practice, by the oldest pottery that has been found. The minimum age is less easily specified, since it is governed by the radioactive dose rate experienced by a particular sample. A very rough guide might be that thermoluminescence will probably not often be of value for pottery less than 300 to 500 years old, and in some cases will not be useful at ages less than 1000 years. In exceptional instances, where the clay has a high radioactive content, ages of 100 years or less can be determined.

It will be appreciated that this dating technique is fundamentally complex, based as it is on a phenomenon that is not well understood and that varies according to several independent sources of radiation. This, together with the uncertainties associated with pottery burial (section 4.7) will probably continue to limit the achievable accuracy. That apart, the work described gives a reasonable basis for dating, allowing for the sort of errors indicated. These are notably greater than with current radiocarbon-dating achievement, for example, and may well turn out to be most useful for earlier periods. Another use might be to check the validity of a stratigraphical association in cases where this is in doubt, or to distinguish between two or more possible ages allowed by the archaeological evidence. The use of TL dating in museum authentication work has already attracted some notice (13, 33).

Table 4.3 summarizes dating work on pottery that has been published so far, with brief indications of the ceramics that have been investigated.

## 4.9
### Sample Collection

It may be useful to summarize a few general points on the collection of pottery samples for thermoluminescent dating, although the particular dating laboratory will certainly want to be consulted beforehand as to its requirements:

(a) For archaeological dating, between 1 and 3 grams is likely to be the minimum sample size. However, it is often useful to the laboratory if more than this can be supplied.

(b) Samples should not be heated significantly above room temperature and must not have been subjected to any form of ionizing radiation. In particular, pottery that has been radiographed cannot be reliably dated. Material in crushed or powdered form should not be exposed to bright light for more than very short periods.

(c) If there is any suspicion during excavation that the ceramic may have been reheated subsequently to its original deposition (perhaps because of the burning of a structure), this fact should be carefully noted.

(d) The burial conditions of the potsherds actually to be dated should be noted, e.g., for homogeneity of the burial situation. Where the dating laboratory is incorporating an environmental radiation factor, it may request a soil sample or, in some cases, it may ask to use a dosimetry capsule methods of estimation. Information about groundwater present may also be requested.

Table 4.3 Published work directed to pottery dating. Only investigations applied to ceramics are entered. Dates in the second column are on archaeological (including sometimes radiocarbon) grounds, except for "unknowns", where the TL dating result is given in parentheses. (Known-age programs are grouped in batches of related work, each batch being separated by a heavy line.)

| Number of Dates | Archaeological Attribution | Dating Work and Results | Other Work | Ref. |
|---|---|---|---|---|
| **Initial Work and General Reviews** | | | | |
| — | — | — | Initial discussion of method | 40 |
| 1 | 3500 B.C. (Greece) | — | Glow curves | 41 |
| 1 | 1300-1000 B.C. (Switzerland) | | | |
| — | — | — | Early discription of method | 42 |
| 1 | Jomon period (Japan) | — | Principles | |
| 1 | Yayoi period (Japan ) | | Glow curves | 44 |
| | | | Apparatus | |
| 1 | 6th mill. B.C. (Japan) ) | — | Glow curves (colorless fraction) | 23 |
| 1 | 1st cent.B.C. (Japan) | | | |
| 1 | Early 8th cent. A.D. (Japan) ) | | Chem. analysis | |
| — | — | Brief review of "colorless" fraction" dating | — | 17 |
| — | — | — | General review of subject | 8 |
| — | — | Description (without detailed results) of fine-grain and coarse-grain techniques. | Review of environmental factors | 12 |

**Table 4.3** continued

| Number of Dates | Archaeological Attribution | Dating Work and Results | Other Work | Ref. |
|---|---|---|---|---|
| **Known-age Dating Programs** | | | | |
| 3 | 5500 to 3500 B.C. (Turkey) | | | |
| 2 | 4500 B.C., A.D. 800 (Iraq) | | Apparatus | |
| 2 | 3000, 1500 B.C. (Jordan and Israel) | "Relative" dating on whole pottery samples (early results). | Estimation of dose rates / Estimation of pottery sensitivities | 7 |
| 1 | 1300 B.C. (Egypt) | | | |
| 4 | 500-100 B.C. (S. Italy and S. France) | | TL/Dose dependence | |
| 6 | A.D. 200-1300 (England) | | Trap depths | |
| 5 | 6000 B.C. (Turkey) | | | |
| 6 | 4500 B.C. | "Relative" dating on whole pottery samples (advance on preceding entry) | "Spurious" TL / Optical bleaching | 10 |
| 2 | 3250 B.C., 1900 B.C. (Cyprus) | | | |
| 2 | 500 B.C., 150 B.C. (S. Italy) | | | |
| 3 | A.D. 250 to 1000 (England) | | | |
| 3 | 5500 to 3500 B.C. (Crete) | "Relative" dating on whole pottery samples (advance on preceding entry) | Apparatus / TL/Dose dependence ($\alpha$ and $\beta$-particles) | 5, 6 |
| 1 | 5500 B.C. (Syria) | | | |
| 1 | 1500 B.C. (Cyprus) | | | |
| 2 | A.D. 130, 1350 (S. France) | | | |
| 5 | 1030 B.C. to A.D. 1570 (Peru) | "Relative" dates (constant dose rate assumed) | — | 43 |

**Table 4.3** continued

| Number of Dates | Archaeological Attribution | Dating Work and Results | Other Work | Ref. |
|---|---|---|---|---|
| 7 | Jomon period (Japan) | "Relative" dating, colorless coarse grains | Some chemical analyses | 32 |
| 3 | Yayoi period (Japan) | See text | | |
| 2 | Tumulus period (Japan) | | | |
| 1 | Asuka period (Japan) | | | |
| 5 | 5500 to 600 B.C. (Iran) | "Relative" dating of whole pottery samples | Principles | 15 |
| 4 | 550 to 300 B.C. (S. Italy) | | Apparatus | |
| 12 | 5500 to 600 B.C. (Iran, Baluchistan) | "Relative" dating of whole pottery samples (advance on preceding entry) | Apparatus | 16 |
| 6 | 550 B.C. to A.D. 330 (S. Italy) | | | |
| 6 | 450 to 100 B.C. (Greece) | | | |
| 1 | A.D. 1350 (Southwest U.S.A.) | | | |
| 25 | See preceding entry | Same results as preceding | TL/Dose relation | |
| 13 | See following entry | Some of results following | Radiocarbon dates | 24 |
| 4 | 7000 to 5000 B.C. (Turkey) | "Relative" dating, whole pottery samples. 19 of samples in ref. 16 redated on improved apparatus. See text | Improved apparatus. TL/Dose relation ($\beta$, $\gamma$, and X radiation) | 13 |
| 12 | 5500 to 600 B.C. (Iran, Baluchistan) | | | |
| 6 | 550 B.C. to A.D. 330 (S. Italy) | | | |
| 1 | A.D. 1350 (Southwest U.S.A.) | | | |

**Table 4.3** continued

| Number of Dates | Archaeological Attribution | Dating Work and Results | Other Work | Ref. |
|---|---|---|---|---|
| 5 | 4000 to 3000 B.C (Denmark) | "Absolute" dating on coarse grains | Dosimetry method for internal dose rate | |
| | | See text | TL/Dose dependence ($\alpha$-radiation | 22 |
| 4 | 3000 to 2000 B.C. (Denmark) | | | |
| 2 | 2000 to 1000 B.C. (Denmark) | | | |
| 9 | 1000 to 1 B.C. (Denmark) | | | |
| 6 | A.D. 1 to 500 (Denmark) | | | |
| 4 | 500 to 1 B.C. (Denmark) | "Absolute" dating on coarse grains (advance on preceding; 10 samples redated | Dosimetry method for internal and external dose rates | |
| | | See text | | 18 |
| 6 | A.D. 1 to 500 (Denmark) | | | |
| 3 | 1530 B.C. (Cyprus) | "Absolute" dating on fine grains; first publication | | |
| | | | | 38 |
| 6 | A.D. 170 to 1370 (France) | | | |
| 1 | 1530 B.C. (Cyprus) | "Absolute" dating on fine grains. Advance on preceding; 9 samples redated | | 11 |
| | | See text | | 21 |
| 2 | A.D. 170, 1370 (S. France) | | | |
| 14 | A.D. 20 to 320 (Gr. Britain) (Several samples to each date) | | | |

**Table 4.3** continued

| Number of Dates | Archaeological Attribution | Dating Work and Results | Other Work | Ref. |
|---|---|---|---|---|
| 3 | 7500 B.C. (Syria) | "Absolute" dating on coarse grains; early work | Variation of relevant properties (e.g., radioactivity) among separated fractions | 19 |
| 4 | A.D. 1 to 1300 (France) | | | 20 |
| 1 | A.D. 600 (Mexico) | | | |
| 22 | A.D. 45 to 350 (Gr. Britain) | "Absolute" dating on coarse grains | Supralinearity corrections | 46 |

## Dating of Unknowns

| | | | | |
|---|---|---|---|---|
| 1 | 1700 B.C. (Iran) | "Absolute" dating on fine grains | — | 39 |
| 2 | 1000 to 200 B.C.; A.D. 950 (Thailand) | | | |
| 4 | 3300 B.C. to A.D. 800 (Gr. Britain) | | | |
| 1 | 510 B.C. (Nigeria) | "Absolute" dating on fine grains | — | 47 |
| 3 | 230 B.C. to A.D. 60 (China) | "Absolute" dating on fine grains (modified for authentication) | — | 33 |
| 6 | Recent (China) | | | |

## Ancillary Investigations

| | | | | |
|---|---|---|---|---|
| 3 | Not given | — | Thermoluminescent effect of various radiations. Nonuniformity of pottery | 28 |

**Table 4.3 continued**

| Number of Dates | Archaeological Attribution | Dating Work and Results | Other Work | Ref. |
|---|---|---|---|---|
| — | — | — | Nonuniformity of TL in pottery | 37 |
| — | — | — | Internal dose rates by dosimetry method | 36 |
| — | — | — | External dose rates by dosime-try method | 35 |
| — | — | — | External dose rates (dosime-try capsule method) | 34 |

(e) Sampling of a complete artifact should, if at all possible, be performed in a dating laboratory. If this is not possible, laboratory advice should always be sought beforehand.

## 4.10
### Dating of Other Materials

Thermoluminescent dating seems to have been confined to terra cotta and various forms of earthenware, though in principle any ceramic (including, e.g., Egyptian faïence and fired brick) should be datable. Other possibilities may be glass (including volcanic glasses), lavas and rocks that have been calcined to a high enough temperature (the most recent heating being the event dated).

Studies on porcelains and other fine ceramics run into at least two difficulties: the minimum sample requirement is likely to be much more onerous with these materials, and they are usually of comparatively young ages, making them less suitable for the technique. Nor is the present accuracy of TL dating sufficient for some of the distinctions drawn in the porcelain field. In the case of a "relative" dating technique, a different calibration graph may be needed for these rather different materials.

Glass is known to show the TL phenomenon (48). A given specimen would, of course, need to contain sufficient radioactivity to be dated in this way. Another objection is that the transparency of glass severely increases the danger of optical drainage (section 4.4), unless it were certain that the specimen had not been exposed to daylight to a significant extent since excavation. It seems probable that fission-track dating may be a more suitable technique for many samples of glass (see chapter 5).

The dating of lava flows, which may sometimes interest the archaeologist, has been attempted (49) but with results that have not so far proved encouraging.* The dating of stone "pot boilers" has been investigated (50) and the distribution of TL present in sandstone around a pit has been used to show that the pit was employed as an oven rather than for some purpose not implying strong heating (51).

## 4.11
### Phenomena Related to TL

Brief mention might be made of three phenomena which also measure electron trapping. None appears to have been used to substitute for TL in pottery dating, but conceivably any of them could be so used.

The first is electron spin resonance, or ESR, also called electron paramagnetic resonance, or EPR (52). An electron has a magnetic moment arising from the fact that it has a spin. In the orbitals of atoms, molecules, and so on, there is a strong tendency for electrons to "pair"; the magnetic moment of each one of the pair are then opposed, thereby canceling each other, and cannot be observed. An unpaired electron, however, can exhibit properties arising from its magnetic moment, one such property being ESR. This is observed by placing the material in a strong magnetic field and allowing the electrons to interact with an applied microwave signal of the correct frequency. Since the metastable electrons that give rise to thermoluminescence are themselves unpaired, they will contribute to an ESR response obtained from that material, although they will not necessarily be responsible for the whole of it. It is therefore possible to use ESR to obtain much the same information that is provided by thermoluminescence. An advantage of ESR would be that the electrons are not displaced from their traps in the course of

---

*For more recent work on this subject, see reference (55).

the measurement, so that repeated experiments on one sample are possible.

The second phenomenon is exo-electron emission (53), the emission of electrons from the surface of a solid as a result of stimulation by heat or light; it is observed in the case of thermoluminescent materials. Typically, the substance would be heated in a high vacuum and the emitted electrons detected and counted. The result obtained often parallels the TL glow curve from the same material. The method seems more sensitive than thermoluminescence, though the results may depend markedly on the surface properties of the material. Applications in the TL dosimetry field have been described (54).

Finally, there is thermally stimulated current, or TSC (55). If a material containing trapped metastable electrons is heated while an electric potential difference is applied across it, the trapped electrons, upon ejection from their traps, migrate in the electric field to form a tiny current which can be measured at the electrodes used to apply the field. The integrated current should represent the total number of electrons ejected. The use of this technique for geological dating has been suggested (56).

## Acknowledgments

The author wishes to thank Miss E. K. Ralph and Mr. M. C. Han for the providing results from the dating program of the University Museum and for figures 4.2 and 4.4, and also Dr. V. Mejdahl for the communication of results in advance of publication.

## References

1. Cameron, J. R., Suntharalingam, N., and Kenney, G. N., Thermoluminescent Dosimetry. Madison: University of Wisconsin Press (1968).
2. Randall, J. T., and Wilkins, M. H. F., "Phosphorescence and Electron Traps I. The Study of Trap Distributions." Proceedings of the Royal Society A184 (1945): 366-389. Kelly, P., and Bräunlich, P., "I. Phenomenological Theory of Thermoluminescence." Physical Review B (Solid State) 3rd Series, 1 (1970): 1587-1595.

**3. Halperin, A., and Braner, A. A.,**
"Evaluation of Thermal Activation Energies from Glow Curves." Physical Review, 2nd Series, 117 (1960): 408-415.

**4. Bonfiglioli, G.,**
"Thermoluminescence: what it can and cannot show." Pp. 15-24 of McDougall, D. J. (Ed.), Thermoluminescence of Geological Materials. London and New York: Academic Press (1968).

**5. Tite, M. S.,**
"Some Complicating Factors in Thermoluminescent Dating and their Implications." (Reference 4): 389-405.

**6. Tite, M. S.,**
"Thermoluminescent Dating of Ancient Ceramics: a Reassessment." Archaeometry 9 (1966): 155-169.

**7. Tite, M. S., and Waine, J.,**
"Thermoluminescent Dating: a Re-appraisal." Archaeometry 5 (1962): 53-79.

**8. Aitken, M. J.,**
"Thermoluminescent Dating in Archaeology: Introductory Review." (Reference 4): 369-378.

**9. Friedrich, K.,**
"Ausleuchtung von Kristallphosphoren mit Ultraschall nach Vorbestrahlung mit UV-Licht und $\beta$-Strahlen." Annalen der Physik 7. Folge 7 (1961): 201-209.

**10. Aitken, M. J., Tite, M. S., and Reid, J.,**
"Thermoluminescent Dating: Progress Report." Archaeometry 6 (1963): 65-75; Idem: Thermoluminescent Dating of Ancient Ceramics." Nature 202 (1964): 1032-1033.

**11. Aitken, M. J., Zimmerman, D. W., and Fleming, S. J.,**
"Thermoluminescent Dating of Ancient Pottery." Nature 219 (1968): 442-445.

**12. Aitken, M. J., Zimmerman, D. W., Fleming, S. J., and Huxtable, J.,**
"Thermoluminescent Dating of Pottery." In Radiocarbon Variations and Absolute Chronology. Proceedings of the Twelfth Nobel Symposium, Uppsala, Sweden, August 11-15, 1969. Almquist and Wiksell, Stockholm (Wiley Interscience Division, John Wiley & Sons, New York, 1970).

**13. Ralph, E. K., and Han, M. C.,**
"Potential of Thermoluminescence Dating." Presented at Symposium on Archaeological Chemistry, 156th American Chemical Society National Meeting, Atlantic City, N.J., September 9-12, 1968. In Science and Archaeology, edited by R. H. Brill, Cambridge, Mass.: The M.I.T. Press (1971): 244-250.

14. Aitken, M. J., Fleming, S. J., Reid, J., and Tite, M. S.,
"Elimination of Spurious Thermoluminescence." (Reference 4):
133-142.

15. Ralph, E. K., and Han, M. C.,
"Dating of Pottery by Thermoluminescence." Nature 210 (1966):
245-247.

16. Ralph, E. K., and Han, M. C.,
"Progress in Thermoluminescent Dating of Pottery." (Reference 4):
379-387.

17. Higashimura, T., Ichikawa, Y., and Sidei, T.,
"Thermoluminescence Dating of Pottery Using Separated Mineral Fraction." (Reference 4): 441-443.

18. Mejdahl, V.,
"Thermoluminescence Dating of Ancient Danish Ceramics." Archaeometry 11 (1969): 99-104.

19. Aitken, M. J., Fleming, S. J., and Zimmerman, D. W.,
"Thermoluminescence Dating of Ancient Ceramics." Pp. 523-530 of
Radioactive Dating and Methods of Low Level Counting. Vienna: Inter-
national Atomic Energy Agency (1967).

20. Fleming, S. J.,
"Study of Thermoluminescence of Crystalline Extracts from Pottery."
Archaeometry 9 (1966): 170-173; Idem: "Thermoluminescent Age
Studies on Mineral Inclusions Separated from Ancient Pottery."
(Reference 4): 431-439.

21. Zimmerman, D. W.,
"Dating of Ancient Pottery by Thermoluminescence." Pp. 858-867 of
Auxier, J. A., Becker, K., Robinson, E. M. (Eds.), Proceedings of
Second International Conference on Luminescence Dosimetry, Gatlin-
burg, Tenn., September 23-26, 1968. (Available from Clearing House
for Federal Scientific and Technical Information, National Bureau of
Standards. U.S. Department of Commerce, Springfield, Virginia
22151.)

22. Mejdahl, V.,
"Dosimetry Problems Related to the Thermoluminescence Dating of
Ancient Ceramics." (Reference 21): 868-882.

23. Ichikawa, Y.,
"Dating of Ancient Ceramics by Thermoluminescence." Bulletin of the
Institute of Chemical Research, Kyoto University 43 (1965): 1-6.

24. Ralph, E. K., and Han, M. C.,
"Potential of Thermoluminescence in Supplementing Radiocarbon
Dating." World Archaeology 1 (1969): 157-169.

25. Aitken, M. J., Alldred, J. C., and Thompson, J.,
"A Photon-Ratemeter System for Low-level Thermoluminescence Measurement." (Reference 21): 248-265.

26. Ichikawa, Y.,
"Thermoluminescence of Roof Tiles Irradiated by Atomic Bombs in Hiroshima and Nagasaki." Bulletin of the Institute of Chemical Research, Kyoto University 42 (1964): 48-53.

27. Labeyrie, J., Lalou, C., and Nordemann, D.,
"A High Sensitivity Apparatus to Detect Thermoluminescence Induced by Very Weak Irradiation." (Reference 4): 175-181. Bonfiglioli, G., Brovetto, P., and Cortese, C., "Apparatus for Thermoluminescence Measurements." The Review of Scientific Instruments 33 (1962): 1095-1100.

28. Burchell, D., and Fremlin, J. H.,
"Relative Efficiency of Different Radiations in Storing Thermoluminescent Energy." (Reference 4): 407-412.

29. Wapstra, A. H., Nijgh, G. J., and Van Lieshout, R.,
Nuclear Spectroscopy Tables. New York: Interscience (1959). Marion, J. B., and Young, F. C., Nuclear Reaction Analysis. Graphs and· Tables. Amsterdam: North-Holland Publishing Co. (1968).

30. Faul, H.,
Nuclear Geology. New York: John Wiley and Sons, Inc. (1954): 12.

31. Lederer, C. M., Hollander, J. M., and Perlmann, I.,
Table of Isotopes, 6th Edition. New York: John Wiley and Sons, Inc. (1968).

32. Ichikawa, Y.,
"Dating of Ancient Ceramics by Thermoluminescence II." Bulletin of the Institute of Chemical Research, Kyoto University 45 (1967): 63-68.

33. Fleming, S. J., Moss, H. M., and Joseph, A.,
"Thermoluminescence Authenticity Testing of Some 'Six Dynasties' Figures." Archaeometry 12 (1970): 57-65.

34. Mejdahl, V.,
"Measurement of Environmental Radiation at Archaeological Excavation Sites." Archaeometry 12 (1970): 147-159.

35. Aitken, M. J.,
"Thermoluminescent Dosimetry of Environmental Radiation on Archaeological Sites." Archaeometry 11 (1969): 109-114; Idem: "Low-level Environmental Radiation Measurements Using Natural Calcium Fluoride." (Reference 21): 281-290.

36. Aitken, M. J.,
"Evaluation of Effective Radioactive Content by|Means of Thermoluminescent Dosimetry." (Reference 4): 463-469.

**37. Fremlin, J. H., and Srirath, S.,**
"Thermoluminescent Dating. Examples of Non-Uniformity of Luminescence." Archaeometry 7 (1964): 58-62. Fremlin, J. H., "Effects of Non-Uniformity of Materials on the Thermoluminescent Method of Dating." (Reference 4): 419-425.

**38. Zimmerman, D. W.,**
"Thermoluminescence from Fine Grains from Ancient Pottery." Archaeometry 10 (1967): 26-28.

**39. Zimmerman, D. W., and Huxtable, J.,**
"Recent Applications and Developments in Thermoluminescent Dating." Archaeometry 11 (1969): 105-108.

**40. Daniels, F., Boyd, C. A., and Saunders, D. F.,**
"Thermoluminescence as a Research Tool." Science 117 (1953): 343-349.

**41. Grögler, N., Houtermans, F. G., and Stauffer, H.,**
"Über die Datierung von Keramik und Ziegel durch Thermolumineszenz." Helvetica Physica Acta 33 (1960): 595-596.

**42. Kennedy, G. C., and Knopff, L.,**
"Dating by Thermoluminescence." Archaeology 13 (1960): 147-148.

**43. Mazess, R. B., and Zimmerman, D. W.,**
"Pottery Dating from Thermoluminescence." Science 152 (1966): 347-348. Idem: "Thermoluminescence Dating of some Peruvian Pottery." (Reference 4): 445-448.

**44. Ichikawa, Y.,**
"Dating of Ancient Ceramic Material by Thermoluminescence." Journal of Nara Gakugei University, Natural Sciences 11 (1963): 55-61.

**45. E.g., Chapter VI of reference 4; Chapter 6 of reference 30.**
Houtermans, F. G., Jäger, E., Schön, M., and Stauffer, H., "Messungen der Thermolumineszenz als Mittel zur Untersuchung der thermischen und der Strahlungsgeschichte von natürlichen Mineralien und Gesteinen." Annalen der Physik 6. Folge, 20 (1957): 283-292. Durrani, S. A., Christodoulides, C., and Ettinger, K. V., "Thermoluminescence in Tektites." Journal of Geophysical Research 75 (1970): 983-995.

**46. Fleming, S. J.,**
"Thermoluminescent Dating: Refinement of the Quartz Inclusion Method." Archaeometry 12 (1970): 133-145.

**47. Fagg, B. E. B., Fleming, S. J.,**
"Thermoluminescent Dating of a Terracotta of the Nok Culture, Nigeria." Archaeometry 12 (1970): 53-55.

**48. Spurny, Z.,**
"A Glass Thermoluminescent Dosimeter." (Reference 21): 18-26, and references cited therein.

**49. Aitken, M. J., Fleming, S. J., Doell, R. R., and Tanguy, J. C.,**
"Thermoluminescent Study of Lavas from Mt. Etna and Other Historic Flows: Preliminary Results." (Reference 4): 359-366.

**50. Srirath, S., and Fremlin, J. H.,**
"Nonuniformity in the Thermoluminescence of 'Pot-Boilers.' " (Reference 4): 427-430.

**51. Aitken, M. J., and Thompson, J.,**
"Determination of Heat Penetration in Archaeological Remains." (Reference 4): 413-417.

**52. Low, W.,**
"Paramagnetic Resonance in Solids." Solid State Physics, Supplement 2. New York: Academic Press (1960), Chapter V. Zeller, E. J., "Use of Electron Spin Resonance for Measurement of Natural Radiation Damage." (Reference 4): 271-279.

**53. Scharmann, A.,**
"Exo-electron Emission." (Reference 4): 281-290. Kramer, J., "Dosimetry with Exo-electrons." (Reference 21): 180-199.

**54. Bräunlich, P.,**
"Thermoluminescence and Thermally Stimulated Current-Tools for the Determination of Trapping Parameters." (Reference 4): 61-88.

**55. Hwang, F. S. W., and Fremlin, J. H.,**
"A New Dating Technique using Thermally Stimulated Current." Archaeometry 12 (1970): 67-71.

**56. Hwang, F. S. W.,**
"Thermoluminescence Dating Applied to Volcanic Lava." Nature 227 (1970): 940-941.

## 5.1
### Uranium and Fission

Uranium is an unusual element. It occurs naturally as a mixture of two long-lived isotopes, composed of 0.7 percent $U^{235}$ and 99.3 percent $U^{238}$. Both isotopes decay in complex chains of events into lead with the emission of $\alpha$- and $\beta$-radiation. These radioactive decays are the basis of the lead-uranium clock which is fundamentally important in geology. The rates of these decays are very slow: the half-life of $U^{235}$ is $0.713 \times 10^9$ years and that of $U^{238}$ $4.51 \times 10^9$ years, the latter roughly the same as the age of the earth. From the point of view of the anthropologist, uranium thus decays so slowly that it can be considered stable and its quantity constant. But uranium also undergoes spontaneous fission. In this process its nuclei split into two fragments without any external stimulus. This type of fission is not to be confused with the neutron-induced fission of $U^{235}$, in which the nucleus splits in two after having been struck by a neutron. Induced fission is the basis of nuclear energy production.

The rates of spontaneous fission are much slower than those of the radioactive decays of these isotopes. $U^{238}$ fissions spontaneously with a half-life of about $8 \times 10^{15}$ years. The half-life for spontaneous fission of $U^{235}$ is even higher by a factor of about 20, so that its contribution to the spontaneous fission can be neglected in our considerations.


## 5.2
### Fission Tracks

The amount of energy released in each spontaneous fission is relatively large (about 200 MeV) and the resulting two nuclear fragments rip into the surrounding material for a distance of the order of 10 microns before they are stopped. Along their path they cause extensive damage, that is, fission tracks (1); this damage can be developed by etching if the material is a nonmetallic crystal or a glass, because the damaged areas are preferentially attacked by solvents. The etched tracks are called fission track etch pits; in most materials these can be visually distinguished from etch pits of other origin (Fig. 5.1).

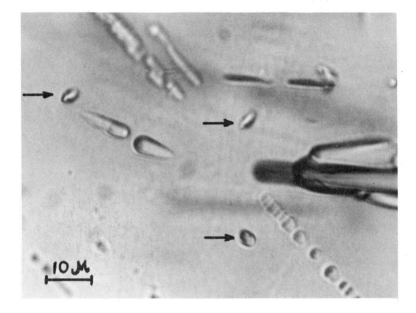

Fig. 5.1 Fission tracks in obsidian, etched in 16% hydrofluoric acid for 3 minutes at room temperature. In addition to the fission tracks, etched scratches and bubbles are visible.

## 5.3

### Fission Track Age

Many minerals and glasses contain enough uranium (of the order of 1 to 1000 ppm) to accumulate statistically significant numbers of fission tracks in time periods of interest to anthropologists. If in a given material all fission tracks are conserved, then the number of accumulated tracks depends only on the accumulation period ("age") and the uranium content. Hence, if the uranium content is known, the fission track age can be deduced from the number of spontaneous fission tracks.

Fortunately the uranium content of many materials can be determined by a technique that is also based on the counting of fission tracks: the tracks of the neutron-induced fission of $U^{235}$. This nucleus splits in two when struck by a low-energy ("slow") neutron, leaving tracks quite similar to those of the spontaneous fission of $U^{238}$. The number of induced fission tracks is proportional to the uranium content and thus to the neutron irradiation dose. Therefore, by counting these tracks we can measure the uranium content of a sample, since the neutron dose is known.

## 5.4
### Track Development and Counting

In practice one polishes a section of the material under study, etches it for the proper length of time with a suitable solvent at the right temperature and observes the fission tracks under a good microscope in transmitted light at a magnification of about 1000X. Then the tracks of the spontaneous fission of $U^{238}$ are counted per unit area. The sample is then annealed at a temperature high enough (see next section) to remove the spontaneous fission tracks and is irradiated in a nuclear reactor with thermal neutrons. Then it is polished and etched again under the same conditions as before and the tracks of induced fission of $U^{235}$ are counted. Thus the dating by the fission-track method consists in principle of the repeated counting of fission tracks, once before and once after the irradiation with slow neutrons.

## 5.5
### Annealing

At room temperature, fission tracks are essentially stable in most materials. As the temperature is raised, however, there comes a point when electrons and ions in the material rearrange themselves and the tracks begin to disappear. After a certain time at that temperature all tracks will be erased. The process is called annealing.

One of the most useful aspects of fission-track work lies in the differential character of the annealing: different materials require different temperatures to erase the tracks in the same length of time. Selected annealing data are shown in Table 5.1. Of the materials shown, apatite is the most easily annealed and zircon the most refractory mineral. In the table the temperatures (in $°C$) are quoted at which the number of fission tracks is reduced to 50 percent in various materials for different annealing times. The annealing temperatures can be dependent upon the chemical composition of the material.

Table 5.1 Annealing Data (Temperatures in °C)

|  | 1 min | $10^2$ min | $10^4$ min | $10^6$ min |
|---|---|---|---|---|
| Zircon | 810 | 700 | 610 | 540 |
| Epidote | 700 | 665 | 645 | 620 |
| Sphene | 680 | 600 | 535 | 480 |
| Mica (phlogopite) | 570 | 440 | 340 | 275 |
| Glass (pitchstone) | 550 | 410 | 320 | 250 |
| Glass (australite) | 470 | 360 | 270 | 210 |
| Apatite | 410 | 335 | 270 | 215 |

Now let us consider a hypothetical granite boulder presumed to have been used in a man-made fireplace in prehistoric times. Granite contains a large number of crystalline minerals. By examining the apatite crystals, one can easily verify whether or not the stone was heated. A study of other minerals (biotite and zircon, for example) may allow an estimate of the maximum temperature reached. The age of the fire can be determined with some confidence by considering the fission-track ages of several minerals with a sufficiently high uranium content. Many such materials exist, and it is only a question of finding them in an archaeologically meaningful context.

## 5.6

### Limitations

The principal limitation for fission-track dating of archaeological and anthropological materials lies in the fact that the uranium content must be sufficiently large to produce a statistically significant number of tracks within the length of time to be measured. "Statistically significant" is hard to define, because track counting is influenced by external factors, such as homogeneity and optical properties. As a rule it is difficult to count tracks if their number is less than about 10 per $cm^2$.

For example, it has been repeatedly stated that the K-Ar ages from Olduvai Gorge (see chapter 6) were "confirmed" by fission-track dating (2). Actually, the uranium content of the volcanic glasses encountered there happens to be rather low. The glass has many bubbles and other imperfections that make track recognition difficult. The resulting theoretical precision is thus much lower than that of the K-Ar dates and the "confirmation" is only rough.

So far the fission-track method has been successfully applied to glasses (natural and manmade), apatites, zircons, sphenes, and micas (3, 4, 5, 6). Several other minerals are being tested. At present there is no way of developing fission tracks in microcrystalline or cryptocrystalline materials. Unfortunately, these include chert, flint, and bone materials.

The fission-track clock is very new and has seen little application in archaeology. It has great promise for the future if archaeologists succeed in finding suitable materials in the right juxtaposition. By now, this is hardly a new problem.

## References

1. Fleischer, R. L., Price, P. B., and Walker, R. M.,
"Nuclear Tracks in Solids," Scientific American 220 (1969): 30-39.
2. Fleischer, R. L., Leakey, L. S. B., Price, P. B., and Walker, R. M.,
"Fission Track Dating of Bed I, Olduvai Gorge," Science 148 (1965): 72-74.
3. Watanabe, N., and Suzuki, M.,
"Fission Track Dating of Archaeological Glass Materials from Japan," Nature 222 (1969): 1057-1058.
4. Naeser, C. W., and Dodge, F. C. W.,
"Fission Track Ages of Accessory Minerals from Granitic Rocks from the Sierra Nevada Batholith," Bulletin of the Geological Society of America 80 (1969): 2201-2212.
5. Wagner, G. A., and Storzer, D.,
"Die Interpretation von Spaltspurenaltern am Beispiel von natürlichen Gläsern, Apatiten und Zirkonen," Eclogae Geologicae Helvetiae 63 (1970): 335-344.
6. Miller, D, and Jäger, E.,
"Fission Track Ages of Some Alpine Micas," Earth and Planetary Science Letters 4 (1968): 375-378.

**Potassium-Argon**              Henry Faul
                               **Dating**

## 6.1

### Principles

The potassium-argon clock is based on the accumulation of radiogenic $Ar^{40}$ produced in the radioactive decay of $K^{40}$. The pertinent constants are shown in Table 6.1. The decay into argon occurs by a process known as electron capture and only part (11.2 percent) of the $K^{40}$ decays that way. The rest decays by $\beta$-ray emission into $Ca^{40}$. Unfortunately, $Ca^{40}$ is the most common isotope of ordinary calcium. There is so much calcium everywhere in nature that the potassium decay can add only negligible amounts to all the $Ca^{40}$ that is already there, and thus a potassium-calcium clock is not practical.

Potassium is fairly common in nature: It is the seventh most abundant constituent of the earth's crust: 2.6 percent by weight, on the average. A material should contain at least 1 percent potassium in order to be useful for a K-Ar clock in anthropology; such materials are common. Micas, feldspars, and volcanic glasses are good examples of materials that contain between 1 and 10 percent of potassium (metal).

In order to be useful as a K-Ar clock, a system must also satisfy three additional requirements:

1. It must contain only a negligible amount of inherited radiogenic argon at the time of its origin, that being the date to be measured. Inherited radiogenic argon cannot be distinguished from radiogenic argon generated in situ.

2. It must fully contain all the radiogenic argon generated within it. In other words, it must be a closed system. A leaky system would not be

**Table 6.1** Constants for Potassium-Argon Dating (after Dalrymple and Lanphere, 1969)

| | | |
|---|---|---|
| Half-life of $K^{40}$ | | $T = 1.31 \times 10^9$ years |
| Decay constants: | Electron capture | $\lambda_e = 0.585 \times 10^{-10}$/year |
| | Beta decay | $\lambda_\beta = 4.72 \times 10^{-10}$/year |
| Natural abundance of $K^{40}$ in potassium | | $K^{40}/K = 1.19 \times 10^{-4}$ mols/mol |
| | | $Ar^{40} = 99.600\%$ |
| Atmospheric argon composition | | $Ar^{38} = 0.063\%$ |
| | | $Ar^{36} = 0.337\%$ |
| | | $Ar^{40}/Ar^{36} = 295.5$) |

useful as a clock because it is not usually possible to make valid corrections for argon leakage.

3. The potassium content of the system must remain constant from the date being measured to the present, except for the slight decrease that is due to radioactive decay. (In samples of interest to archaeologists this decrease is essentially zero.)

The first requirement is particularly serious in archaeological samples because the time spans involved are short compared to the decay rate of potassium. Radiogenic argon is constantly being produced in all rocks that contain potassium; these include the magma inside volcanoes. One could imagine various volcanic processes that could generate a system which already contains inherited argon at the time of its formation and thus would give an unreal K-Ar "age." Such anomalous "ages" have been observed and studied in detail, but it is clear that they are rare and generally restricted to unusual minerals and uncommon geologic conditions. The minerals beryl, cordierite, tourmaline, and other cyclosilicates usually contain inherited argon. Basalts that erupted on the deep-sea floor under high hydrostatic pressure in historic times are known to have given spurious K-Ar "ages" of some tens of millions of years. It is amply demonstrated, however, that surface basalt flows are sufficiently well degassed by the volcanic process to be free of inherited argon and thus give true K-Ar ages. The same is true for ash falls and explosively ejected volcanic materials in general. The water escaping from the materials as pressure is released is the major agent in sweeping out other gases, including argon.

The dry atmosphere contains 0.734 percent Ar by volume and this argon consists of the three isotopes 36, 38, and 40 (see Table 6.1). Various materials may adsorb some of this argon on their surface and thus serve to introduce it into our samples. Atmospheric argon, however, can be recognized by its isotopic composition, and it is not too difficult to correct for it if the amount present is not overwhelming.

## 6.2

### What is Time Zero?

The K-Ar clock is reset every time the system is degassed, but it is reset to zero only if the degassing is complete. This is the crucial factor.

Incomplete degassing produces unreal "mixed ages" which are not a measure of time at all but reflect primarily the degree of degassing.

Complete degassing requires high temperatures, for most materials high enough to melt them. Volcanic ash falls and surficial lava flows are, as a rule, completely degassed in the process of ejection. On the other hand, a granite boulder may be heated in a man-made fire for a very long time and yet would lose only a fraction of its old argon in the process. Its K-Ar age would be greater than the age of the fire. Some materials (notably tektites) melt to highly viscous glasses and have to be vaporized in vacuo before the last traces of argon are released.

## 6.3
### Datable Materials

Thus, with few exceptions, the K-Ar dating materials of interest to anthropologists are limited to volcanic ash falls and lava flows. The time measured then is the time when these materials last cooled.

In geology, the K-Ar clock is probably the most useful method of measuring time, but applications to anthropology and archaeology are still very few. The reason lies partly in the difficulty of finding datable materials relevant to anthropological research and partly in the slowness of the potassium decay and the resulting problems with the measurement of very small amounts of $Ar^{40}$

Yet if one were to pick the one series of K-Ar measurements that has caused the greatest stir in scientific circles, one would probably select the celebrated determinations of the age of the hominid remains of Olduvai Gorge in Equatorial East Africa. Measurements on volcanic rocks (basalt and trachytic pyroclastics) by Curtis and Evernden [1] first indicated that the skull called Zinjanthropus boisei by Leakey in 1959 [2] was about 1.75 million years old, about twice as old as was generally believed at the time. A lively controversy ensued and more K-Ar determinations were made in several laboratories. There was much debate among anthropologists, evolutionists, stratigraphers, and geochronologists until the matter was finally resolved about 1965 [3], largely by meticulous stratigraphic studies. The original K-Ar age of Zinjanthropus was confirmed.

It is very likely that the K-Ar clock will find more and wider applications in the study of early hominid and prehominid fossils. As techniques improve, younger and younger samples will become measurable. There is little doubt that useful measurements can be made in the range from 10,000 to 100,000 years and that the K-Ar clock can be made to take over where $C^{14}$ leaves off.

## 6.4
### Selection of Samples

It is difficult to list all the criteria that go into the selection of a good sample. Any sampling process is essentially a compromise between what is desired and what can be collected. Some basic rules are generally observed:

1. The sample must be fresh. It is true that some minerals may withstand much weathering without significant loss of argon or change in potassium content. Other minerals may lose both of these constituents but in proportion to the amounts present, so that the K/Ar ratio does not materially change and a correct age can be measured. Most rocks and minerals, however, are severely altered by weathering and their K/Ar ratio is not preserved. Unless the unaltered minerals can be cleanly separated from the weathered mass, the resultant age will be suspect. Whole-rock measurements on weathered samples are rarely meaningful.

2. The material must be in situ. It is essential to confirm the origin of each sample by independent field study. When dealing with volcanic materials one must be certain that they were deposited by volcanic processes and not moved about by water and thus possibly contaminated in transport. It has been demonstrated that a few flakes of Precambrian muscovite could ruin the finest Pleistocene tuff for K-Ar dating.

3. The material must be mineralogically identifiable—i.e., it must be either crystalline or glassy. Some materials, notably some feldspars, most glasses, and most glauconites are known to lose argon at room temperature and thus give anomalously low ages. It is true that some samples of strange, unidentified substance have given reasonable ages, but serious investigators are not likely to accept such results.

4. The sample must contain a fair amount of potassium. The younger

the sample, the higher the potassium content should be. Samples a million years old or younger should contain at least 1 percent of potassium to permit meaningful analysis of the argon.

## 6.5

### Potassium Analysis

Numerous methods are available for the analysis of potassium, but the flame photometer or the atomic absorption spectrophotometer are most frequently used.

An aliquot of the sample is dissolved in boiling hydrofluoric acid with a few drops of sulfuric acid or perchloric acid and evaporated to dryness. The residue is taken up in a little hydrochloric acid, made up to a given volume with water and introduced into the flame of the atomic absorption spectrophotometer. For flame photometry, a known amount of lithium is added to the solution as an internal standard and the sample is then atomized into the flame of the photometer. With proper calibration, either method permits rapid potassium analysis with a precision better than $\pm$ 1 percent (standard deviation).

## 6.6

### Argon Analysis (by Isotope Dilution)

A few grams of the sample are placed in a molybdenum crucible inside a vacuum system. (For very young samples the amount may be a few tens of grams). The system is evacuated to a pressure less than $10^{-8}$ torr, sealed, and a known small amount of $Ar^{38}$ tracer (the "spike") is introduced through a gas pipette. The sample is heated to about 1400-1500° C either by internal coils or with an induction heater, and the evolved gas is purified. Water is absorbed on artificial zeolite (molecular sieve), hydrogen and hydrocarbons are oxidized on hot copper oxide (about 500° C), and all other reactive gases are removed with hot titanium sponge (900° C). The remaining argon is captured on activated charcoal chilled with liquid nitrogen and transferred to a gas mass spectrometer. The ratio $Ar^{38}/Ar^{40}$ is measured to determine the amount of $Ar^{40}$, and the ratio $Ar^{36}/Ar^{40}$ is measured to determine how much of the $Ar^{40}$ comes from air-argon contamination.

## 6.7

### Calculating the Age

On the basis of the potassium and argon analyses, the age of the sample is calculated from the equations

$$t = \frac{Ar^*}{K} \ 1.436 \times 10^{14} \ \text{years} \tag{6.1}$$

and

$$Ar^* = Ar^{40} - 296 \ Ar^{36} \tag{6.2}$$

where Ar is the amount of radiogenic argon-40 in the sample, $Ar^{40}$ is the total amount of argon-40, $Ar^{36}$ is the amount of argon-36 (air contamination), and K is the amount of potassium (metal). All amounts are given in mols (atomic). The numerical constant is derived from the decay constants of potassium and the abundance of $K^{40}$ in common potassium, as given in Table 6.1. Equation 6.1 is valid only for young samples because it ignores the decay of potassium since the formation of the deposit. Ages suspected to be greater than 20 million years should be calculated with the unabridged equation

$$t = 1.885 \times 10^9 \ \ln \left(7.62 \times 10^4 \ \frac{Ar^*}{K} + 1\right) \tag{6.3}$$

where ln stands for natural logarithm (log to the base e).

## 6.8

### Sources of Error

A skillful analyst can determine any of the factors in these equations with an accuracy of about ± 2 percent or better. The error limits are usually given as the standard deviation, which means that if any of the measurements were repeated a large number of times, about 2 out of 3 results would fall within the limits. This does not mean that any K-Ar age is accurate to within 2 percent. Note equation 6.2. Now picture that factor 296 $Ar^{36}$ becoming larger, approaching equality with the factor $Ar^{40}$. That means that the calculated value of $Ar^*$ would become smaller and smaller, but the error expressed in absolute value would remain constant. Expressed as a fraction or a percentage of $Ar^*$

the error would soar. When the calculated value of Ar is about the same as the error in the determination of either $Ar^{40}$ or 296 $Ar^{36}$, the calculation no longer has any meaning and represents the basic limitation on the measurement of very young samples.

As a rule one should not blame spurious age results on analytical error. If the laboratory work is competently done, the sources of the discrepancy are more than likely elsewhere. When a measured age is different from what was expected or when it does not check with the results obtained on other samples presumed to be of the same age, then the discrepancy should be regarded as a clue to some unsuspected natural phenomenon. The thoughtful researcher will learn much that is new by investigating such possibilities instead of just blaming the analyst.

## References

1. Leakey, L. S. B., Evernden, J. F., and Curtis, G. H.,
"Age of Bed I, Olduvai Gorge, Tanganyika." Nature 191 (1961): 478-479.
2. Leakey, L. S. B.,
"A New Fossil Skull from Olduvai." Nature 184 (1959): 491-493.
3. Evernden, J. F., and Curtis, G. H.,
"The Potassium-Argon Dating of Late Cenozoic Rocks in East Africa and Italy." Current Anthropology 6 No. 4 (1965): 343-364.

## Annotated Bibliography

Dalrymple, G., and Lanphere, M. A.,
Potassium-Argon Dating, W. H. Freeman & Co., San Francisco (1969) 258 pp.
A comprehensive discussion of all aspects of K-Ar dating principles, techniques, and applications.
Faul, H.,
Ages of Rocks, Planets, and Stars, McGraw-Hill, New York (1966) 109 pp.
Brief survey of the principles of geochronology.
Faul, H.,
Nuclear Clocks, U.S. Atomic Energy Commission, Division of Technical Information, Oak Ridge, Tenn. (1968) 60 pp.
Elementary review of geochronological methods and results.

Obsidian Hydration     Joseph W. Michels and
Dating                 Carl A. Bebrich

## 7.1
## Introduction

Obsidian hydration dating is a relatively new technique now available to archaeologists. It has produced useful results when applied to a variety of archaeological problems. The importance of dating controls in archaeology makes the discovery and development of new dating techniques a matter of great interest. In the case of obsidian hydration dating, however, interest and enthusiasm are especially great due to its wide range of applications in archaeological analysis and its low cost.

## 7.2
## History of Obsidian Hydration Research

In 1948, Irving Friedman and Robert L. Smith, geologists with the U.S. Geological Survey, began to collaborate on research designed to demonstrate the high water content of volcanic glasses that have become hydrated since formation by absorption of meteoric water (1). Between 1958 and 1960 they demonstrated that this hydration process is continuous and that the rate at which water diffuses into the stone's interior is uniform. They called upon Clifford Evans and Betty J. Meggers, archaeologists with the Smithsonian Institution, to supply specimens of ancient obsidian of known age. It was with these specimens that Friedman and Smith were able to demonstrate the continuous and uniform rate character of this process and to provide a new, rapid, and inexpensive dating method for archaeology. The principal strategy underlying this early research in obsidian dating was to establish an absolute dating technique along the lines of radiocarbon dating.

After Friedman and Smith had measured some 600 archaeological specimens from various geographical areas and of differing age, it became apparent to them that the rate of hydration is not uniform throughout the world. After examining a number of factors that might be capable of affecting the rate, they discovered that one of the principal variables was atmospheric temperature. Since the specimens submitted had assigned to them a calendrical date by correlation with independently derived chronological information, such as radiocarbon dates, historical records, archaeological estimates, and tree-ring dates,

Friedman and Smith were able to plot the assigned age of each specimen against the thickness of the hydration rim. As soon as a few relatively reliable reference points were established for selected regions of the world (Alaska, the U.S. Southwest, coastal Ecuador, Egypt, and so on) visually estimated trend lines were graphed, thus arriving at tentative hydration rates for a series of given climatic zones. Once the slope of the trend lines was established, the thickness of the hydration rim of any given specimen could be correlated with a calendrical date by consulting the graph representing the appropriate climatic zone (2).

An archaeological evaluation (3) of the research of Friedman and Smith involved a critical review of the degree of correspondence between obsidian dates and their respective archaeological association and resulted in useful precautions regarding the interpretation of obsidian dates. Generally these precautions conformed to those associated with the application of radiocarbon dates. The evaluation, however, did not include consideration of novel applications of obsidian hydration data. The yardstick of success or failure remained one of comparison with radiocarbon dating.

In 1959, Donovan Clark, while a graduate student in archaeology at Stanford University, obtained a National Science Foundation grant to examine central California obsidian materials for the purpose of establishing a regional hydration rate. In order to develop obsidian dating as a chronometric dating tool, Clark analyzed obsidian artifacts from five California sites which possessed radiocarbon dates. Like Friedman and Smith, he plotted each radiocarbon date against the hydration rim thickness of corresponding artifacts. Since the sites were all within a climatically and petrologically homogeneous region, all the data were placed on a single graph and a "rate" or trend line slope was calculated (4).

Clark was now able to undertake a statistical evaluation of some aspects of the technique and to demonstrate that "within-lot" variance is significantly less than "between-lot" variance. Applying the trend test, Clark showed that there is less than 1 percent of doubt that the increase in hydration values with corresponding archaeological estimates is meaningful.

In further work, Clark appealed to many archaeologists to submit well-documented specimens for analysis. The comprehensive objectives included (1) determination of the nature of all possible factors which control or modify rates of hydration, (2) classification of obsidian artifacts and obsidian rock from natural sources on a worldwide basis according to differences in composition and texture, (3) establishment of definitive regional rates of hydration from which absolute dating can be derived, and (4) standardization of the techniques of the method for routine use in the fields of archaeology and geochronology (5). Clark terminated his relationship with the project prematurely, late in 1962, but several graduate students from George Washington University assisted Evans in completing some of the objectives of the two-year project (6).

Between 1962 and 1964 there was a virtual halt to all research on obsidian hydration dating and use of the technique because of several major difficulties that discouraged immediate acceptance of the new technique. First there was the discouraging knowledge that an important determinate of the hydration rate is atmospheric or soil temperature, and since this is variable around the globe, separate rates of hydration would have to be established for each microenvironment; second, different kinds of obsidian proved to have different hydration rates under identical temperature regimes; finally, archaeological application of the technique uncovered wide-ranging patterns of artifact re-use among prehistoric communities which can interfere with the interpretation of the data.

During the next six years, however, re-examination of the obsidian dating technique has proved extremely fruitful, and solutions of the several difficulties have been found. The second phase of research began with the establishment of the UCLA obsidian dating laboratory in 1964. Clark donated the bulk of his research records and microslide collection to the UCLA laboratory at that time. The first real utilization of the laboratory for strictly substantive research began in August of 1964 when the present authors proceeded to date the 453 artifacts that constituted the data upon which Michels' doctoral dissertation was based (7). Departing from earlier research, it explores and illustrates the uniqueness and versatility of the obsidian dating technique in its application to archaeological material.

To avoid the problems connected with the determination of hydration rates for specific archaeological areas, the new method was treated as a highly precise tool for relative dating. Relative dating programs such as seriation of artifacts or site components require large numbers of samples, a requirement that radiocarbon dating cannot meet since the cost of dating is still high. Obsidian dating, however, is inexpensive and fast. For the cost of one commercially processed radiocarbon date the archaeologist can obtain fifty or more obsidian dates. Instead of securing two or three dates from a single site, as is the pattern for radiocarbon dating, the archaeologist can now obtain anywhere from 60 to 500 dates. Sampling from a single site was originally massive for the purpose of seriating artifact types. Many applications of sampling on such a large scale, however, soon began to emerge. These are discussed in detail in a separate section of this chapter.

Archaeological analysis of 3000 specimens from the Valley of Mexico revealed the presence of two different rates of hydration which corresponded to two basic types of obsidian visually contrasted as green and gray (8). This discovery together with Leroy Johnson's work on a hydration rate for the Klamath Basin of California and Oregon (9) stimulated new interest in using the technique as a chronometric tool.

The Pennsylvania State University obsidian dating laboratory has accounted for 90 percent of all dates produced since 1966 (see Table 7.1).* Between 1964 and 1968 the authors supervised the establishment of seven additional laboratories and provided training of student technicians. Most of the new laboratories were established at universities under the sponsorship of archaeologists who were principally concerned with dating large numbers of specimens in connection with a single research program. As a result, many of these laboratories operate only on an intermittent basis. Two laboratories that have consistently been in operation over the past six years have been those at UCLA and Pennsylvania State University and account for the greater bulk of dates.

By the end of 1970, 10,000 obsidian hydration dates have been produced, 60 percent of them at The Pennsylvania State University laboratory since 1966. This large volume and the opportunity they

*The authors gratefully acknowledge financial support for this work from the National Science Foundation.

**Table 7.1** Summary of Sites and Number of Artifacts Dated by Obsidian Hydration as of July 1970

| Geographical Area | Number of Artifacts Dated | Number of Sites Sampled |
|---|---|---|
| North America | | |
| Alaska | 375 | 18 |
| Oregon | 400 | 6 |
| California | 1500 | 60 |
| N.W. Plains | 800 | 50 |
| U.S. Southwest | 53 | 16 |
| Ohio | 21 | 6 |
| Mesoamerica | | |
| Chihuahua | 77 | 1 |
| West Mexico | 520 | 13 |
| Basin of Mexico | 3500 | 30 |
| Coastal Guerrero | 99 | 4 |
| Puebla | 48 | 5 |
| Oaxaca | 19 | 4 |
| Hidalgo | 108 | 3 |
| Highland Guatemala | 1500 | 150 |
| Pacific Coast of Guatemala | 60 | 1 |
| El Salvador | 100 | 1 |
| Honduras | 100 | 1 |
| South America | | |
| Ecuador | 424 | 14 |
| Near East | | |
| Syria | 200 | 1 |
| Egypt | 18 | 3 |
| Africa | | |
| East Africa | 29 | 10 |
| Asia | | |
| Japan | 65 | 35 |
| New Zealand | 140 | 14 |
| Easter Island | 125 | 6 |
| Totals | 10281 | 452 |

have provided for intensive archaeological evaluation have contributed a new, solidly based level of confidence in the technique. A factor contributing to the early lack of interest in the method was the belief that it was only of regional concern. Archaeologists have since begun to notice that many of the most critical areas of prehistoric research feature heavy utilization of obsidian: the Arctic, western North America, Mexico, Central and South America, East Africa, Egypt, the Near East, the Classic world of the Mediterranean and parts of Japan, to name but a few (Fig. 7.1). Moreover, we have discovered that materials other than obsidian do hydrate. One now being analyzed by Bebrich is Los Angeles County fused shale, a material similar in fracturing properties to obsidian that was used for the manufacture of tools by the prehistoric residents of southern California.

The few years that have elapsed since the discovery of this technique have witnessed important developments in evaluation and application and have secured for it a permanent place among the dating programs now available to archaeology.

## 7.3
### Petrographic Characterization of Obsidian

### 7.3.1
#### Petrogenesis
The solidification of molten lavas under differential rates of cooling results in all structural gradations from amorphous glass to completely crystallized rock. Obsidian is one of the glassy products of volcanic activity formed by the rapid cooling and solidification of silica-rich components of the extruded lava, which prevents crystallization of the principal component, silica ($SiO_2$), although other constituents may be found suspended in various stages of crystallization.

Because of their more viscous nature, lavas of high silica content tend to form thicker, more lenticular bodies on cooling rather than thinner, but more extensive flows, as do basalts. Obsidian may also manifest itself as a domelike structure at the conduit. Often these thick veins and domes of obsidian are subject to erosion, and concentrations of rolled and battered nodular pieces, called "float" obsidian, can be found some distance from their point of extrusion.

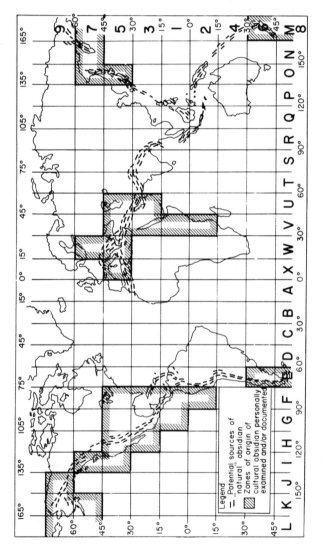

Fig. 7.1 World obsidian hydration zones (after D. L. Clark, 1964, Fig. 14) (4).

## 7.3.2
### Chemical Composition

Obsidian is not a specific chemical compound but a potentially variable mixture of many substances drawn from the parent magma (10). Its physical properties, such as refractive index and specific gravity, therefore, differ according to its composition. The constituents for any given specimen are numerous, and their respective contributions to the total composition may range from less than a few parts per million for the rarer elements to more than 75 percent by weight for a major constituent such as silica. Constituents of rhyolitic obsidian that contribute more than 0.01 percent by weight include: $SiO_2$ (72-76%); $Al_2O_3$ (10-15%); $Na_2O$ (3-5%); $K_2O$ (1-7%); $Fe_2O_3$ (<0.5-2.6%); $FeO$ (1-1.8%); $CaO$ (0-1.2%); $TiO_2$ (0-0.5%); $MnO$ (0-0.1%); $MgO$ (0-0.4%); $H_2O$ (0.2-0.9%); $P_2O_5$ (0-0.1%).

## 7.3.3
### Microcrystalline Properties

When the process of solidification of a molten magma is accelerated through rapid cooling, chemical compounds which tend toward crystallization may assume the form of crystallites, microlites, and other light-refracting structures with definite mineralogical identities. These are embryonic crystals that represent a stage between the amorphous state and the crystalline. Figure 7.2 illustrates a variety of such microcrystalline inclusions. Some glasses contain several such types; belonites, for example, are almost invariably associated with bacillites and feldspar microlites. Other glasses contain only one type or none at all.

There is a possibility that these structures can affect the rate of hydration either directly or indirectly. Clark (4) observed the incompatibility of hydration values obtained from apparently contemporaneous gray and green obsidian artifacts from the Valley of Mexico. On the basis of a correlation of color with significant differences in the observed frequencies of microcrystalline structures, Clark postulated that the two varieties of obsidian hydrate at different rates; a hypothesis later confirmed by Michels (8). Whether the presence or absence of these structures serves merely to signify systematic differences in chemical composition between the gray and green obsidians or whether they are themselves active agents in the hydration process remains to be determined.

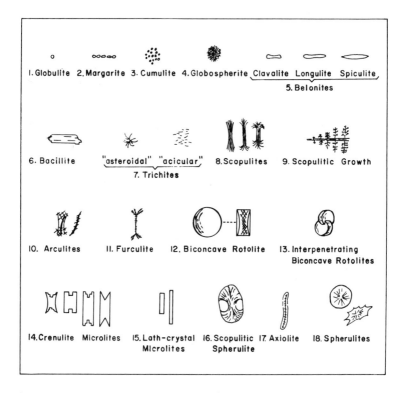

Fig. 7.2 Types of crystallites and microlites (after D. L. Clark, 1961, Fig. 14) (4).

## 7.3.4
### Classification

Natural glasses as well as other volcanic solids may be subdivided according to relative silica contents and proportions of light to dark minerals. Volcanic glasses take their names from the lavas that, upon cooling, form the various igneous rocks. Thus there exist rhyolitic, latitic, dacitic, andesitic, trachytic, and other varieties of obsidian. Most of these are so rare in occurrence that aboriginal populations have seldom made use of them. Rhyolitic obsidian, however, is geographically widespread (see Fig. 7.1) and is virtually the only one reported from archaeological sites. Trachytic obsidian was also used during prehistoric times (e.g., in Egypt) but is more limited in geographical distribution. Unless otherwise specified by context or explicit statement, further discussion thus refers only to rhyolitic obsidian.

## 7.3.5
### Macroscopic Properties

In the hand, obsidian may exhibit many degrees of mottling and banding. Depending on the kind and degree of crystallization, the surface texture of obsidian may vary from mirrorlike to coarse granular, sometimes pocked with vesicles. The color of obsidian may range from black through gray, green, and red to clear with all variations of reddish browns to reddish blacks. These variations are a function of chemical composition and of physical properties that are a product of the cooling history.

## 7.3.6
### Source Identification

Obsidian flows are so limited in number in any given archaeological provenience that it is feasible to attempt to identify them through analysis of chemical composition. In recent years this has become an important archaeological objective since we have come to appreciate the prominent role obsidian trade has played in the economy of some prehistoric societies. Extensively traded, obsidian documents social contact among often widely separated communities. Control of obsidian quarries could bring wealth and prominence to communities; it could also invite political subjugation by more powerful and envious neighbors.

Using neutron activation analysis, X-ray fluorescence, and optical emission spectroscopy, investigators have begun to characterize discrete obsidian flows in many parts of the world (11). In order to accomplish this, some investigators concentrate upon minor or trace elements such as beryllium, calcium, manganese, and zirconium, while others focus on combinations of such minor elements with major elements, such as sodium. In all cases the investigators are looking for element sets whose relative concentrations are uniquely characteristic of a particular obsidian flow. Once all obsidian flows for a particular archaeological region have been "fingerprinted" in terms of characteristic concentrations of chemical constituents, archaeological specimens of obsidian can be traced to their original sources, and patterns of distribution can be worked out.

The chemical elements selected for source identification are not necessarily those that affect rates of hydration. In fact, it is more probable that the relative concentrations of the major chemical constituents, rather than those of trace or minor constituents, play the principal role in causing differences in rates of hydration.

## 7.4
### The Hydration Phenomenon

All glasses, natural or artificial, are thermodynamically unstable and undergo progressive alteration through the slow absorption of atmospheric or soil moisture. Initially, rhyolitic obsidian contains 0.1 to 0.9 percent water by weight, with a modal tendency of 0.2 to 0.3 percent, acquired from the parent magma under pressure (12). Thereafter, molecular water drawn from the surface advances into the obsidian as a sharply demarcated concentration gradient (diffusion front); this can be seen through a petrographic microscope as a rim of uniform thickness at any given point of time (2). The water content of the hydrated layer increases tenfold, to about 3.5 percent by weight. This absorption also increases both the density and the volume of the hydrated layer, altering in different ways the character of light passing through a thin section of the obsidian surface cut at right angles to the plane of the hydrated rim. An increase in density raises the index of refraction, while an increase in volume produces mechanical strain within the layer and at the interface between the layer and nonhydrated portion of the obsidian, imparting to the hydrated rim the property of birefringence (the power of double refraction). It is both the strain-produced birefringence and the higher index of refraction that clearly differentiate the hydrated rim from the unaltered glass under microscopic observation. And, it is the apparent sharp demarcation of the diffusion front that permits accurate measurement of the rim thickness.

Theoretically, hydration continues until a critical point of cumulative strain is reached, whereupon the rim spalls (i.e., physically separates) along the diffusion front from the nonhydrated interior. It has been estimated that hydration penetration in the range 40 to 60 $\mu$ can establish sufficient internal strain to effect spalling under the influence of "fortuitous mechanical agencies" (2). The hydration process then begins anew on the surface of the unhydrated interior. Through periodic spalling, the obsidian is progressively altered into another petrological substance, known as perlite (1). Thus, while thermodynamic instability is reduced by the absorption of water, the hydration process ultimately results in physical decomposition. Assuming that physical separation occurs typically in a range of 40 to 60 $\mu$, the frequency of spalling may vary from once in one hundred thousand years to once in over 3 million years, depending on the environmentally determined effective hydration temperature and chemical composition. The temporal range over which hydration dating may thus be applied in all probability includes the entire span during which obsidian has been used by man.

Decomposition of obsidian does not halt with spalling, however; mechanical strain also results in microfractures within the spall where further decomposition and crystallization may be initiated. This process, known as devitrification, operates on a time scale of millions of years and represents the final phase of decomposition (10). It is probably for this reason that pre-Tertiary obsidians are extremely rare. This is perhaps fortunate for the archaeologist, for the number of possible sources of obsidian is thereby reduced, thus making source identification easier.

In the optical microscope, using either white or monochromatic light, the diffusion front ideally appears as a very fine line running parallel to the edge, and the hydrated rim as a uniform band in distinct phase contrast to the nonhydrated interior (under cross-polarized light the rim may appear luminescent as a result of birefringence; see Fig. 7.3). Under the electron microscope, however, acetate peel carbon-platinum replicas of a surficial cross-section of hydrated obsidian suggest that this luminescence does not express the true nature of either the band or the diffusion front (13). These replicas are negative casts of the surface analogous to plaster casts but on a much finer scale. They are sensitive to dimensional differences on the order of 30 Å. High-magnification electron photomicrographs show that the rim lacks a sharply demarcated front and suggest that it is characterized by a series of closely spaced parallel microfractures of unequal lengths, more or less perpendicular to the edge (Fig. 7.4). It is believed that the volume increase consequent to the absorption of water produces sufficient strain to fracture the glass at roughly regular intervals. The termini of the microfractures appear to be coincident with the edge (surface) and with the

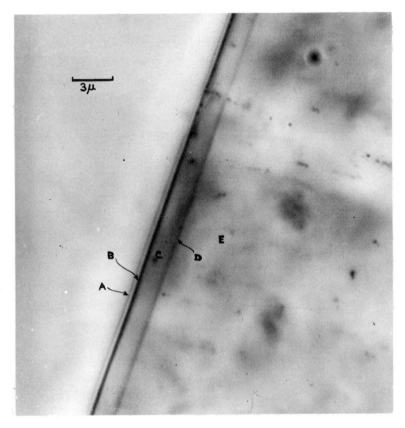

**Fig. 7.3** Photomicrograph of hydration rim. A: Beckett line; B: edge of specimen; C: zone of hydration; D: diffusion front; E: unaltered glass.

water-concentration gradient (diffusion front); i.e., they are of the same depth of penetration as the diffusion front. Variability in the lengths of microfractures is probably a function of small, localized differences in the composition of the glass and the concentration of water in that region. Thus, the optically observed edge and diffusion front are not really straight lines but optical illusions created by the inherent limitations of the light microscope. Electron photomicrographs show that both are nonuniform in contour. Neither the microfractures themselves nor the relatively small differences in their lengths can be resolved by ordinary optical systems, and as a result light refracted from the microfractures is "smeared" in the microscope. Moreover, although only a

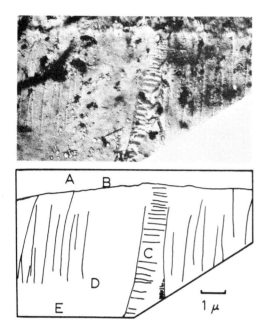

**Fig. 7.4** Electron micrograph of hydration rim. A: balsam outside obsidian; B: outer edge of sample; C: crack formed on fracturing of sample; D: approximate extent of cracking due to hydration, about 4.7 $\mu$ from edge; E: unaltered glass (from D. L. Gibbon and J. W. Michels, 1967, Fig. 2) (13).

single plane is theoretically viewed, the microfractures lie in three-dimensional space and those beneath the viewing plane compound the smearing effect. Variability in the lengths of the microfractures approximates a normal distribution, but even if the distribution were skewed, the result would be the same: the density of light refracted from either terminus is a function of the number of microfractures that terminate in any given plane, and high-frequency planes show a central tendency with relatively small dispersion. This dispersion is so small when viewed optically, and the smearing effects so compounded by the 30 $\mu$ or more of wedge thickness through which the light must pass, that both the edge and the diffusion front appear as fine lines of low light intensity.

The hydration of obsidian is a weathering process peculiar to fused silicate materials. Although it is sometimes referred to as patination, the latter term, most commonly used to designate the weathering of flints, actually involves a complex of processes including but not restricted to hydration. Patina is formed by the interaction of at least three different processes acting principally on impurities in the flint: oxidation and hydration; dissolution and leaching; and chemical and mechanical de-segregation (18). The hydration process involves water as the only externally supplied, chemically active agent, whereas patination generally involves chemical agents in addition to water. The greater uniformity of the weathering process so characteristic of hydration is largely a function of differences in physical structure and the distribution of chemical impurities. Obsidian is a uniform, noncrystalline silica medium in which chemical "impurities" constituting the driving force for hydration are more or less homogeneously distributed. The role of hydration is therefore controlled primarily by temperature and composition. Flint, in contrast, is a crystalline silica of variable grain size, in which chemical impurities may be inhomogeneously distributed. The patination rate is influenced not only by temperature and over-all composition but also by silica grain size and the distribution of chemical impurities between grains.

## 7.5
### Variables Controlling Hydration Rates

In order to yield chronometric dates, the rate of obsidian hydration must be established. Physical scientists (2, 14) have argued on theoretical grounds that the diffusion of water into obsidian should follow the diffusion law $M^2 = Kt$, where M is the depth of penetration of water in microns, K the diffusion coefficient, and t the time in years. Research on obsidian hydration has focused on one or another of the multiple components of K in order to evaluate their effects on the rate of hydration.

### 7.5.1
### Dependence of Diffusion Upon Temperature

The effect of temperature on the rate of obsidian hydration was recognized at an early stage. Using archaeologically dated obsidian specimens from various parts of the world, Friedman and Smith (2) demonstrated that there were systematic differences in the rate of hydration between different climatic zones. In order to clarify and further validate the temperature dependence of obsidian hydration, Friedman, Smith, and

Long (15) induced hydration of obsidian under controlled laboratory conditions. They suspended freshly chipped rhyolitic obsidian in a furnace maintained at a constant temperature of $100° \pm 5°$ C and at 1 atm. of $H_2O$ pressure. Samples were removed at intervals over a four-year period, thin sections were cut and the depth of hydration measured.

The results of their study confirmed that hydration proceeds according to the diffusion law and aided in defining the relation between K and the effective hydration temperature T; this relation is given in the equation (15)

$$K = Ae^{E/RT}$$

where A is a coefficient dependent upon the physical and chemical properties of the glass, e = 2.71828 is the base of the natural logarithms, E the activation energy in Kcal/mole, R the universal gas constant, and T the effective hydration temperature. As this equation makes clear, the temperature is only one of several variables that affect K, since the coefficient A is not a constant.

Although Friedman et al. used a known temperature in their experiment, archaeologists have to cope with ambient temperatures that vary not only from place to place but also from season to season and at different times in a single day. In order to relate the effective temperature to ambient temperature, Friedman et al. (15) have formulated the concept of "effective hydration temperature," which is not the average temperature but rather an estimated temperature at which hydration would proceed at the indicated rate if this temperature were maintained constant. They cite, as an example, the temperature regime of their experiment. At the experimental $100°$ C point, the ambient and the effective hydration temperature are identical because the temperature was constant during the entire period. If it had been held at $100°$ C for half of the time of the experiment and at $20°$ C for the other half, the effective hydration temperature would probably have been about $90°$C; in other words, the same degree of hydration would have resulted had the experiment been run at $90°$ C the whole time. Thus, the effective hydration temperature is conditioned by the length of time temperatures are maintained; this is disproportionately true for higher temperatures.

We do not at present possess a formula for converting ambient temperature data into effective hydration temperatures, but even if we did, the effective hydration temperature of an archaeological area would not be sufficient for calculating a rate of hydration, since the value of A would also have to be known.

Thus the six worldwide hydration rates calculated by Friedman and Smith (2) (Arctic, Sub-Arctic, fast temperate, slow temperate, fast tropical, slow tropical) cannot be taken literally. They serve principally to illustrate the role of temperature, but variability in chemical composition, even among rhyolitic obsidians within a single temperature zone, can produce differences in rate equivalent to those between temperate and tropical climates (8).

## 7.5.2
### Dependence of Diffusion Upon Composition

Obsidians of different compositions can have different rates of hydration. This was recognized in the early stages of obsidian hydration research with respect to major compositional classes such as rhyolitic versus trachytic. Friedman and Smith reported as early as 1960 that evidence from archaeologically dated obsidian artifacts found in Egypt permitted them to conclude that trachytic obsidian hydrated at an estimated rate of $14 \mu^2/1000$ years, while rhyolitic obsidians in the same climatic environment hydrated at an estimated rate of 8.1 $\mu^2/1000$ years (2). As mentioned earlier, compositional variation within a single class of obsidians was discovered to affect hydration rates just as significantly. Michels (8) reports that green rhyolitic obsidian hydrates almost three times as fast as the gray type in the Central Mexican highlands under uniform temperature conditions ($11.45 \mu^2/1000$ years versus $4.5 \mu^2/1000$ years.)

Not enough information is available to define the nature of this dependence at the present time. Friedman and Smith (2), Friedman, Smith, and Long (15), and Haller (16) all stress the dependent nature of the diffusion process upon water concentration. The absorption rates for two glass ores of comparable composition except for initial water content (3.14 versus 5.33 percent) were found by Haller to differ by 40 percent, indicating that higher initial water content results in a greater absorption rate. This is presumably a function of the smaller concentration gradient between the artificially hydrated portion and the water content of the original glass. The hydration rate may thus be expected to vary with the water content of the pristine obsidian as well as with other constituents.

Brill (8), in drawing an analogy with artificial glass, suggests that higher silica and alumina contents in obsidians, coupled with lower alkali contents, could inhibit hydration, whereas the reverse could facilitate it. He argues further that variations of only a few percent in the silica and alumina concentrations could possibly affect hydration rates. Matson (17) suggests also that "$Na_2O$ increases and $Al_2O_3$ decreases the hygroscopic property of synthetic glass."

Further research into the physical chemistry of diffusion dependence in obsidian is urgently needed to determine which constituents account for the variations in hydration rates.

### 7.5.3

### Relative Humidity

Another factor potentially affecting the rate of hydration is relative humidity, although it has been argued both on theoretical and empirical grounds that it does not affect the rate of hydration (2). The surface of obsidian has a strong affinity for water, and any water absorbed on it maintains a molecular film of moisture at the saturation point which is constantly replenished. Moisture from this source is drawn into the body of the obsidian by the diffusion process; yet the hydrated zone of obsidian thus produced never exceeds a water content of about 3.5 percent. This is the "limiting boundary" to water absorption at atmospheric temperature and pressure. Thus, as long as the air or soil environment of obsidian contains sufficient moisture to facilitate absorption, diffusion can occur normally at rates dependent upon other factors. Furthermore, almost any environment on earth does contain sufficient humidity. Extremely humid environments including total submersion in water cannot increase the rate of absorption since surface saturation is reached under even very dry conditions.

We have a wide variety of empirical evidence suggesting that approximately uniform rates exist in climatic zones that contrast markedly in relative humidity. Dry caves in Utah share hydration rates with moist soils of Ohio; Egyptian tombs, with sites in tropical Ecuador; and sites submerged under shallow lakes, with dry land sites in the arid environment of the Valley of Mexico.

### 7.5.4
### Soil Chemistry

The role of soil chemistry as a potential factor affecting hydration rate is poorly understood at the present time. Highly alkaline conditions, in particular, may interact with the diffusion process in some significant way. However, in the authors' experience, such conditions do not appear common in archaeological contexts.

### 7.5.5
### Solar Radiation

Obsidians found on the surface of the ground, particularly in areas of sparse or absent vegetation may hydrate at rates considerably faster than do equivalent specimens shielded from direct exposure to the sun. The direct absorption of the sun's energy by the exposed obsidian specimen alters the effective hydration temperature and thereby the rate of hydration, all other factors being equal. Although a systematic investigation of this phenomenon has yet to be conducted, informal recognition of such effects is widespread among investigators.

### 7.5.6
### Summary

Our current knowledge points to temperature and composition as the principal variables that affect the diffusion coefficient K in the equation $M^2 = Kt$. Special situations may arise where soil chemistry or solar radiation will affect the coefficient. Relative humidity does not appear to function as a variable under any circumstances.

Focusing on temperature and composition as primary if not exclusive determinants of hydration rates does not bring us very close to a convenient determination of the value of K in any given case. A great deal of basic research into the physical chemistry of obsidian must precede any useful formulation of the relation of these factors to the hydration phenomenon.

### 7.6
### Estimation of Rates of Hydration

Empirical studies involving hundreds and sometimes thousands of obsidian hydration measurements have clearly indicated that gross controls for temperature and composition can provide an adequate basis for comparisons of hydration values. Such conditions can usually be found within a given archaeological subregion, such as a river valley, a highland plateau, or a coastal strip. In such circumscribed areas the likelihood of more than one or two variants in the composition of obsidian that affect hydration rate are slight. Furthermore, the effective hydration temperature is likely to be more or less uniform. Under these conditions intrasite and intersite chronometric dating can be pursued with confidence.

### 7.6.1
### Estimation of Hydration Rates by Averaging

A convenient method for estimating the rate of hydration for an archaeological subregion is one in which the hydration-rim thickness is correlated with an independent chronometric scale, such as radiocarbon dating or dendrochronology, as used by Johnson (9) for the Klamath Basin of California and Oregon. He calculated the rate from data acquired during the excavation of the Nightfire Island site (4Sk4) in Siskiyou County, northern California. A deep, well stratified excavation pit was selected, and radiocarbon samples and obsidian flakes were obtained from ten excavation levels. In Table 7.2 the results of radiocarbon dating and hydration-rim measurements for the samples obtained are compared.

As a first step, prior to the actual calculation of the rate, Johnson tested for the validity of his data. He started with the exponential equation

$$y = a \cdot x^b,$$

which can be transformed to the linear equation

$$\log y = \log a + b \cdot \log x.$$

From the ten data points, with the hydration-rim thickness substituted for y, and time in years for x, the regression coefficients can be calculated. In Johnson's example, they were found to be log a = $-1.2679$ (the y-intercept of the regression line) and b = 0.512 (the

**Table 7.2** Carbon-14 Dates and Hydration-Layer Measurements for Obsidian Samples from Ten Levels of the Nightfire Island Site (4SK4), California

| Years (B.P.) | Sample No. | Number of Specimens | Level Mean ($\mu$) | Level S.D. ($\mu$) |
|---|---|---|---|---|
| 1540 ± 100 | GaK-1841 | 5 | 2.4 | 0.3 |
| 2180 ± 80 | GaK-1831 | 5 | 2.4 | 0.7 |
| 2340 ± 100 | GaK-1832 | 8 | 2.7 | 0.6 |
| 2180 ± 90 | GaK-1833 | 5 | 3.1 | 0.7 |
| 3470 ± 80 | GaK-1834 | 11 | 3.5 | 0.8 |
| 3450 ± 90 | GaK-1835 | 15 | 3.7 | 0.8 |
| 4260 ± 100 | GaK-1836 | 18 | 3.8 | 0.7 |
| 4750 ± 110 | GaK-1837 | 14 | 4.1 | 0.4 |
| 4030 ± 90 }* | GaK-1838 } | 16 | 4.2 | 0.9 |
| 4500 ± 110 } | GaK-1839 } | | | |
| 5750 ± 130 | GaK-1840 | 10 | 4.4 | 0.6 |

*$\overline{X}_{activity}$ = 4265 years (B.P.)

slope of the regression line). These values result in the exponential equation

$$y = 0.054 \cdot x^{0.512}.$$

The diffusion equation $M^2 = K \cdot t$, discussed in section 7.5, can be written as

$$M = K^{\frac{1}{2}} \cdot t^{\frac{1}{2}},$$

which is the equivalent to the exponential equation, with $y = M$, $a = K^{\frac{1}{2}}$, $x = t$, and $b = \frac{1}{2}$. Johnson used a statistical method based on the time distribution for two regression lines having the same intercept (19) to test whether the value b = 0.512 is significantly different from the universally established value of 0.5 (15). With his data this was not the case, and he therefore substituted b = 0.5 in the exponential equation

$$y = a \cdot x^{\frac{1}{2}}$$

and its logarithmic equivalent

$$\log y = \log a + \frac{1}{2} \log x.$$

The average value of a can now be found from the ten data points. If we then substitute the values of y and x in the equation, we get ten values for a (Table 7.3) which are averaged to yield a value of a =

Table 7.3 Data for Hydration Rate Averaging (See Table 7.2)

| No. | y | x | $a = \dfrac{y}{\sqrt{x}}$ |
|-----|-----|------|------|
| 1 | 2.4 | 1540 | 0.061 |
| 2 | 2.4 | 2180 | 0.051 |
| 3 | 2.7 | 2340 | 0.055 |
| 4 | 3.1 | 2180 | 0.068 |
| 5 | 3.5 | 3470 | 0.059 |
| 6 | 3.7 | 3450 | 0.063 |
| 7 | 3.8 | 4260 | 0.058 |
| 8 | 4.1 | 4750 | 0.059 |
| 9 | 4.2 | 4265 | 0.063 |
| 10 | 4.4 | 5750 | 0.058 |

$0.059_5$. Alternatively, we could have used the formula

$$\log a = \frac{\Sigma \log y - \tfrac{1}{2}(\Sigma \log x)}{n} \quad (n = 10)$$

to obtain $\log a = -1.2249$, which also yields $a = 0.059_5$.

The exponential equation now has the form

$$y = 0.059_5 \cdot x^{\frac{1}{2}},$$

and we can solve for K in the diffusion equation $M^2 = Kt$:

$$K = a^2 = (0.059_5)^2 = 0.00354.$$

Thus, the hydration rate for Klamath Basin was established as 3.54 $\mu^2/1000$ years.

This method gives no consideration to the standard deviations of either the radiocarbon dates or the obsidian hydration measurements.

## 7.6.2
### Establishing a Rate by Least-Squares Regression

A method which will establish a more reliable hydration rate is now under consideration. Here the data consist of a set of chronometric dates and the corresponding hydration-rim thicknesses together with the standard deviations of both.

As before, we start with the equation

$$\log y = \log a + b \cdot \log x.$$

A computer is programmed to find the regression coefficients log a and b. The mean values of y and x may yield a b value quite different from the established theoretical value of 0.5. By varying the values of x and y within the range of their standard deviations, new values for the regression coefficients are computed. If the data are reliable, a systematic search will finally yield the value of b = 0.5, and the corresponding value of a can be used to solve for the diffusion coefficient $K(K = a^2)$. This value of a is a least-square value, rather than one of simple averaging.

One of the advantages of this procedure is that there is no danger of rejecting good data. In most cases the standard deviations of radiocarbon dates and hydration measurements are quite large. It is therefore entirely conceivable to have a set of data points whose mean values yield unsatisfactory results, while valid results can be obtained by varying the points within their allowable ranges. By the same token, one can conclude that if the value of b = 0.5 cannot be reached, the data are invalid.

### 7.6.3
### Rate Approximation

The archaeologist is sometimes handicapped by not having any independent chronometric scale with which to calculate the hydration rate through least-squares regression analysis or averaging, or else he may wish to work with hydration values as chronometric data before any results from radiocarbon or some other independent dating means are available. In such cases the hydration rate can sometimes be approximated with the aid of preliminary archaeological estimates of age based on such evidence as ceramic phasing, colonial documentation, or architectural cross-dating. If, for example, the archaeologist knows that the site was not occupied prior to a certain period nor after some later period, and if he can furnish fairly reliable estimates of the absolute dating of these periods, it is possible for him to discover a hydration "rate" that places a fairly large number of obsidian samples within the archaeologically estimated limits.

The procedure begins with the arbitrary correlation of a fixed point in time with a specific hydration-rim thickness (essentially one point along an imaginary regression line). This is not always so arbitrary, for a particularly good association of obsidian with a cross-datable feature within a site can suggest an especially plausible correlation.

A rate is then calculated using the hydration equation $M^2 = Kt$. The resulting rate is then tested by comparing the obsidian dates with archaeological age estimates. If no satisfactory correspondence is observed, another arbitrary point in time and another hydration-rim thickness are correlated, thereby establishing a second "rate." A test of correspondence between these dates and archaeological expectations of age is again undertaken. These procedures are repeated until the obsidian dates correspond well with archaeological age estimates throughout the full chronological range of occupation of the site.

The rate ultimately accepted serves as a basis for calibration. Because of the nature of diffusion, a small error in the calculation of the rate can produce gross anomalies in age determinations in areas containing more than a 3-to-5-$\mu$ dating range. Thus, even though a rate may yield what appears to be an acceptable date when calculated for a hydration rim of 3.9 $\mu$, it may be discovered that this is an invalid rate because it would require the chronometric value of a hydration rim 1.2 $\mu$ thick to fall outside the estimated limits of time.

The success of this approach to hydration rate determination rests upon the extent to which archaeological estimates of age are reliable, the presence of a significant range of thicknesses within the obsidian collection dated, and a suitably large number of obsidian samples.

An example of the "rate approximation" approach is provided by Michels (8) for green obsidian from the Valley of Mexico. In this case the arbitrary "known" point was established for the Chiconautla site by associating a tight, high-frequency cluster of obsidian measurements (47 in all) with the primary occupational component (Aztec) and coordinating the approximate terminal date of that component (ca. A.D. 1518) with the lowest hydration rim measurement value of the cluster (2.34 $\mu$), less 0.07 $\mu$ for measurement error (2.27 $\mu$). Thus, from the formula $M^2 = Kt$ we have

$$K = \frac{(2.27)^2}{450} = \frac{5.153}{450} \mu^2/\text{yr}$$

$$K = \frac{5.153}{450} \cdot 1000 = 11.45 \ \mu^2/1000 \text{ yrs.}$$

Subsequent evaluation of the resulting correspondence between obsidian dates and conventional dating for green obsidian from as many as twenty sites within the Valley of Mexico provides empirical support for the validity of the new rate.

## 7.7
### Applications to Archaeology:  Some Case Studies

One of the most intriguing aspects of obsidian hydration dating is its versatility as a tool in archaeological analysis. This versatility stems from the facts that a cultural item is itself being dated, that there is an opportunity to undertake dating of many samples, and that obsidian is often an ubiquitous yet highly valued item in the material culture of many prehistoric societies. In this section a number of applications are described.

### 7.7.1
### Testing Stratigraphy

Archaeologists are often handicapped by their inability to test the chronological sequence of midden deposits. Most excavation procedures and controls are applied with some thought to preserving some measure of chronologically significant artifact or feature associations. All such controls and procedures are based on the geological principle of super-position, which states that younger units of deposition overlie older ones in serial order. The archaeologist, while making use of the prin-ciple of superposition, is often unable to make use of the geologists' techniques for detecting disturbances. The problem of detecting and evaluating such disturbance is especially acute in midden archaeology, where no architectural clues are available.

Mixing and artifact reuse are the two primary situations in midden deposits that set a limitation to the effectiveness of stratigraphic analysis. A stratified deposit is one in which the deposits are super-imposed and also leave contrasting cultural contents. Midden deposits are often excavated by means of artificial vertical units, largely because of the absence of any observable clues that point to natural physical partitions in the deposit. This method is also used in those cases where the physical partitions are so gross or so unsystematic that intrastrata partitioning by means of artificial levels is required. More often than not, the cultural contents of the arbitrary deposition units will differ. They therefore appear to be stratified as well as superimposed, permitting the archaeologists to assume that the order of deposition of the units accurately reflects the order of cultural succession.

The problem then is to untangle features that may contribute to confusion in stratigraphic analysis. For midden deposits, the following three features should be distinguished: superposition of the deposition units; artifact mixing; and the net stratigraphic value of the deposition units. The latter is the concept used to refer to the degree to which the subdivisions of the midden deposit recognized accurately reflect the order of cultural succession.

Obsidian hydration dating can contribute to a solution of the problem of the unknown amount of mixing and also to the determination of net stratigraphic value. The procedures (20) apply to any site containing a sufficient quantity of worked obsidian. The analysis involves plotting on a three-dimensional scatter diagram the frequency distribution of hydration-rim values against the deposition units from which the artifacts were recovered. Fig. 7.5 is such a diagram concerning artifacts from the Mammoth Junction Site, Mono County, California; the vertical axis represents the thickness of the hydration rim. Maximum thickness (thus maximum age) is located at the bottom of the axis and intervals of reduced thickness are expressed by the micron values progressing toward the top. The horizontal axis represents the deposition units. The deepest units are located at the juncture of these two axes, and progressively shallower units are arranged toward the outer end. In this case, a range of 1 to 8 $\mu$ is represented on the vertical axis. The deposition units at this site were ten arbitrary 15-cm levels.

Mixing is clearly present in all deposition units, as evidenced by the overlapping of time sectors by all of the units of deposition. The extensiveness of mixing can be observed by noting the length of the vertical column. One fourth of a micron represents approximately 250 years at this site [based on the hydration rate set by Clark for central California (4)]; thus, a vertical column extending more than 1 micron reveals that the deposition units include artifacts ranging over 1000 years in age. In this case, where all deposition units have large segments of their

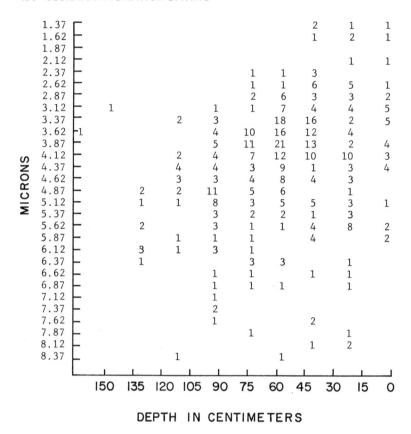

**DEPTH IN CENTIMETERS**

**Fig. 7.5** Summary of dated artifacts from the Mammoth Junction Site, California (after J. W. Michels, 1969, Fig. 1) (20).

respective vertical columns overlapping with all of the others, it is reasonable to predict that the net stratigraphic value will be negligible. Using an analysis of variance, and Scheffe's S-method of multiple comparison (21), it was possible to subdivide the Mammoth Junction site deposit into four stratigraphically significant units of deposition. (It was necessary to ignore the top and the bottom 30 cm of the deposit.) The four units are 30 to 61 cm, 61 to 76 cm, 76 to 107 cm, and 107 to 122 cm; they reveal heavy representation of distinctive segments of the micron range. The ranges for each unit are considerable, however, and the inventories thereby associated with each represent the refuse of over a millennium of cultural activity.

## 7.7.2

### Testing Artifact Reuse

Members of a community may have been systematically collecting previously fashioned implements, intending them to be used in tasks for which they had not themselves manufactured suitable implements. This might result from the interruption of trade relations between areas. Obsidian has a long history as an important commodity in trade relationships (7, 22). A breakdown in the trade network at any point would result in alternative behavior; one alternative pattern might have been the systematic reuse of the obsidian chips and discarded artifacts that lay upon the ground in the vicinity of communities that had previously imported fresh obsidian.

Evans and Meggers (3) postulated that there was extensive reuse of obsidian artifacts at the Chorrera R-B-1 site, Ecuador. Samples of obsidian artifacts from varying excavation levels have been dated from this site, and evidence of systematic reuse of obsidian could be detected by the scatter-diagram technique. A scatter diagram (Fig. 7.6) reveals a scatter of hydration-rim values that is excessive, appears bifurcated, and is not closely comparable to that of the Mammoth Junction site. The trend line documents a tendency toward superposition. The fluctuations of the median line above the trend line reveal deposition units that have experienced heavy intrusion by younger refuse. And the very pronounced dip of one segment of the median line below the trend line indicates that a disproportional amount of older refuse has somehow intruded up into the younger deposits. This was not observed at the Mammoth Junction site.

The question arose whether the anomalous features on Fig. 7.6 could be interpreted as evidence of systematic artifact reuse during a certain cultural period. A provisional definition of the features that will indicate the existence of a pattern of artifact reuse during a specific period of time was established. These features are a positive slope of the trend line, a pronounced dip of a segment of the median line below the trend line at some vertical sector, and a horizontal sector of the scatter diagram, located on or above the trend line, that is largely or completely vacant. The first feature reveals the general chronological integrity of the site deposit; the second that a proportionally significant number of

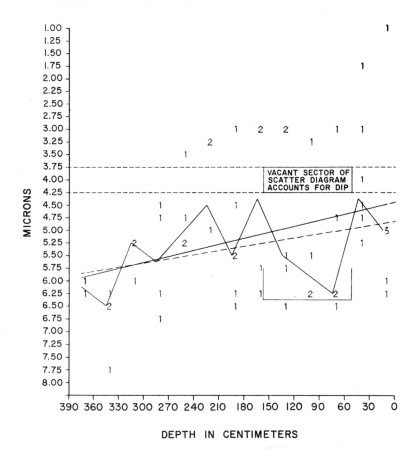

**Fig. 7.6** Dated artifacts from site R-B-1, Chorrera, Ecuador. This figure illustrates the presence of all three features indicative of artifact reuse: a positive slope to the trend line, a pronounced dip of a segment of the medium line below the trend line at some vertical sector, a horizontal sector of the scatter diagram located on or above the trend line which is largely or completely vacant (after J. W. Michels, 1969, Fig. 11) (20).

artifacts of older age has intruded into levels of a deposit laid down later. The third feature indicates that for some measurable period of time there is evidence that few, if any, artifacts of the kind under consideration were being manufactured. Figure 7.6 shows all three of these features. The largely vacant horizontal sector lies between 3.75 and 4.25 $\mu$, representing the latter half of the Tejar phase at this site (A.D. 460 to 710), a period approximately 250 years long on the basis of the hydration rate determined by Friedman's scale B (2).

Particular artifact reuse can also be determined. When an obsidian core or a flake struck from such a core is fabricated into a tool, the surfaces of the obsidian forming the tool are freshly fractured (1). The hydration associated with earlier periods is no longer present. We are thus measuring only the period of time between the production of the tool, when fresh surfaces are exposed, and the archaeological recovery of the specimen. If, however, after several hundreds or thousands of years after its manufacture the object is reused by a new artisan, the analyst may well discover hydration rims that date to the initial manufacture of the artifact as well as to the subsequent reuse. Multiple rims of varying thickness can often be found on a single wedge removed from an artifact, because a wedge may represent both the immediate working edge of the tool and a portion of two connecting surfaces. If the latter (the sides or faces of the tool) were the original surfaces, then they should still exhibit the hydration rim that dates the initial manufacture. However, the working edge may have been further abraded by reuse, in which case the sector that refers to the working edge would have a thinner hydration rim, which will tell us approximately when the tool was re-used.

An artifact that was simply crushed under foot may of course also have this secondary hydration rim. Fortunately the archeologist can generally tell whether the spalling of the edge looks sufficiently systematic to indicate wear or incidental fracture.

### 7.7.3
### Perceramic and Nonceramic Archaeological Components
While the valleys of Oaxaca and Tehuacán in highland Mexico have yielded substantial information about the food-gathering and incipient agricultural periods (23), the basin of Mexico has remained largely a

mystery for periods antedating the regular use of pottery. The period
spanning from 7000 to 1500 B.C., which marks the gap between
hunters and well-established agriculturists has continued to defy the
efforts of many archaeologists. William Sanders (24), during an extensive survey of the Teotihuacán valley, recorded close to 300 sites but
was unable to identify a single locality dating to the above-mentioned
period. By inference from the Tehuacán and Oaxaca data, there was no
question that the basin of Mexico, like its sister valleys, possessed a
local population during this early era. But where were the sites?

Some 30 to 40 previously excavated sites in the basin of Mexico were
reexamined with the aid of obsidian hydration dating (25). Approximately 3000 selected specimens were dated and their chronometric
placement was established with the aid of Friedman and Smith's scale E
rate ($4.5 \mu^2/1000$ years) for the gray obsidian (2) and Michels' rate of
$11.45 \mu^2/1000$ years for the green obsidian (8). Many of the sites under
study were understood to be multiple-component sites, that is, more
than one episode of occupation was represented. Some were known to
have been continuously occupied over very long periods of time and to
have witnessed profound transformations of the political, social, and
religious life of the population. However, none of the sites was known
to have contained any manifestation of a pre-Formative, that is,
Archaic occupation. The dating of these 3000 specimens showed that
the greatest portion of the obsidian specimens dated to phases that
would have been predicted anyhow on the basis of ceramic evidence,
but there was a residue of specimens from several sites which exhibited
far older dates than anticipated, some dating to the Archaic era.

The discovery of this collection of artifacts established for the first
time that an Archaic population did exist in the basin of Mexico, and
by analyzing the kinds of implements represented, we can make some
provisional observations about the ways of life associated with this population. A study of these artifacts is still continuing and a full report on
this research will be published in the near future. One important point
already established is that obsidian hydration dating has made the discovery of several early and hitherto undetected components of culture
in this region of Mexico possible.

A different kind of discovery is illustrated by a consideration of the

Chiconautla site in the Teotihuacán valley, located on the edge of Lake Texcoco in the basin of Mexico and known to have been a very important town during the Aztec and early Colonial periods. It was excavated in the 1930s by George Vaillant, and the materials recovered were deposited with the Museum of Natural History, New York City. Michels undertook an analysis of the obsidian which included obsidian dating. Slightly over 100 artifacts from the Chiconautla site were dated with very perplexing results at first. This site contained Aztec ceramics and some Colonial materials exclusively, and there had been every reason to believe that this town came into existence during the late Post-Classic, or Aztec, period and continued into the early Colonial era.

The obsidian dates, however, revealed a more complex picture. Half of the 100 dates fall precisely within the period representing the Aztec era and approximately 10 percent fall within the Colonial period. The surprising discovery, however, is the very large percentage of artifacts, between 22 and 25 percent, that date to the Classic era. There was no other archaeological evidence to support the newly discovered occupation. Virtually not a single sherd of Classic-period pottery was found during excavation. The mystery of this anomalous distribution of obsidian dates was cleared up however, when Michels analyzed the functional characteristics of the Classic-period artifacts. Over 70 percent of them were rasp end-scrapers, believed to have been used in connection with maguey cultivation and maguey fiber extraction. Only 18 percent of the Aztec-period obsidian assemblage consisted of rasp end-scrapers. The maguey plant is economically very important in the highlands of Mexico and it was already cultivated during the Classic, Post-Classic, and Colonial eras. The anomaly in the distribution of dates can be explained by the hypothesis that during the Classic Period the locality of Chiconautla was being utilized for the farming of maguey by a population residing elsewhere.

### 7.7.4
### The Construction of Artifact Assemblages

Perhaps the most fundamental contribution of the technique is its use by archaeologists to associate artifacts with each other for the purpose of forming artifact complexes in the absence of reliable stratigraphy. For the first time there exists a perfectly unbiased procedure for segregating surface materials and materials from poorly stratified or unstratified sites into analytically useful units of association. Segregation is accomplished by establishing arbitrary micron ranges and by treating all artifacts having hydration values falling within an established range as in some sense associated. Artifacts having hydration values falling outside the range belong to other, similarly constituted, units of association. For very large artifact collections an added advantage is achieved by constituting "dead" spaces between micron range units. All artifacts having such intermediate hydration values are excluded from analysis. This has the effect of creating artifically what can be figuratively described as "sterile layers" between deposits of cultural refuse so that all contamination is eliminated.

The cultural history of the Valley of Mexico has been amplified through many years of archaeological research and continues to be further developed. One era, however, which has been sadly neglected has been the Colonial era of Indian life. The presence of recognizable colonial archaeological sites in the Valley of Mexico has been difficult to establish. As a result, virtually all our information concerning the Colonial era comes from the archival records prepared by Spanish colonials. Many very important aspects of Indian life for comparative studies are ignored in the records, because the Spanish chroniclers did not consider them significant.

A very good example of this has to do with the obsidian industry. We have been able to establish that obsidian was a very important commodity in the civilization of highland Mexico, especially in the societies that flourished in the basin of Mexico. We know, for example, that obsidian was used in the production of artifacts that played important roles in religious ritual, and as symbols of status. It has been employed to prepare weapons for warfare, as tools in the production of other objects, and for various subsistence activities, as well as to make ornaments for personal adornment and to serve as a valuable commodity in trade relationships. Anthropologists are therefore very anxious to know what role obsidian played in the postconquest Indian culture. Did the wide range of utilization of obsidian persist?

The dating of 3000 obsidian specimens in the Valley of Mexico (8) resulted in a large number of specimens being ascribed to the Colonial

Period. These specimens were studied as a group, as an assemblage constructed from varying site locations, but all essentially contemporaneous for the purposes of analysis and comparison. On the basis of this
assemblage, consisting of close to 200 artifacts that could be demonstrated as belonging to the Colonial Period, Michels was able to describe
what kinds of obsidian were most popular, what techniques of processing were used, the geographic range of distribution, the range of products manufactured, and the social and economic impact of the industry.

## 7.7.5
### The Compatibility of Hydration Dating and Ceramic Phasing

An important question is the degree to which obsidian dating is com-
patible with the kinds of evidence provided by ceramics. A very good
test of this was conducted with Valley of Mexico material. The La
Venta site, excavated by Juan Vidarte, has been fully analyzed using
conventional techniques, including ceramic phasing. An analysis of the
relative frequencies of various ceramic types was undertaken as an indicator of the occupational intensity, phase by phase, of this multi-
component site. One hundred specimens of obsidian were submitted for
dating. The resulting distribution of dates by period at the site was as
follows: 25 percent of the dates fell within what is referred to as the
late Formative period, 47.9 percent of the dates fell within the Classic
period, and 18.8 percent of the dates fell within the early Post-Classic
period. Juan Vidarte (26) reports that percentages based on ceramic
sherd frequencies are as follows: 20 percent for the late Formative
period, 40 percent for the Classic period, and 20 percent for the early
Post-Classic period. This is an example of the precision with which there
can be compatibility between the results of obsidian and ceramic dating. In this case, the techniques independently suggest that the most
prominent period of occupation at the La Venta site was the Classic
period but that there was an important Late Formative and also an important early Post-Classic component. The relative intensity of occupation is illustrated by these percentage values.

This kind of test is being repeated at many other sites with the object
to explore fully the compatibility of these two categories of data. If the
compatibility turns out satisfactory, then many of the observations
made of preceramic or nonceramic sites with the aid of obsidian dating

can be regarded as fully comparable to statements being made about
ceramically analyzed sites. This would certainly augment the range of
comparison available to the cultural historian.

### 7.7.6

### The Treatment of Obsidian Artifact Attributes as Time Series Data

Artifacts measured by the obsidian dating technique possess absolute
and discrete hydration depth values expressed numerically, on the basis
of which they can be ordered as a series with relative position determined by successive increments of numerical value: 1.3, 1.9, 2.5 $\mu$, and
so on. Such an ordering permits the various culturally significant
attributes of each specimen to be chronolgoically situated relative to
those of every other specimen. Thus a collection of obsidian artifacts
taken from a single site or from several sites within the same general
locality can be analyzed as a set of ordered observations on a number of
variables through time. A given artifact can be characterized with respect to its form, its physical dimension, its typological affiliation, its
provenience within the site deposit, its method of manufacture, and so
forth. All such variables can be treated independently as time series
data. This approach to the analysis of obsidian artifacts was explored
with a collection of artifacts excavated by Michels (7) from the Mammoth Junction site, which appears to have been a popular station for a
number of activities: obsidian quarrying, manufacturing, hunting, traveling, and summer residence, largely because of its ecological and geographical provenience. Some 450 artifacts classified as projectile points,
knives, scrapers, and choppers were measured. A number of intriguing
patterns emerged when their attributes were studied as time series data
with the seriation based on their hydration values. Thirty-seven different projectile point types were identified in the collection, and these
were ordered serially by their hydration values, permitting the appraisal
of the history of style in projectile-point manufacture over an extended
period of time. It became possible to note which periods witnessed the
introduction of new types and to observe the rhythm of typological
transformations and innovations over a long period of culture history.
Focusing on the gram weights of the projectile points as time series data
revealed periods in the history of the site when there was a considerable
variability in weight and other periods when there was remarkable uni-

formity in weight. Probably, however, the most interesting discovery using the attribute of gross weight was that all of the last half-dozen point types to develop in time had weights of one gram or less, clearly demonstrating that the last episode of innovation in point styles in this locality was associated with the use of arrows and bows. Another important discovery using the time series approach was the identification of a period when a considerable amount of attention was being given to the production of large, lenticular biface pre-forms (blanks) for distribution in a wide trading arc that connected highland California piedmonts with areas as far away as the Pacific coast.

## 7.8
### Procedures for Dating

In the following sections we provide specific instructions for microslide preparation and measurement procedures. These are described in detail in order to enable the reader to conduct his own hydration measurements.

### 7.8.1
### Sample Selection

The sample of obsidian artifacts selected for dating should be determined with a clear idea of the problem or problems to be solved in mind. A general rule, however, is to try always to submit recognizable utilized objects rather than débitage. There are two reasons for this. First, the dating technician is guided by utilized edges in the selection of a suitable locus for removal of a wedge for thin-sectioning. Secondly, regardless of what research problems are primary, dating of recognizable tools automatically increases the anthropological value of the obsidian by supplying time series data on artifact function.

### 7.8.2
### Sample Size

The size of the artifact sampling to be dated must also be considered. Although each date is reliable within the margin of its standard error, the portability and reusability of obsidian provides for the possibility of depositional mixing (see section 7.7.6.) This fact, together with the likelihood that a site may contain the remains of multiple-occupational episodes, argues for the desirability of dating a quantity of obsidian specimens. The number necessary depends on the complexity of the history of site utilization. A good illustration of the problems of dating a complex multiple-component site is provided in Fig. 7.7, which depicts frequency distribution curves for the Maquixco site, Valley of Mexico. A curve based on a total of 233 dated obsidian artifacts serves as a standard. Beginning with a random sample of 20 artifacts, an attempt is made to approximate the curve produced by the total sample. Not until the size of the random sample is increased to 100 specimens is the total-sampling curve approximated. Maquixco has an unusually long and complex history of occupation, stretching from the pre-Classic to the Colonial period—a duration of more than 3500 years. Other sites with only one component or at least only one principal component may yield satisfactory histographs of occupation with smaller numbers of samples. Dating specific features, such as rooms, burials, or artifact caches, may require no more than five or ten deter-

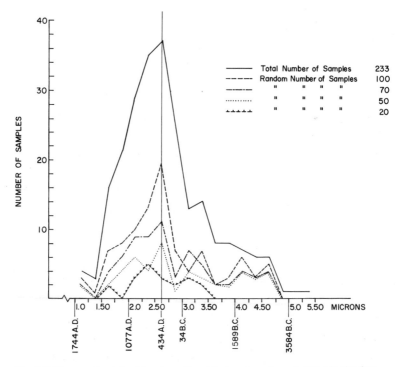

**Fig. 7.7** Histograph of the Maquixco Site, Mexico, based on obsidian hydration measurements.

minations. It is important to emphasize that we are not suggesting that obsidian dates for a given site be averaged. On the contrary, the date spread is a real and important fact about the chronology of the site. Averaging will merely distort the chronological picture.

### 7.8.3
### Sample Characterization

Laboratories that process obsidian specimens must be informed as completely as possible about many aspects of the artifacts.

Provenience: Included in this category of information are the site name and location and the archaeological provenience of each specimen. Site location is identified by (1) country, (2) state, province, or district, and (3) geographic coordinates. Archaeological provenience is provided by a catalog listing, including an identification number for each specimen and the archaeological unit (mound, structure, house, trench, level, and so on) from which each specimen was recovered.

Climate: Climatic data are particularly important for preliminary evaluation of the behavior of hydration values and for a provisional determination of hydration rate. Desirable information includes seasonal length and variation in mean daily temperature, as an index of effective hydration temperature, and such modifying factors as the quantity and seasonal variation in rainfall, site altitude, site location (hilltop, piedmont, valley floor, and so forth), flooding and groundwater level in relation to the excavated deposit.

Soil: Since soil chemistry cannot be excluded from the possible set of variables affecting the hydration process, the measurement of pH is desirable. If additional information concerning, in particular, the relative abundance of alkaline compounds is available, it should also be included.

Cultural Horizons: The laboratory should also be informed of what periods or cultural horizons the investigator suspects his sample derives from, indicating specific associations between individual specimens or lots of specimens and periods or horizons.

Collateral Dating: In order to attempt a precise determination of hydration rate, the results of other dating techniques, such as radiocarbon, potassium-argon, and archaeomagnetic dating, should be reported in full and the association of the samples dated by other means with obsidian objects noted. Moreover, note should also be made of datable materials associated with obsidian which have been recovered but which have not been dated.

Sources of Obsidian: Insofar as possible, the source or sources of the obsidian to be dated should be identified. However, if no correlation between source and sample can be made on the basis of available information, sources of obsidian should nevertheless be identified whenever possible. The ratio of obsidian to other lithic artifacts in the site should also be included in a statement of sample characterization.

### 7.8.4
### Sample Shipment

Since obsidian samples may undergo considerable deterioration involving chipping and breakage during shipment, each specimen should be wrapped individually in a paper or plastic envelope clearly labeled with the catalog number. The envelopes should then be placed in a sturdy, well-padded container for shipping.

### 7.8.5
### Artifact Identification

In addition to the investigator's catalog designation, the dating laboratory also assigns its own identification number to each artifact. At the Penn State Laboratory the identification number has two parts: a collection number that can be used in a variety of ways (for example, to designate all artifacts submitted by a particular investigator or all those from a particular site); and an individual number that uniquely identifies each specimen processed. The two number series are independent and run sequentially.

### 7.8.6
### Cutting of the Wedge

The first step in sample preparation involves cutting a wedge from each artifact. Two parallel cuts are made along an edge of the specimen using a watercooled, continuous-rim diamond-impregnated copper-alloy blade of approximately 0.4-mm thickness and 10-cm in diameter. The blade is powered by a ½-hp motor producing 3600 rpm cutting speed with minimal lateral vibration. Careful consideration should be given to the cut locations on the specimen. Whenever possible, flaked areas should be used for cutting purposes to insure that culturally derived hydration is being secured. Both cuts from the blade must be made perpendicular to at least one surface on the artifact. In general, the cuts are made to a depth of 4 to 5 mm so as to produce a wedge about 1 mm in thickness, to insure that a sufficient perimeter is acquired for measuring purposes. Normally, the specimen is held by hand during cutting and only rarely is a mechanical vise used. Sufficient control of the angle of the cut can be acquired with practice so that the perpendicular requirement is met. The specimen is pushed slowly into the blade, without twisting to execute each cut, and then withdrawn slowly so that no grab is encountered in pulling the specimen away from the blade. Normally 20 to 40 specimens are cut in this manner before the next phase of sample processing is begun.

The sample wedges thus formed by the cutting process are removed individually as each artifact is processed. They are removed with the aid of a dull razor blade. Normally, one of the two parallel cuts is slightly deeper than the other. The technician should insert the razor blade in the shallower of the two cuts and press the blade gently in the direction of the deeper cut to fracture the wedge at the base of the cut. From the time the wedge is removed from its parent specimen until it is mounted on a prenumbered glass microslide the numeric ordering of the specimens, based on assigned laboratory numbers, must be maintained so that the relationship between the wedge and the parent specimen will always be known.

### 7.8.7

#### Initial Grinding

Initial grinding involves the use of American Optical Co. 303-½ corundum abrasive, and a horizontal lapidary that rotates at 300 to 450 rpm. After experimenting with a number of different lapidary surfaces we have come to the conclusion that the most desirable surface upon which to conduct both the preliminary and the final grinding operations is a window-glass surface. Lapidary machines do not come equipped with such surfaces; however there is no difficulty in having an appropriate disc of window-glass 6.4-mm thick cut to specification. Glass is affixed to the standard metal lapidary surface by any one of a number of different adhesives.

Glass is not as hard a surface as the standard metal lapidary surfaces and will show grooving under intensive use; broad over-all concave surfaces will begin to develop. To economize, the plate glass can be turned over. The cost of this glass does not exceed $3.50 to $5.00.

Glass appears to be more effective as a lapidary surface than metal because of its resistance to developing traps or grit pockets that can tear apart the specimen. The result is considerably lower frequency of rejects due to the destruction of the specimen during grinding.

Selection of the 303-½ corundum power as our slurry abrasive is based on considerable experimentation with a variety of grain sizes. Large-grain abrasives increase the reject ratio because of too rapid cutting which restricts the precision with which the grinder can control the point at which grinding should be terminated. Finer abrasives reduce the efficiency by requiring more grinding time.

The purpose of the initial grinding stage is to remove the edge chipping created by the cutting operation and also to provide an optically flat finish on the wedge surface. Initial grinding of the wedges is accomplished by the following set of procedures: A slurry mixture consisting of corundum abrasive in water is so prepared that it has a moderate to thick viscosity. The lapidary wheel is set in motion and a continuous flow of water is provided from a suspended container with a drip rate of about one drop per second; this is important because if the water drips too fast the slurry will be quickly washed away, and if it drips too slowly it will dry on the plate. The slurry is applied to the central portion of the rotating wheel and centrifugal motion will gradually move it toward the edge, leaving a fairly even coverage of the plate.

Grinding of the wedge is accomplished by first moistening the fingers and then applying the wedge to the ball of the index finger. Provided the wedge is small enough, say about 3 by 3 mm, it will not become easily dislodged when the finger is applied to the rotating lap. The finger is put down in such a way that the fingernail almost makes contact with the rotating glass, and the wedge is held behind this opposite to the direction of the rotating plate. A light to moderate pressure is maintained by the finger on the wedge against the wheel. It is important that the wedge be ground parallel to the cut made with the saw in order to maintain uniform thickness. This helps prevent deviation from the perpendicular which may result in an increase of measurement error.

After the wedge has been ground to approximately half its original thickness, eliminating the chipped edge created by the sawblade, it is removed from the wheel. Then, with a sharp pencil, a mark is made on the freshly ground surface in order to identify it and the wedge is washed in clean water and placed into a wedge tray consisting of a compartmented plate with anywhere from 20 to 40 cells, approximately 6.4 mm or less in depth, which serve to isolate each wedge processed through the initial grinding phase.

### 7.8.8
Mounting of the Wedge

A diamond stylus is then used to inscribe the collection and specimen number on the slide on which the wedge will be mounted. Slides 45 by 25 mm and slightly more than 1 mm thick were found most suitable because those of larger size can be more difficult to handle, especially during the final grinding phase.

The wedge is cemented to the slide with Canada balsam. This medium is used in preference to other products such as Lakeside cement because of its ease of handling, its optical properties (which most closely approximate that of obsidian), and because it provides a more plastic medium which does not deteriorate as readily under the stress of grinding. The Canada balsam is used in conjunction with a hot plate to drive off the solvent and provide a solid but plastic compound for mounting. The hot plate must be thermostatically controlled. It has been our experience that a temperature of $76°$ C is most appropriate for use in mounting wedges with Canada balsam. Correct heating time of the balsam can be determined after cooling of the slide by running the fingernail over it. If the fingernail depresses the balsam without etching it, it probably has not been heated long enough. If the fingernail can just etch without chipping the balsam, the appropriate time has been used. If flaking of balsam takes place, there is a possibility that it may have been heated too long.

The amount of heating time required in mounting the wedge varies depending upon the freshness of the balsam. A fresh bottle may require a heating time in excess of two minutes, perhaps as many as three to three and one-half minutes, before the relatively solid medium is achieved. However, after a bottle has been open for an extended period of use, the heating time may be reduced to between ½ and 2 minutes. It is important to avoid prolonged heating of the balsam for fear that it may become brittle and tend to chip off during the final grinding phase. A correct combination of heating temperature and time will insure the proper combination of plasticity and solidity necessary for success in the final grinding stage and for prolonged storage of the slide.

Normally as little balsam as possible is used—just enough to insure a secure mount and to protect the edges of the wedge but no more. The area covered by balsam should not exceed 1 cm in diameter. It is applied using a small, fine-tipped paintbrush held with the tip touching the slide so that the balsam drains down onto the slide.

Next, the wedge is transferred from the slide tray to the slide by a pair of tweezers, and the pencil-marked surface is placed in the balsam matrix. It is heated in this matrix for a specified period of time and then is pressed against the glass with a medium-to-heavy pressure using the tips of a pair of tweezers in such a motion that it slides forward and backward, seating it close to the glass. This is done in order to place the wedge as closely as possible to the glass while still maintaining a slight adhesive film between them. This must be done with uniformity so that all wedges have approximately the same distance between their lower surfaces and the glass, so that in the final grinding phase a uniform thickness of about 50 $\mu$ is maintained.

After the wedge has been seated on the microslide, the latter is taken off the hotplate and placed on a flat glass platform for rapid cooling. The wedge is then immediately pressed against the microslide for approximately 15 seconds to insure that it remains close to the glass slide during cooling.

### 7.8.9

**Final Grinding**

Dating an obsidian artifact depends primarily upon accurate measurement of certain optical characteristics within the wedge of the specimen. Any distortion due to improper thickness can interfere with the transmission of light through the specimen or cause the absence of a satisfactorily parallel set of planes perpendicular to the surface of the artifact. The final grinding phase therefore is to prepare optimum optical condition for microscopic measurements in the wedge. These conditions are met by grinding the wedge to a thickness of 30 to 50 $\mu$. Specimens of greater thickness will tend to interfere with light transmission, and the hydration rim may become obscured by crystalline inclusions in the wedge; also, refraction lines such as Becke lines will increase in frequency and tend to distort the image. Wedges thinner than 30 $\mu$, although desirable, are technically not feasible with the equipment normally used. The range of 30 to 50 $\mu$ has proven adequate for our purposes and the use of more sophisticated instrumentation does not seem warranted. Maintenance of perpendicular surfaces is not difficult at this stage as the plane of the glass microslide aids in this process by providing greater angular control over the positioning of the wedge.

Preparatory to the final grinding, the slide is immersed in water. A suction-tipped plastic dart of the kind used in toy guns is attached to the surface of the slide opposite the wedge. It aids in gripping and manipulating the slide securely during the final grinding phase. As in the initial grinding phase, the abrasive composition is a relatively viscous slurry made of American Optical Co. 303-½ corundum and water. The grinding must be checked frequently, because the grinding process proceeds very rapidly and the specimen may be obliterated altogether if not checked frequently.

Basically, there are three techniques of determining the thickness. One is to use a machinists' dial indicator which gives a direct and absolute measurement of thickness. In practice, however, these instruments have been found to be inconvenient. The second technique involves the determination of thickness by touch; running a finger tip over the glass surface onto the Canada balsam wedge surface and estimating the difference between the two. With some training, the thickness of 30 to 50 $\mu$ can be determined with ease. In a third method, the slide is held against a strong light and its transparency determined. If it is insufficient, then inclusions in the obsidian will probably obscure the hydration rim beyond recognition or at least beyond accurate measurement. In such a case further grinding is necessary. Normal practice is to apply both the finger test and the transparency test, because one serves as a check on the other. After the desired thickness has been achieved, the slide is thoroughly washed and dried. (If the balsam is not of sufficient hardness, it may pick up corundum abrasive during the final grinding which may cloud the slide during mounting and make accurate measurement of the hydration rim more difficult.)

## 7.8.10
### Mounting of Cover Slip
Following the rinsing and drying operation, the slide is brought to the hot plate which is still held at 76° C, and fresh balsam is applied uniformly over an area approximately 1.5 x 1.5 cm. The glass cover slips used in covering the wedge preparatory to microscopic measurement are 18 x 18 mm. They are held between the index finger and the thumb and one edge brought against the microslide surface and up to the area of the balsam. The cover slip is then allowed to fall into the balsam on top of the area to be covered. Then, with a pair of tweezers, it is depressed very gently and the balsam spread evenly over the entire area underneath. At the same time, by rotating the cover slip horizontally, bubbles that may have formed by solvent vaporization may be driven to the edges and dispersed from the balsam medium. Any bubbles left around the edges of the wedge may interfere with accurate measurements.

The length of time that the slide is held on the hot plate is not as critical as in the initial mounting phase. However, a period of not less than 2 minutes is required, but this time may be extended in order to handle 6 to 8 specimens simultaneously. Likewise, the seating operation that took place in the initial mounting phase is not required here.

Finally the specimen is cooled by removal from the hot plate and placement on the cooling glass. Cooling takes one to two minutes. Light pressure should be applied to the cover slip. It is important that the cover slip be close to the wedge surface because the magnification used in the measuring procedure calls for a relatively short focal depth.

## 7.8.11
### Rejects
If the procedures outlined are followed carefully, a rejection rate of no more than 5 percent can be expected. Although this rate is relatively low, rejections must be expected to be derived from several sources.

These include:

1. Total absence of hydration for any reason whatever. For example, a "recently" flaked specimen that has not had sufficient time for hydration or one that evidences recent accidental fracturing of an old surface.

2. Loss of identification of the wedge during preparation.

3. Initial grinding incomplete, with the zone of shatter created by the saw blade not completely removed, obscuring the hydrated portion of the wedge.

4. Improper cutting angle, when the cut is not perpendicular to the surface of the artifact. To cause rejection, the angle of skewing is usually in excess of $10°$. As the angle increases, the error incurred in measurement also increases. For values in the range 1 to 10 $\mu$, deviations of $10°$ or less will result in an error of less than 0.5 $\mu$, which is within the standard error.

5. Angle skewing in the initial grinding phase, when the angle of cut is not maintained constant during grinding. If, additionally, the initial cutting was not parallel, the angular error may become enlarged during the grinding phase.

6. Prolonged heating of the balsam during the initial mounting phase. This results in overhardening and a brittle matrix which, under stress during the final grinding phase, may result in deterioration of the mounting medium and thus the obliteration of the hydration edge.

7. Final grinding to less than 30 to 50 $\mu$. The stress created by the lapidary is sufficient to break down the balsam mounting matrix and to damage the outer edges of the specimen when the thickness becomes 20 $\mu$ or less.

8. Final grinding too thick. This results, particularly in specimens with a high microlite and crystallite content, in obscuring the hydration rim completely or at least to the point that accurate measurement cannot be obtained.

9. Pulverization of the wedge during application of the cover slip through excessive pressure. Occasionally, this is detected only under the microscope.

10. Compositional abnormalities. This includes a number of conditions that can interfere with hydration measurement: exposure to fire, low silica content, chemical leaching of the surface, an irregular diffusion front, and other factors.

## 7.8.12
### Microscope Requirements

The petrographic microscope should have the following specifications: the capability of accepting a I-IV order quartz wedge; a polarizer and condenser, a rotatable stage, a 100X oil immersion lens, a 50X dry lens, a high-intensity variable light source, and a Vickers image-splitting measuring eyepiece. The dry lens is used only when the hydration rim is very thick, that is, when it exceeds the field of view provided by a 100X objective or when rapid scanning of the hydration rim over large sections of a wedge is desired.

## 7.8.13
### Resolution and Visual Contrast

Most specimens will be viewed and measured with the 100X objective using oil immersion. Preparatory to viewing the slide, a small drop of immersion oil is applied to the area directly over the wedge. The first step is to focus on the upper surface of the wedge with the fine adjustment. This can be accomplished most easily by focusing on selected microlites and crystallites near the surface of the wedge. A high contrast is desired but with a background of strong lighting. Normally the light diaphragm must be adjusted at approximately half open, and light intensity at some point below maximum output. The iris must be held open during the measurement procedures in order to maximize the light input. The polarizing mechanism must be in operation at all times, both during initial focusing and during the location of the hydration rim and its measurement. The image-splitting eyepiece must be set at zero shear; i.e., the two images used in measurement of the hydration rim must not be separated but superimposed. After these adjustments, the examiner should be ready to move the specimen by hand manipulation in such a way that he can begin to track along the edge in search of a hydration zone.

## 7.8.14
### Location of the Hydration Rim

Generally the hydration rim can be detected as a combination of two parallel lines at some point along the edge of the specimen; the distance separating them may vary considerably. Occasionally the band may appear as a luminescent strip along the edge due to the birefringent properties of the hydration rim. In such a case, rotation of the stage may be necessary in order to bring out the parallel-line effect. One often encounters certain shadowlike lines in the viewing field, one of which is referred to as a Becke line. There are others, and sometimes a pair of such lines may confuse the observer into believing that they enclose the zone of hydration, although such lines are generally of weaker intensity, more diffuse, and of larger dimensions than either the edge or the diffusion front.

The hydration rim will not necessarily run along the entire perimeter of the wedge. The section that is broken out from the interior of the wedge will have no hydration at all; normally triangular wedges thus will have one side lacking hydration altogether. Moreover, due to irregularities in the grinding process, some sections of the hydration rim may have been inadvertently removed. One has therefore to search carefully along the entire perimeter of the wedge. It may also happen that one or more hydration rims of different thicknesses are found on the same wedge due to reuse or some other factor. Most hydration rims we have encountered in dating almost 6000 artifacts have been in the range of about 1 to 10 $\mu$. This would account for perhaps one eighth or less of the field of view provided by a 100X oil immersion lens.

The presence of a hydration rim can be almost invariably confirmed by removing the quartz wedge and viewing the edge under cross Nicol prisms while rotating the stage; at some point the edge will become luminescent in the zone having hydration whereas the interior of the obsidian will for the most part remain dark. However, once the technician has gained experience in the identification of hydration rims, he will be able to recognize the properties without this procedure. The discovery of the two parallel lines is a good indicator and will enable the technician to identify most hydration rims.

While tracking along the edge of the specimen it may become necessary to make minor adjustments in focus and lighting in order to maintain maximum contrast and maximum resolution of the upper surface of the wedge. At this point both polarization and the quartz wedge will normally be in operation. The red background created by the I-IV order quartz wedge was found generally most effective in enhancing visual contrast and in aiding in the detection of both the edge and the diffusion front. Once the hydration rim is located or suspected, the stage is rotated to the position permitting maximum contrast and resolution. It may be necessary either to stop down further or to open up the diaphragm.

### 7.8.15

### Selection of Measurement Locations

The most consistent results in hydration measurement were obtained by selecting only those areas where the rim is absolutely parallel. Areas where the diffusion front curves in relation to an edge which is perfectly straight are not appropriate.

In summary, the criteria for the selection of measurement location on a specimen are: (1) the presence of an extensive segment of the hydration rim in which the edge and the diffusion front run absolutely parallel to one another; (2) the resolution of the edge and the diffusion front to or very near optimum conditions, meaning that the lines are resolved as finely as possible and approximate the concept of "line" in geometry (i.e., no thickness, only length); (3) the lack of microlite and crystallite inclusions and other structural features which may lead to the obscuring of either of the two images created during the image-splitting measuring process.

### 7.8.16

### Use of the Image-Splitting Eyepiece

The image-splitting eyepiece permits one to obtain an accuracy actually greater than the resolving power of the optics used (27). It is claimed that an accuracy greater than $\pm 0.125 \mu$ (this is the Vickers announced setting accuracy at 100X objective magnification) can be obtained under certain conditions, particularly in the comparison of circles and lines. Another important feature of the image-splitting eyepiece is the absence of parallax error, such as is the case with the filar screw micrometer. Since one is actually viewing in the plane of the object, the object itself serves as the measurement indicator, whereas in the case of the filar micrometer a hairline is tracked across the viewing field, incurring a parallax error that results in a standard error of measurement as much as twice that of the image-splitting eyepiece.

Up to this point the image-splitting eyepiece has been maintained at zero shear. The exact value of zero shear on the instrument scale may vary with the instrument involved and has to be determined by laboratory experience. A thousand measurements with the Penn State laboratory eyepiece have demonstrated that the value is $9810 \pm 1$ unit. This means that instrument precision is about $\pm 1$ unit on the scale of the image-splitting eyepiece measurement drum. This is on the order of less than $\pm 0.01\ \mu$ (using the 100X immersion objective and the 1.5X-by 10X image-splitting eyepiece for a total magnification of approximately 1500X).

The axis of the image-splitting eyepiece must now be aligned with that of the stage in order to permit a shear that is perpendicular to the rim—perpendicular so that only the minimum distance between specimen edge and diffusion front is measured; a shear not perpendicular will result in a larger measurement. This can easily be controlled by using some reference point such as a microlite or crystallite and rotating the drum several times across the edge of the specimen. The reference point should then form a line in its motion perpendicular to the edge of the hydration rim.

The highest precision can be obtained if a microlite of very small size can be found (on the order of the size of the diffusion-front thickness or slightly larger) actually situated on or very close to the diffusion front itself which can serve as a point of focus while shearing. If a microlite cannot be found on the diffusion front then the normal measuring procedure is followed, and that is to shear the edge of one image onto the diffusion front of the other, thus shearing across one hydration rim width.

It takes a fair amount of time to gain skill in placing the edge precisely on the diffusion front, because due to the refractive index of the Canada balsam the edge will normally appear slightly thicker than the diffusion front. The objective is to shear the edge over onto the diffusion front in such a manner that the edge is bisected by the latter. A test of this condition is to move the edge over the diffusion front and then slightly beyond; the technician will be able to detect some difference in light intensity as the edge shears first, to the diffusion front, second, over the diffusion front, and third, passes the diffusion front. Once the edge has sheared past the diffusion front, the light intensity will rapidly pick up and this will be a warning that the edge has moved too far. The technician should shear up to and on the diffusion front, back off a short distance, rotate the drum again, and follow this procedure repetitively until he feels that the edge is directly on top of the diffusion front.

After two measurements following the above procedures have been accomplished at the same locus on the hydration rim segment, the technician proceeds to locate another appropriate rim segment for measurement and then begins to perform the same operations. In this manner at least two measurements are obtained for two locations. We recommend, however, that three or more locations be measured and up to eight or more measurements be recorded.

### 7.8.17

### Calibration Factor Determination

In order to convert the drum units recorded in the measuring process to the metric scale, the microscope must be calibrated. For each set of optics a different calibration factor is used to convert the units into microns, either by use of a stage micrometer slide inscribed with a set of uniform lines of known distance, or by means of a diffraction grating, which is a slightly more accurate device. Either technique is at least an order of magnitude greater in potential accuracy than the capability of the image-splitting eyepiece or the microscope, so that variation in the stage micrometer slide or in the diffraction grating standard do not constitute a significant source of measurement error. At a 1000X magnification, the technician will be able to view a field on the order of approximately $80\,\mu$. The segment of the stage micrometer slide used in the calibration amounts to $50\,\mu$, that is, 5 intervals on the stage micrometer slide.

For this procedure, again, the eyepiece is set to zero shear. In addition, both eyepiece color filters are used—the red and the green. The scale is placed in the field for maximum light intensity, the image-splitting eyepiece is oriented so that it shears perpendicular to the line, and the first line in the series is brought onto the fifth line, shearing a distance of $50\,\mu$. Once the superposition is obtained, the drum value is recorded, and the procedure is repeated four times at that location. These operations are then performed four additional times at two other locations. The mean value of the 12 measurements taken is then divided into the 50 $\mu$ that have been sheared, thus yielding the number of microns per drum unit. In Penn State laboratory, this value varied only slightly for each technician, indicating that individual operator variation is only about 0.01 $\mu$ or less. We conclude that different observers do not vary significantly in their visual abilities and that significant factor differences are almost solely due to instrument variation.

## 7.8.18

### Example of Micron Value Determination

Consider the following example: The drum measurement recordings of the superposition of the edge on the diffusion front are 9440, 9439, 9441, and 9432. Each of these four values is then subtracted from zero position shear value of 9810, yielding 370, 371, 369, and 378, respectively. The average of these drum values, 372, is then multiplied by the technician's factor, which in this case is 0.0081, yielding a micron value of 3.01.

## 7.9

### Measurement Precision

As with all dating techniques, a margin of error is associated with obsidian hydration dating. Unlike some other techniques, however, the extent of error does not vary significantly from one date to another. Technician and instrument errors affect all specimens in a given series equally. For this reason, each laboratory computes a standard error that applies to all measurements produced by that laboratory.

## 7.9.1

### Optical Resolution and the Photodensitometer

A second measurement technique was developed in an effort to evaluate the subjectivity inherent in the image-splitting method, and to crosscheck the degree of precision obtainable. The preparation is the same as previously described, except that no cover slip is cemented on after final grinding. The sample is cleaned in acetone to remove excess Canada balsam and a temporary cover slip is mounted with an oil with an index of refraction equal to 1.52. This index is slightly above that of the hydration rim ($\eta \sim 1.505$ for obsidians studied here) but it gives a high contrast in practive. Again, a good sample area is chosen, lighting and filters are adjusted for maximum contrast, and a photograph is taken using a maximum-contrast film. A print is made solely for use as a "map" of the sample during measurement, and the negative is put on the stage of a scanning densitometer and so oriented that the densitometer slit is parallel to the edge of the sample image; the slit is stopped down to minimum width, and the sample is scanned. The output of the photometer is recorded on a strip chart, as shown in Fig. 7.8. The character of the peaks is strictly dependent upon the operator's having made a proper choice of areas for the photograph. The system is calibrated by scanning a photographic negative of a replica of a 15,000-line/inch diffraction grating taken under the same conditions as the sample photos.

Rim width is determined by measuring the distance on the chart recording between the peaks marking the advancing edge of the hydration rim and the outer surface of the artifact. The standard deviation for measurements made photographically is $\pm 0.04\,\mu$, and that between mean values obtained by the image-splitting eyepiece and by the photodensitometer is $\pm 0.11\,\mu$. This is virtually identical with the published setting accuracy of the A.E.I. image-splitting eyepiece $(0.125\,\mu)$ and may be taken as an indication of the magnitude of the instrument error.

**7.9.2**

**Human Error**

Human error, the extent to which one or more technicians fail to reproduce the measurement of a single hydration rim exactly, has been found to be the result primarily of the following four variables: light

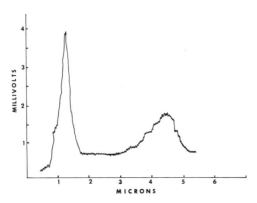

**Fig. 7.8** Photodensitometer graph.

intensity, focus, orientation relative to the polarization plane, and the quality of the slide.

In order to assess the extent of technician error, we had three well-trained laboratory technicians replicate the measurement of a single series of 18 microslides. Each measured separately three loci on all microslides, the loci being the same for all three.

Single-technician error was determined by calculating the standard deviation of differences between measurement values for loci #1, #2, and #3 of each specimen for each technician. Thus a series of 162 observations were made.

Intertechnician error is expressed as the standard deviation of differences between measurement values at a single locus of a single specimen by the three technicians. Again, a series of 162 observations support the value arrived at (Table 7.4).

### 7.9.3
### Dating Error

For chronometric applications of obsidian dating a second kind of dating error exists: that associated with the calculation of the rate of hydration. This can be substantial or modest, depending on the quality of the evidence used.

### 7.10
### Computer Applications

To date, there are five important applications of computer methods used in the process of obsidian hydration dating.

Table 7.4 Summary of Measurement Error[*]

| | |
|---|---|
| Setting accuracy of A.E.I. image-splitting eyepiece (as reported by manufacturer) | S.D. ± 0.125 $\mu$ |
| Difference between mean values obtained by the image-splitting eyepiece and by the photodensitometer | S.D. ± 0.11 $\mu$ |
| Single-technician error | S.D. ± 0.064 $\mu$ |
| Intertechnician error | S.D. ± 0.068 $\mu$ |

[*]Standard measurement error adopted by Penn State laboratory        S.D. ± 0.10 $\mu$

### 7.10.1

### Determining the Hydration Rim Measurement

The drum measurements for each sample are punched on computer cards. A simple program reads these values and, using a precalibration factor, calculates the mean rim thickness. A list of all the samples, their identification, provenience, and hydration measurements is produced.

### 7.10.2

### Obsidian Dates Storage and Retrieval

The same program that calculates the rim measurements for a set of samples also punches up a deck of cards that contains the information for each sample. A central file of all such data will make it simple for any investigator to obtain duplicates of any desired set.

### 7.10.3

### Frequency Graph

Once the hydration measurements for a given excavation have been established and punched on cards, a frequency graph can be produced by the computer. With the rim measurements (in intervals of $0.1 \mu$) along the x-axis, and the frequency of occurrence along the y-axis, the graph provides a clear and useful over-all view of the distribution of obsidian dates at the site.

### 7.10.4

### Hydration Rate

A computer program that enables calculation of the hydration rate from the rim measurements and chronometric values was described in section 7.6.2.

### 7.10.5

### Constructing a Translation Table

Once a hydration rate for a specific site or locality has been established by one of the methods discussed in section 7.6, a table can be produced that enables easy conversion of micron readings to years. It will list micron values from 0 to 20 in intervals of $0.01 \mu$, the B.P. dates corresponding to the mean micron values, the mean values plus the standard deviation, and the mean values minus the standard deviation. The B.C. or A.D. dates are likewise listed.

# References

1. Friedman, I., and Smith, R. L.,
"The Deuterium Content of Water in Some Volcanic Glasses." Geochimica et Cosmochimica Acta 15 (1958): 218-228.

2. Friedman, I., and Smith, R. L.,
"A New Dating Method Using Obsidian: Part I, The Development of the Method." American Antiquity 25 (1960): 476-522.

3. Evans, C., and Meggers, B. J.,
"A New Dating Method Using Obsidian: Part II, An Archaeological Evaluation of the Method." American Antiquity 25 (1960): 523-537.

4. Clark, D. L.,
"The Application of The Obsidian Dating Method to the Archaeology of Central California." Doctoral dissertation, Stanford University (1961): 1-160. "Clark, D. L., Archaeological Chronology in California and The Obsidian Hydration Method: Part I." Annual Report of the Archaeological Survey, Department of Anthropology, University of California, Los Angeles (1964): 143-211.

5. Clark, D. L.,
"The Obsidian Dating Method." Current Anthropology 2 (1961): 111-114.

6. Dixon, L. E.,
Catalog of Obsidian Hydration Measurement Data for Mexico. Washington: Smithsonian Institution (1969): 1-137.

7. Michels, J. W.,
"Lithic Serial Chronology Through Obsidian Hydration Dating." Doctoral dissertation, University of California, Los Angeles (1965): 1-279.

8. Michels, J. W.,
"The Colonial Obsidian Industry of The Valley of Mexico." In Science and Archaeology, edited by R. Brill, Cambridge, Mass.: The M.I.T. Press (1971): 498-546.

9. Johnson, L., Jr.,
"Obsidian Hydration Rate for the Klamath Basin of California and Oregon." Science 165 (1969): 1354-1356.

10. Johannsen, A.,
A Descriptive Petrography of the Igneous Rocks 1, 2nd Edition, Chicago (1939): 8-27. Marshall, R. R., "Devitrification of Natural Glass." Geological Society of America Bulletin 72 (1961): 1493-1520.

11. Green, R. C., Brooks, R. R., and Reeves, R. D.,
"Characterization of New Zealand Obsidians by Emission Spec-

troscopy." New Zealand Journal of Science, 10 (1967): 675-682.
Gordus, A. A., Fink, W. C., Hill, M. E., Purdy, J. C., and Wilcox, T. R.,
"Identification of the Geologic Origins of Archaeological Artifacts: An
Automated Method of Na and Mn Neutron Activation Analysis."
Archaeometry 10 (1967): 87-96. Renfrew, C., Dixon, J. E., and Cann,
J. R., "Obsidian and Early Cultural Contact in the Near East." Proceed-
ings of the Prehistoric Society 32 (1966): 30-72. Weaver, J. R., and
Stross, F. H., "Analysis by X-Ray Fluorescence of Some American
Obsidians." Contributions of the University of California Archaeologi-
cal Research Facility (1965): 89-93.

**12. Ross, C. S., and Smith, R. L.,**
"Water and Other Volatiles In Volcanic Glasses." American Mineralo-
gist 40 (1955): 1071-1089.

**13. Gibbon, D. L., and Michels, J. W.,**
"Electron Microscope and Optical Observations of Obsidian Hydration," Proceedings of the Electron Microscopy Society of America 25
(1967):

**14. Katsui, Y., and Kondo, Y.,**
"Dating of Stone Implements By Using Hydration Layer of Obsidian."
Japanese Journal of Geology and Geography 36 (1965): 45-60. Haller,
W., "Kinetics of the Transport of Water Through Silicate Glasses at
Ambient Temperatures." Physics and Chemistry of Glasses 1 (1960):
46-51.

**15. Friedman, I., Smith, R. L., and Long, W. D.,**
"The Hydration of Natural Glass and The Formation of Perlite." Bulletin of the Geological Society of America 77 (1966): 323-330.

**16. Haller, W.,**
"Concentration-Dependent Diffusion Coefficient of Water in Glass."
Physics and Chemistry of Glasses 4 (1963): 217-220.

**17. Matson, F. R.,**
"Hygroscopicity of Soda-Lime-Silica Container Glasses." Journal of the
American Ceramic Society 32 (1949): 121-128.

**18. Hurst, V. J., and Kelley, A. R.,**
"Patination of Cultural Flints." Science 134 (1961): 251-256.

**19. Griffiths, J. C.,**
Scientific Method in Analysis of Sediments, New York: McGraw-Hill
(1967): 446-647.

**20. Michels, J. W.,**
"Testing Stratigraphy and Artifact Reuse Through Obsidian Hydration
Dating." American Antiquity 34 (1969): 15-22.

**21. Scheffe, H.,**
The Analysis of Variance, New York: John Wiley & Sons (1959)

**22. Renfrew, C., Dixon, J. E., and Cann, J. R.,**
"Obsidian and Early Cultural Contact in The Near East." Proceedings of the Prehistoric Society 32 (1966): 30-72.
**23. MacNeish, R. S.,**
"Ancient Mesoamerican Civilization." Science 143 (1964): 531-537. Flannery, K. V. et al., "Farming Systems and Political Growth in Ancient Oaxaca." Science 158 (1967): 445-454.
**24. Sanders, W. T.,**
The Cultural Ecology of the Teotihuacan Valley. Department of Anthropology, Pennsylvania State University (1965): 1-210.
**25. Michels, J. W.,**
The Structure and Function of the Prehispanic Obsidian Industry of the Basin of Mexico. National Science Foundation Grant Number GS-1256 (1966).
**26. Vidarte, J.,**
Personal communication, Mexico City (1969).
**27. Dyson, J.,**
"Precise Measurement by Image Splitting." Journal of the Optical Society of America 50 (1960): 754-759. Idem, "The Precise Measurement of Small Objects." AEI Engineering 1 (1961): 1-5. Duffy, F. C. H., "Optical Methods of Helix Measurement for the VX. 4164 Traveling Wave Tube." AEI Rugby Research Laboratory Report, No. L 4758, (1960): 1-10.

# Index